THE PINEAPPLE

1. A pineapple, by Johann Christoph Volckamer, 1708.

THE PINEAPPLE

King of Fruits

FRAN BEAUMAN

Chatto & Windus
LONDON

Published by Chatto & Windus 2005

2 4 6 8 10 9 7 5 3 1

Copyright © Fran Beauman 2005

Fran Beauman has asserted her right under the Copyright, Designs
and Patents Act 1988 to be identified as the author of this work

First published in Great Britain in 2005 by
Chatto & Windus
Random House, 20 Vauxhall Bridge Road,
London SW1V 2SA

Random House Australia (Pty) Limited
20 Alfred Street, Milsons Point, Sydney,
New South Wales 2061, Australia

Random House New Zealand Limited
18 Poland Road, Glenfield,
Auckland 10, New Zealand

Random House (Pty) Limited
Endulini, 5A Jubilee Road, Parktown 2193, South Africa

The Random House Group Limited Reg. No. 954009

www.randomhouse.co.uk

A CIP catalogue record for this book is available from the British Library

ISBN 0 7011 7699 7

Papers used by Random House are natural,
recyclable products made from wood grown in sustainable forests;
the manufacturing processes conform to the environmental
regulations of the country of origin

Typeset by SX Composing DTP, Rayleigh, Essex
Printed and bound in Great Britain by
William Clowes Ltd, Beccles, Suffolk

Contents

Illustrations

1. A plate from *Nurnbergische Hesperides* by Johann Christoph Volckamer, 1708 (British Library).
2. A Tupí-Guaraní family with a pineapple. From *History of a Voyage to the Land of Brazil* by Jean de Léry, 1578.
3. A wild pineapple (Duane Bartholomew).
4. *An Indian Cacique of the island of Cuba addressing Columbus* by Benjamin West, 1794 (Bridgeman Art Library).
5. A drawing of the 'Indies' by Honorio Philopono, c.1621.
6. The earliest known illustration of a pineapple. From *Historia General y Natural de las Indias* by Gonzales Oviedo, 1535 (Huntingdon Library, San Marino, California).
7. *Farming Large Pineapples in China*, 1690 (Bridgeman Art Library).
8. A detail from *Theatrum Botanicum* by John Parkinson, 1640 (British Library).
9. A detail from *A True and Exact History of Barbados* by Richard Ligon, 1653 (British Library).
10. A plate from *Byzondere Aaemerkingen* by Pieter de la Court, 1737 (Wageningen UR Library).
11. A detail from *Treatise of Husbandry and Gardening* by Richard Bradley, 1721 (British Library).
12. A pinery. From *The Gardener's Dictionary* by Philip Miller, 1731 (British Library).
13. A tradecard for Henry Scott's nursery in Weybridge, 1754 (British Museum).
14. Sir Joseph Bank's pinery. From *Tod's Plans of Hot Houses* by George Tod, 1807 (British Library).
15. A tradecard for Dominic Negri's shop on Berkeley Square, c.1785 (British Museum).
16. A Coade pineapple gatepost at Ham House (Ham House, The National Trust/Jonathan Button).
17. A garden temple. From *Grotesque Architecture* by William Wrighte, 1767 (British Library).

Preface

It is 9.30 at night on a drizzly Sunday evening in October. Taj Stores, a Bangladeshi supermarket on Brick Lane in east London, lures me inside with its display of jack-fruit the size of footballs, as beguiling as they are baffling in terms of how they are actually supposed to be eaten. Distracted by the glare of the neon strip lighting, I weave my way up and down the aisles in search of . . . I am not sure what. It does not take long to spy it, though. There amongst the ten-high stacks of tinned peaches, pears and other plebeian fruit picked from the fields many moons ago sits a gaudy can of what was once considered 'the king of fruits' – the pineapple. Beheaded and flayed, sliced and diced, the only vestiges of its former incarnation are to be found on the can's label, in a crude illustration of a tropical paradise somewhere far, far away. Oh, how it has fallen from grace! The reason? The pineapple's ever-changing and always complex relationship with Man.

The relationship was sparked the moment a hungry Tupi-Guarani hunter-gatherer deep in the Amazon rainforest first stumbled upon this dirty yellow jewel. From these humble beginnings, the pineapple became a potent status symbol in Europe and North America. A greenhouse filled with the fruit was, by the 1770s, an essential feature of the country house garden, despite the extensive labour involved: the three years the plant took to fruit were years of incredibly hard work for some unfortunate garden boy – stoking the stoves, raking the manure, even sleeping amongst the plants to make sure that they did not burst into flames by mistake. The expense was extortionate, with the cost of producing a single pineapple matching that of a new coach.

Yet the glory that ensued from this taste of Paradise beneath chilly grey skies made it all worth it – for the master of the house, at least. The Prada handbag of its day, the pineapple functioned as a response to a condition that today might be deemed 'status anxiety' – the most impressive specimens made the rounds of urban dinner parties for weeks at a time, only finally consumed once they had begun to rot. The mania soon spread to the other side of the Atlantic, to be adopted with zest by colonial American gentlemen anxious to copy fashions back home.

Why did the pineapple capture first the British then the American imagination? In appearance it is the oddest of all the imports from the New World; it was rumoured that a surfeit could kill you; it is not a stimulant like other popular exotics – tea, coffee and tobacco. And yet, innumerable representations of the pineapple – on gateposts and teapots, in poems and plays, in royal portraits and scenes from Dickens – show that the cultural resonances it has accumulated over the five centuries since its 'discovery' by Christopher Columbus have consistently reflected the various dreams, desires and anxieties of the British and American psyches.

So what is 'the angel at the center of this rind', as the modernist poet Wallace Stevens inquired of it? I hope that by the end of the book, you will feel that you have really got to know the pineapple – its strengths and its weaknesses, its likes and dislikes, its needs and wants. For this is, in the truest sense of the word, its biography.

THE PINEAPPLE

I

'Every fruit has its secret'

D. H. Lawrence (1923)[1]

Brazil.

The rainforest.

Screeeeeeeeeeeeech!

55° west longitude at the Equator.

Crack!

About five o'clock in the afternoon.

Drip.

Drip.

Drip.

It has rained every day for forty days. Even the sloths are impelled to seek shelter. Off they lollop to the only canopy they know, the trees, many up to 120 feet tall. Light is scarce. Occasionally a solitary beam weaves its way through the leaves to reach the muddy soil, but mostly the animals that live on the ground – the armadillos, jaguars, beetles and the rest – manage without this luxury. A parrot screeches overhead: the branches shake with a dash of colour as it flees for safety from an anaconda. A vampire bat follows it, confused. With mosquitoes everywhere, streams teaming with piranhas and a desperately unforgiving climate that sees an average of a 150 inches of rainfall a year, this is one of the most extreme environments on earth.

Peer through the trees. They are dense, I know. But look closely, past the Swiss cheese plants and the sweetheart vine and the other exotics that inhabit this curious place, and you might chance upon a plant that makes you marvel. Most of what is visible is long, stiff leaves like a sculpture of swords. But nestling in the centre, raised a few inches off the ground to deter predators, is the plant's one precious fruit. Wrapped up in an all-but-impenetrable dirty yellow shell, each scale of the carapace is the shape of a diamond, eyed with a black ring.

A pineapple!

Before the arrival of Christopher Columbus in the Americas, the pineapple was South America's precious little secret. Nowhere else on earth had yet had the privilege of even a taste or a smell, let alone of producing this extraordinary fruit from beneath its soil. For all but the tiniest proportion of the earth's history, South America had it all to itself.

The pineapple originates from the area now recognised as Brazil and Paraguay.[2] It is the leading edible member of the relatively young family *Bromeliacae*, of which there are a total of over 2,000 species.[3] These are found mostly in the tropical and subtropical regions of America, apart from one rogue species which grows only in western Africa. Diverse in form, they range in size from Spanish moss to the ten-foot-tall *Puya Raimondii*, whose most distinctive feature is that it takes 150 years to flower. Most bromeliads grow perched on other, larger plants like trees, a feature known in botanical terms as *epiphytic*.

The pineapple is not epiphytic, however, but terrestrial: it grows with its roots in the soil, independent and apart, shunning the support of its fellow plants. Nonetheless, it has retained some of the characteristics of the epiphytes. For example, its ability to store water in its leaves helps it endure long periods of drought. A throwback to its epiphytic ancestry, it seems a little eccentric that the pineapple has clung on to this adaptation, in view of the fact that a lack of rainfall has rarely been a problem for it. Clearly, Nature was determined to ensure its survival.

The pineapple plant is a perennial: it grows all year round. It has the capacity to live indefinitely; but once it does become adult and bear fruit, usually after two to three years, it develops little side shoots, leaving the original plant slowly to die. The changing seasons affect it little, while it does not seem to care how much rain falls. Instead, temperature is the crucial factor. It cannot tolerate frost and is pretty much unable to flourish when soil temperatures drop below about 70°F, while it must have an air temperature of 60–70°F and a high percentage of sun and light. It also likes a soil rich in minerals.

Pineapple reproduction tends to take place vegetatively – that is, by planting its crown (the shoot on top of the fruit), its suckers (side shoots that develop from the main stem at ground level) or its slips (side shoots just below the fruit). When a pineapple is grown in this way, it turns out exactly the same, genetically, as the plant from which it came in the first place. The genes simply repeat themselves.

While most pineapple reproduction is thus asexual, the plant also has the ability to reproduce sexually, through either self-fertilization or cross-fertilization. This means that it harbours the features of both the male and the female: in other words, it is a hermaphrodite. Cross-fertilization, however, means that the fruit will contain seeds, an undesirable attribute amongst today's consumers. Because of this, the humble hummingbird is banned from the island of Hawaii – flying from flower to flower with pollen in its unusually long beak, it was once the primary culprit of the unplanned cross-fertilization of the island's pineapple crop.

Much of the appeal of the pineapple lies in the peculiarity of its physical makeup. The plant itself grows from a terminal bud surrounded by a thick rosette of concave leaves close to the soil surface. These leaves allow the plant to collect water in the rosette, where it can be absorbed by the aerial roots that grow along the stem or through the epidermis of their sheath. Leaf colour ranges from light or dark green to dark red or purple, depending on the species and the conditions. It is from the terminal bud that the pineapple's fibrous flowering stem emerges, usually to a height of about three feet and accompanied by more leaves, these ones often armed with spiked edges (depending on the variety).

The stem eventually bears flowers, each of which ripens into a fruitlet. A fruitlet contains all of the parts of a complete flower including sepals, petals, stamens and a pistil with a stigmatic surface where pollination takes place, as well as an ovary where the fruitlet's seeds develop. On most bromeliads each fruitlet survives independently, but on the pineapple and its close relatives they are fused together to produce a single fruit. The biological term for this sort of fusion, in which a single fleshy fruit is made up of a crowd of flowers, is a *sorosis*. It derives from the Greek word *soros*, meaning a heap, and there is a certain romance in the idea that the pineapple is really just a heap of flowers dressed up to look like some kind of tough guy.

The shell is composed of sepal and bract tissues and the apices of the ovaries. These are the remains of the flowers which persist after the fruit is formed and each one manifests itself as a different one of the fruit's 'eyes'. It also means that the core of the fruit is in fact the stalk, which is why it sometimes tastes a little chewy. Yet the pineapple's most distinctive physical feature is its crown. The numerous short stiff leaves are the continuation of the stalk that penetrates up through the fruit, then peeps its head over and above the top. So why has the physical form of the pineapple evolved in such a singular fashion? The crown, the armour and the rosette of leaves are not simply a fashion statement. Most probably, they are to protect it from casual predators, a major problem for the pineapple since it grows at ground level.[4]

Perhaps the most extraordinary aspect of the pineapple's physical makeup lies in its mathematical proportions. It forms one of the most perfect examples in nature of a phenomenon known as Divine Proportion. In the ancient world, great importance was attached to this concept, which was also known as the Golden Mean: it affected the layout of buildings, the composition of art and even literary structure. The basis is a constant called *phi* (1.6180339). Discovered by the Greek mathematician Euclid, *phi* emerges from a geometrical theorem that generates a series of numbers in which each number is the sum of the two preceding numbers: 0, 1, 1, 2, 3, 5, 8, 13, 21, and so on. It was later named the Fibonacci series in honour of the great thirteenth-century Italian thinker Leonardo Fibonacci (also known as Leonardo of Pisa).[5]

In the 1820s it was discovered that, amazingly, the Fibonacci series frequently occurs in nature, illustrated particularly clearly in the pineapple (as well as a snail's shell or a sunflower's florets, amongst other examples). The 'eyes' on its shell are arranged in curving rows: one set goes one way from base to top, the other crosses the first row at an oblique angle. The number of rows of each always, but always, conforms to two consecutive numbers from the Fibonacci series: usually 5 and 8 or 8 and 13, depending on the variety. Every single fruit is the same in this respect. In practical terms, this minimises the amount of mechanical stress exerted on it during growth.[6] But it also means that it fulfils the properties of Divine Proportion – it is, mathematically, perfect.

And the taste? While this might seem like the pineapple's very reason for being, in reality it is seen by most theorists as merely a social construct. On a personal level, when I am asked whether I do actually eat a lot of the stuff, I am afraid that the answer is no. People always look disappointed. Surely I have pineapple whenever possible: pineapple yoghurt for breakfast, pineapple salad for lunch and pineapple pie for supper? Well, no. On a beach on the island of Koh Pha Nang in Thailand, aged eighteen, I succumbed to the charms of a passing fruitseller to buy armfuls of the freshest, juiciest pineapple I had ever had. After wrestling with it for some time with my tiny penknife, in the process penetrating more of my own flesh than that of my stubborn new friend, I finally indulged in a taste; then another one; and another one. This was my downfall. The roof of my mouth began to burn. My lips itched. My tongue smarted. It felt like it had been attacked by paint-stripper. In retrospect though, lucky me. I have witnessed a particularly vicious pineapple make someone's lips actually bleed. There is a scientific reason for this phenomenon. It lies in its chemical composition.

The pineapple is the only known source of bromelein, an enzyme that digests protein – it is, literally, flesh-eating. Not only does this mean that it often features in weight-loss diets (in the 1980s a woman named Judy Mazel made over six million dollars with her Beverly Hills Diet that advocates eating a pineapple after every meal), but it also helps to tenderise meat, which is why it is so often married with ham or gammon. In addition, bromelein is an effective natural remedy. Because it helps in the breakdown of proteins into amino acids, much like the stomach's own gastric juices, it can relieve gastrointestinal problems. By inhibiting the action of chemicals in the body that contribute to pain and swelling, it has an anti-inflammatory effect, while it also has the ability to improve respiratory ailments like catarrh and bronchitis by reducing the thickness of bronchial secretions.

As well as containing high levels of vitamins A, B1, B2 and C, another unusual aspect of the pineapple's chemistry is that, unlike most fruits, it has no starch reserves of its own. This means that the sugar content that makes up 15 per cent of the fruit must be accumulated before it is harvested – otherwise, it does not have the resources to sweeten any further. In other words, it has to be picked when it is already ripe, unlike a banana or a peach, for example, which ripen the most after they are picked. Remember this next time you are dithering in the supermarket. The way to tell that a pineapple is ready to eat is to smell it, then to check that the leaves look fresh and green.

The first humans to encounter the fruit were the Tupí-Guaraní Indians. The inhabitants of greater Amazonia before the arrival of European explorers represented four major language groups: Tupí-Guaraní, Gê, Carib and Arawak. The Tupí-Guaranís were the largest contingent: under a variety of tribal names (Tupinambas, Potiguaras, Tabajaras, Castes and Guaranís), they dominated the Brazilian coast from the mouth of the Amazon river all the way south to Cananéia in the state of São Paulo, as well as along sections of the Amazon basin, throughout a large region of the tropical forests along the coastal floodplains and along the major rivers of the Parana–Paraguay system. By domesticating the pineapple, they were also its earliest champions, so it is worth investigating the workings of the tribe. For this was the pineapple's first ever glimpse of human society.[7]

Our knowledge of the Tupí-Guaranís is relatively extensive: since they lived primarily in the coastal areas of Brazil, they were the first inhabitants of the New World to be encountered by the Portuguese explorers of the sixteenth century. They tended to be short and stout (just five feet tall on average) with a light skin colour and straight black hair. A description of two members of the Tupinamba tribe (a division of the Tupí-Guaranís) encountered by the Portuguese sailor Pero Vaz de Caminha at the mouth of the Rio Cahy in 1500 demonstrates a prudishness typical of European explorers.

In appearance they are dark, somewhat reddish, with good faces and good noses, well shaped. They go naked, without any covering; neither do they pay more attention to concealing or exposing their shame than they do to showing their faces, and in this respect they are very innocent.[8]

As for the women of the tribe, Caminha thought them a very beautiful sight – though after three months at sea, he probably would have said the same of a friendly warthog.

Three quarters of a century later, a French priest named Jean de Léry landed in Brazil as a member of the first and only Protestant mission to the area. His vivid, observant and engaging descriptions of the Tupí-Guaraní tribe in *History of a Voyage to the Land of Brazil* form a rare portrait of a people just before they are engulfed by the multiple and terrifying forces of colonisation. The main flaw in his account is that he assumed that the way the Tupí-Guaranís lived was the way all the tribes of the continent lived, when in fact the Gê, the Caribs and the Arawaks differed greatly. Yet despite this, de Léry is an invaluable source. What struck him most was the Tupí-Guaranís' devotion to decorating themselves:

[They] paint their bodies in motley hues; but it is especially their custom to blacken their thighs and legs so thoroughly with the juice of a certain fruit, which they call genipap, that seeing them from a distance, you would think they had donned the hose of a priest . . .[9]

DE L'AMERIQVE.   121

2. A Tupí-Guaraní family with a pineapple. From Jean de Léry's *History of a Voyage to the Land of Brazil*, 1578.

De Léry also recounted how they despised wearing clothes: they argued that it takes too much time dressing and undressing, a logic I completely understand.[10]

The Tupí-Guaranís lived in semi-permanent settlements of about six hundred people. Their primary means of finding food was hunting and gathering, though agriculture was also practised. It was one of the tasks of the men of the tribe to clear the land of as many of the large trees as possible, then burn down the undergrowth, so that the women could then plant, tend and harvest whatever crops they thought might flourish. Yet conditions were difficult. Agriculture in the sense we know it was all but impossible: the soil of the Amazon rainforest was porous and full of parasites and, when it was cleared, it was burned by the sun and washed away by floods. So they just cultivated what was vital to their sustenance, then moved on to a new site as soon as the soil was worn out, usually after two to three years – a technique known to ethnologists as *slash and burn*.

Day to day, the main preoccupation for the men was warfare, not only against their Tupí-Guaraní neighbours but also against tribes of different tongues. There existed a real passion for it, with the aim being to capture prisoners rather than to occupy land or win loot. They travelled stealthily in canoes, with bows and arrows their principal weapons, and of all the tribes of the area, the Tupí-Guaranís were notoriously one of the most aggressive. Perhaps this is why the pineapple appealed to them so much: it too is rather aggressive in appearance, with its leaves like swords and rind like armour.

Supper consisted mostly of manioc, also known as cassava. The main cultivated crop, it had many uses but it was most commonly made into flour. The tribe also grew various kinds of corn, beans, squash, potatoes, peppers, tobacco, cotton, peanuts and, of course, pineapples. Fruits were gathered from the forest, while the men silently stalked monkeys, tapirs, armadillos and birds. Every meal was a ritual: they ate in silence, squatting on the ground around a gigantic cauldron.

Yet the most unusual element of the tribe's diet was human flesh, with the dish of choice prisoners of war. Following a successful raid, prisoners were escorted back to the village, fattened up for a few weeks, then, in an elaborate ritual, executed (painlessly, at least) by a blow to the head from behind, cooked and skinned. A piece of flesh was then served to each member of the tribe to help them gain the spiritual strength of the unfortunate. This explains why the primary purpose of warfare was purported to be the capture of prisoners – a central concern since political power derived primarily from their ritual consumption. This fundamentally violent culture was the one into which the pineapple was first introduced and it was inevitably to inform the way it later came to be perceived.

The earliest form of pineapple to become known to Man, from which all domestic varieties derive, was the wild pineapple. Brazil is the only country that can still boast them growing in the wild, but I had the chance to see some in the (now-defunct) Delmonte Variety Garden just outside Honolulu in Hawaii, a strangely lovely spot despite the fact that it was perched in between two lanes of a motorway. Accompanied by Professor Duane Bartholomew, one of the world's leading experts on the botany of the pineapple, I spent a hot afternoon wandering around the exhibits on display. The wild pineapple is a very different fruit to the one most of us know. It is full of seeds, small (about the size of an English apple), stringy and very sour – horrid, all in all. Had it stayed this way, it would have been a very different story. Luckily though, it did not.

3. A wild pineapple.

The wild pineapple acquired the size and taste of the fruit familiar to us today through its gradual domestication – human intervention, in other words. Since the process of 'slash and burn' meant that they were forced to replant all they needed for sustenance every couple of years, the Tupí-Guaranís were only likely to choose those specimens that most fulfilled their requirements. Not such an innocent player after all, the pineapple pandered to these as much as possible in order to entice them to incorporate it into their limited agricultural activities – by (amongst other developments) increasing its size to make itself a more rewarding food source, changing its reproductive methods to rid itself of nuisance seeds, and even adapting its chemical composition to bring the way it tasted more in line with Man's sweet tooth. Even its leaves are shaped in such a way that they are perfect for collecting rain water. It was (in part) to please the Tupí-Guaranís that it evolved thus, and in this way the properties of the domesticated pineapple serve as a rich archive of cultural information about the qualities the tribe most valued in a foodstuff.[11]

There is little evidence for precisely when or where the pineapple evolved from a wild species to a domesticated one. The process is likely to have begun as soon as the tribes of the Amazon established a settled village life – around 2000 BC. Since this also corresponds with accepted dates for the onset of manioc cultivation, it seems reasonable to take this as a reference for pineapple cultivation, thereby making it a practice that is at least 4,000 years old.[12] A number of factors point to it being one of the earliest components of the lowland complex of cultivated plants, along with the sweet potato, the peanut, the potato, maize, and many more. Its wide distribution is one; the natives' intimate knowledge of its properties is another – it takes years and years to discover that a food is a source of wine or useful in medicine. The absence of a recognisable wild progenitor also suggests that its current form has existed for quite some time.[13]

Gradual domestication meant that the fields became an increasingly important source of the fruit. The women were responsible for sowing, tending and harvesting, with the latter a particular challenge: you not only have to be strong, but also have inordinately tough hands since the leaves will shred your skin to ribbons in a second. There was no chance of the pineapples that grew in the wild being neglected, however: in yet another trick employed (among other purposes) to attract Man's attention, de Léry recalled how 'they have such a fragrance of raspberry that when you go through the woods and other places where they grow, you can smell them from far off'.[14] The women then brought their haul back to the village in huge baskets called *panacons* that they balanced precariously on their heads.[15]

While the pineapple was not a staple in the Tupí-Guaraní diet, it was a frequent supplement, both fresh and in jam.[16] But it really came into its own when it was used to make alcohol, for which it is eminently suitable due to its richness in sugar. The combination of this with the fact that the pineapple, unlike most fruits, is available all year round may explain its relatively prolific cultivation.[17]

Thus firmly assimilated into Tupí-Guaraní society, it now demanded a name. De Léry was the first to record that the Tupí-Guaranís used the term *anãnã*, meaning *an excellent fruit* or *fragrance*, as well as *nãnã* to refer to just the plant part.[18] Presumably its etymology reflected prevailing native attitudes to the fruit. The term, most commonly in the form of *ananas*, subsequently conquered all vernaculars of Africa, India, and most of the languages of Europe too. It does seem only fair that in the main the term *anãnã* has stuck, that the Tupí-Guaranís receive some credit for domestication, that in most languages every reference to it gives a nod to its earliest champions. The term also forms the basis of its botanical name, *Ananas Comosus*. *Comosus* comes from the Latin word *comos* that means hairy, with long hair or, in the case of plants, leafy.

Highly skilled navigators, the Tupí-Guaranís travelled the length and breadth of the continent's waterways in canoes made from the largest logs available and manned by thirty to sixty men. They moved villages periodically, not only to ensure a continuing supply of new land and food, but also because these tribal migrations were believed to generate spiritual renewal. Border trading between tribes allowed the pineapple to scatter itself throughout South America: by the time Christopher Columbus dropped anchor, the pineapple as a cultivated plant had spread throughout Brazil, Columbia, parts of Central America, the West Indies and possibly beyond.[19]

The inhabitants of these areas developed a wide variety of different ways to incorporate the pineapple into the indigenous culture. The Spanish Jesuit priest Joseph de Acosta noted that in the 1570s in Peru, 'they eate it being cut in morcells, and steeped a while in water and salt . . . I have seene in New Spain, conserves of these pines, which was very good.'[20] Tribes in Colombia and Venezuela boiled them with manioc starch for breakfast.[21] But like the Tupí-Guaranís, others appreciated its potential to liven up a party. Pineapple wine was observed in Panama in 1503,[22] while the Spanish writer Gonzalo de Oviedo recorded that 'I have drunk some of it and it is not very much like real wine, for the great part because it is very sweet. No Spaniard or Italian would drink it while he had that of Castile or even of Spain though it were not of the choicest.'[23] The Nambicuara, a tribe of eastern Bolivia, made an alcoholic drink out of wild pineapple mixed with water (as they still do today), while others used it as an ingredient in medicine.[24] What is interesting in many of these accounts is the extent to which the pineapple was adulterated in order to make it palatable – whether spices, salt or sugar was used, the suggestion is that while evolution had gone a long way towards making the taste of the pineapple appeal to Man, Man himself still had to do the rest.

For a long time, however, the pineapple plant has been much more than merely a source of nourishment. Its leaf fibres can be used to manufacture a cream-coloured rope that is as lustrous as silk and extremely strong: sometimes used to make clothes (a popular practice in the Philippines even today), in pre-colonial South America its most common application was in bowstrings.[25] It is not unlikely that the bowstrings used to shoot arrows at the invading Europeans of the fifteenth and sixteenth centuries were made in this very way – as if it were the pineapple's last attempt to maintain the insularity of the comfortable world it had known for the past few thousand years. In addition, the rotten fruit was used to poison the tips of the arrows themselves.

There is scarce evidence that the pineapple played a more symbolic role within primitive South American society, in the way that many other foodstuffs did. The single exception is to be found in Mexico. De Acosta described an Indian god named Vitzilipuztli depicted with a white target with five pineapples made out of white feathers and set in the form of a cross that he held in his hand.[26] It is also possible that the fruit was a feature in the tribal affirmation rites of young men. Not only did you have to be physically strong to pick it and to penetrate its skin to eat it, but when unripe it is a drastic purgative.

Let us examine the state of the pineapple as it lay on the cusp of a new life. Its thousands of years of existence had shaped its meanings: raised in the rainforests of northern Brazil, the only world it knew was one of fecundity, ferocity and intense heat – here, Nature was the dominant force. Once assimilated into Tupí-Guaraní culture, further associations were layered on top of these, among them, the high regard for the fruit manifested in the name bestowed upon it: *anãná*. Take a moment to savour the taste of the pineapple in its near-virginal state. For South America was soon to be forced to share its secret. With the arrival of an exhausted Spanish crew in the autumn of 1493, the pineapple was finally thrust on to the world stage.

'There is not a nobler fruit in the universe'

Jacob Bontius (1629)

Christopher Columbus is most famous for the voyage he made across the Atlantic in 1492, during which he landed in the Americas, stumbled across a multitude of new plants such as maize and potato and revealed a race of people Europe did not know existed. Undoubtedly, these were momentous events. And yet for the pineapple, they were a mere precursor to the real action. For while Columbus's subsequent voyage in 1493 tends to be assigned to a footnote in his career, to the pineapple, this was the one that really mattered. It was to transform its existence for ever.

The astonishing success of the first voyage meant that Columbus had little difficulty raising funds for the second. Queen Isabella of Spain, for one, was immediately keen to contribute. She liked the idea that he might be able to convert some of the natives to Christianity; she also hoped a colony might be established. That the popularisation of the pineapple was even enough to merit a scribbled addition to his 'To Do' list following his final audience with Her Majesty is unlikely. But whatever the motives behind the trip, on a dazzlingly sunny day in September 1493 Columbus set sail once again. His fleet of seventeen ships was escorted out of Cadiz harbour by huge Venetian galleys, accompanied by the triumphant sound of trumpets and harps and the deafening firing of cannon.[1]

And so, to sea. The sailors settled in for the long haul: the first time around, it had taken nine weeks to reach land. Pretty much all they had for entertainment were the flying fish and their diet was meagre and dull, every day the same meal of salted meat, lentils and hardtack (a snack made from flour and water that was said to remain edible for up to fifty years). This was washed down with red wine or, when it ran out, water that had usually gone off in the casks. At night the captains sheltered inside a cabin with a bunk, but the rest of the crew slept wherever they could on the cold, hard, damp deck.

But on this voyage, after just three weeks Columbus was struck by a hunch that land was not far off. Sure enough, on 3 November 1493, an island was glimpsed in the distance. 'Albricias! Que tenemos tierra!' (The reward! For we have land!) hollered the lookout. It turned out to be the Caribbean island later named Dominica: on his second attempt, Columbus had navigated the shortest and speediest route across the Atlantic. The following day another island appeared, and the Captain was quick to bestow upon it the name of Guadeloupe, in honour of a promise made to the monks of Santa Maria of Guadeloupe during a pilgrimage he had made there before he left Spain.

Guadeloupe in 1493 was a truly spectacular sight. A letter from Guglielmo Coma, a nobleman from Aragon and one of Columbus's closest companions on the trip, described how it 'held the seamen close in its spell', with its 'wide and lovely plains and the indescribable beauty of its mountains'.[2] A constant in almost all contemporary accounts is how awestruck Columbus's crew were by the landscape before them: even though most were used to new people and places, the New World was more extraordinary than anything they had ever seen. Guadeloupe's inhabitants concurred: they called it *Karukera*, the Island of Beautiful Waters.

Guadeloupe was populated by members of the Carib tribe – originally from South America, they had, like the pineapple, gradually migrated north.[3] A typical Carib was of medium height, with olive skin and very black eyes and hair. They washed every morning (a habit that must have seemed bizarre to the Europeans, for whom anything more than a bath a year was deemed incredibly virtuous). None, however, had beards, for these were considered a deformity. They also differentiated themselves from other tribes with a unique style: wearing two cotton bandages, one above the knee and one on the ankles, to make the calves look more bulky than they really were, a practice about which Columbus's expedition doctor Diego Alvarez Chanca commented sniffily: 'it appears that they regard this as an attraction'.[4] Most of the women in the tribe were of Arawak origin, brought back from raids on nearby islands to bear the Carib men children. As a result, the sexes spoke (literally) a different language. When they were forced to communicate, the women had to attempt to do so in Carib.

The staple food was crab, supplemented by fish, bird and lizard meat. They cultivated a similar range of plants to the Tupí-Guaranís: mainly manioc, in addition to sweet potatoes, beans and peppers. But they also loved fruit and many had their own fruit gardens. The usual method of preparing pineapple differed from tribes further south: it was pounded vigorously with a mortar into a thick paste, then seasoned with capsicum peppers. This concoction was used to accompany meat. Another popular use for it was once again in the manufacture of wine. The Caribs consumed this in epic quantities and this was in part what encouraged the pineapple's widespread domestication: ensuring a constant supply of intoxicating substances was one matter that the natives were reluctant to leave to chance.

Yet, not unlike the Tupí-Guaranís, the Caribs were famous for their cannibalism: it is from the word *Carib* that we get the word *cannibal*. Columbus had heard rumours of these terrifying warriors on his first westerly trip. Again, war was their favourite form of sport, the taking and slaughtering of prisoners a matter of pride. At the ensuing party, the bravest warriors were given the heart, the women the arms and the legs, with the rest shared out amongst everyone else – sometimes washed down with pineapple wine, no doubt.

Despite the grisly reputation of Guadeloupe's inhabitants, Columbus was determined to venture ashore. He commanded the fleet to land in the harbour of what is now Grande Anse and, having made my own pilgrimage there, I am able to vouch for Guglielmo Coma's sense of awe at the stunning vista. While today it has a busy road running behind it and a thatched hut with ice-creams for sale, to the European, Grande Anse still retains the air of a blissful New World, with long stretches of white sand, immensely tall coconut trees and bright, bright blue sea. Inland, its appearance has been transformed by the introduction of the banana, the coconut and sugarcane, all unknown in the Caribbean until brought over by Europeans. However, the coconut tree does not differ so drastically in appearance from the Caribbean's wide variety of indigenous palm trees, while sugarcane is similar to the native reeds that grow near the mouths of rivers – in sum, the view from a distance has altered only a little since first glimpsed by Columbus.[5] It takes just a small leap of imagination to picture the Spanish crew tired, hungry but excited, wading through the sea and collapsing ashore into the unknown.

What dangers lurked? What wonders beckoned? Fortunately, the Carib warriors were away on a slave raid and Columbus's men went unchallenged as they forged their way inland to see what they might be able to plunder. They faced considerable pressures from investors back in Spain to return with riches: above all else, their mission was to establish what elements of the island might be exploited for commercial gain.

It was immediately clear that this island held a trove of treasures that the Europeans had never even dared to imagine. They found a wide variety of plants that were soon to infiltrate our culinary world forever, including peanuts and sweet potatoes, as well as cloth made from cotton, hammocks, pottery, mallard ducks and tame parrots. In a hut near the shore they also stumbled across a less appealing prospect: roast baby. Dr Chanca later wrote in a letter to the city council of Seville that:

> They say that the flesh of a man is so good that there is nothing like it in the world, and it certainly seems so, from the bones that we found in their houses, they had gnawed at everything that could be gnawed, so

that nothing was left on them except what was too tough to be eaten. In one house a neck of a man was found cooking in a pot.[6]

Why a man's neck, of all things? Presumably it is not the tastiest part of the human body. Nonetheless, there is no doubt that the world into which Columbus's crew had stumbled was a violent and bloodthirsty one.

Soon came the pineapple's turn to manifest itself – a moment that Ferdinand Columbus used his father's log books to recreate, since Columbus's account of the second voyage was, alas, lost.

> They also saw calabashes and some fruit that looked like green pine cones but were much larger; these were filled with solid pulp, like a melon, but were much sweeter in taste and smell. They grow on plants that resemble lilies or aloes . . .[7]

The key adjective here is 'sweeter'. The sensation of sweetness was still a real luxury in Europe due to the high price of sugar – to discover it in a cultivated plant like the pineapple signified the prospect of significant financial reward.

An additional eyewitness report has been handed down to us by Michele de Cuneo. De Cuneo was born into a noble family in Savona, near Genoa, and was in all likelihood a childhood friend of Columbus. Lucky enough to accompany him on the second voyage, his letter to a friend, Hieronymo Annari, written on 28 October 1495, was the first published account of the pineapple.

> There are also some like artichoke plants but four times as tall, which give a fruit in the shape of a pine cone, twice as big, which fruit is excellent and it can be cut with a knife like a turnip and it seems to be very wholesome.[8]

Like many discoveries from the New World, the pineapple is here compared to a variety of fruit and vegetables already within the European realm of experience, a tactic that was to recur in almost all early accounts of the fruit. The most common point of reference was the pine cone, understandably, but the artichoke and the aloe are also frequently employed in order to translate this new experience into a more familiar cultural setting.[9]

Yet for anything really to exist to us, it requires a name. In order to be able to think about it, talk about it or write about it, Europe had to decide on what this should be. The pineapple was known to the Caribs by the same word as to the Tupí-Guaranís, *anãnã*, but the explorers were not content to accept another culture's linguistic decisions: 'Your Majesty, language is the perfect instrument of empire,' wrote the Bishop of Avila to Queen Isabella in 1492.[10] For this reason, there was no attempt at all to incorporate its existing name into Spanish. Instead, the pineapple was renamed *immediately* in order to recast it into an all-new European incarnation. Since the only element of it that was familiar was that it looked a little like a pine cone, it was named after the Spanish term for this, *piña*. In this way, Europe took possession of this oddity.

While the pineapple clearly caused something of a stir the moment it was discovered, a number of other pressing matters had to be addressed. A group led by one of the crew's captains, Diego Marquez, got lost in Guadeloupe's dense rainforest for six days, amongst trees so tall that even the stars were obscured from view. Though they eventually turned up on the beach, to much rejoicing, subsequent myth has it that they had been so busy devouring pineapples that they failed to take note of their bearings. There is no evidence to support this, but it is an enticing idea, certainly, that the pineapple has the power to obliterate all thoughts of the world outside. After spending nearly a week exploring Guadeloupe, on 10 November Columbus reluctantly decided that it was time to move on. He sailed for Hispaniola (now Haiti) where he founded the colony of Isabella, named after his benefactor, followed by sojourns in Cuba and Jamaica. Wherever he went, the pineapple was offered up as a local treasure.

Many months later, the crew stopped off in Guadeloupe on the way back from Hispaniola to stock up on provisions for the voyage home. Among these were a few ripe pineapples to present to King Ferdinand

4. *An Indian Cacique of the island of Cuba addressing Columbus* by Benjamin West, 1794.

and Queen Isabella. Columbus set sail again on 20 April 1496, but the journey home was slow, mostly beating to windward. After a month at sea, everyone was restricted to meagre rations of six ounces of cassava bread and one cup of water a day. Just south of the Azores they were lucky enough to catch a westward breeze, yet the crew were getting hungrier and hungrier and a couple of them even suggested eating the Indian captives for breakfast. The captives objected, not surprisingly, and the debate was still raging when land was spotted. On 11 June the voyage ended in the Bay of Cadiz. Banners were erected, the city band turned up and so did the crowds – but they found it a sad spectacle, what with the battered ships and the miserable crew, described by an onlooker as frighteningly thin and with 'faces the colour of saffron'.[11]

The sailors faced one final task before they were allowed down to the taverns to indulge in some much-missed beer and women. As the loot was unloaded, it was discovered that all the precious pineapples had rotted on the journey – except for one single specimen that had managed not to collapse into a pulp. Columbus immediately headed to the Spanish court to offer it to His and Her Majesty. According to Ferdinand Columbus, 'he presented a great quantity of things and specimens that he brought from the Indies, including various birds, animals, trees and plants, as well as such implements and things as the Indians have for their use and pleasure'.[12] Amongst this bevy of curiosities snuggled the pineapple. Since the reaction of the King and Queen was crucial to its future success (or otherwise) in Europe, it was a nerve-racking moment. Happily, it was captured by a man named Peter Martyr.

Peter Martyr was an Italian who worked at the Spanish court as tutor to the royal princes. Though he never actually saw the New World for himself, he learned all he could from talking to those with first-hand experience. It is thought that he even had Columbus's diary of the second voyage to assist him. The first three parts, or 'Decades' as he called them, of his major work De Orbe Novo were first published in 1516. A unique collation of contemporary perceptions of the Americas, it contains the most widely disseminated account of the pineapple to emerge from the earliest explorations.

The most invincible King Ferdinand relates that he has eaten another fruit brought from those countries. It is like a pine-nut in form and colour, covered with scales, and firmer than a melon. Its flavour excels all other fruits. This fruit, which the King prefers to all others, does not grow upon a tree but upon a plant, similar to an artichoke or an acanthus. I myself have not tasted it, for it was the only one which had arrived unspoiled, the others having rotted during the long voyage. Spaniards who have eaten them fresh plucked where they grow, speak with the highest appreciation of their delicate flavour.[13]

That 'the King prefers [it] to all others' was to be quoted to death in future accounts. In this era of Divine Rule, in which unquestioning deference to the monarchy was a given, no more effective recommendation existed. Stamped with the royal seal of approval, it was from the beginning cast on the world stage as worthy of royalty (in contrast to, for example, the potato, a more democratic foodstuff shunned by the upper echelons of society for many years).

Sadly, Queen Isabella's reaction to the pineapple is lost to us. In fact, the way women reacted to the pineapple was rarely recorded, at least up until the nineteenth century. It is not impossible that the pineapple might have become the Queen of Fruits, rather than the King of Fruits, had Isabella been heard more vociferously. After all, since both Isabella and Ferdinand had crowns of their own, ostensibly giving them equal footing, why was the pineapple cast as a male rather than a female? Perhaps it reveals that these two were not quite the equal powers on the throne that some historians have believed them to be. A crown was still viewed as an inherently male decoration.

And so the pineapple emerged into the confused world that was turn-of-the-century Spain. Spain was in the midst of a whirlwind period of cultural advance ushered in by Ferdinand and Isabella. It was a nation on the threshold of a global empire, but few were aware of it at the time: apart from some gold and exotics, there was nothing in the New World that had really made an impact on the cultural landscape. Only with hindsight was the significance of Columbus's voyages truly appreciated.[14]

The rest of Europe was no different. With many predisposed to be suspicious of the new and the exotic, the pineapple's place within the continent's dietary sphere was by no means assured – especially since tales of this kingly fruit spread infinitely more quickly than specimens of the fruit itself. Those who had seen it were keen to share their experiences: amongst both sailors and scholars, it was thought about, talked about and written about far more rapturously than any of the other New World discoveries. Drawings also appeared, though these varied wildly in the way they depicted the size, botany or colour of the fruit. For most, it was years before it manifested itself in any other way but in the medium of words and pictures.[15]

Fortuitously for the pineapple, its arrival coincided with the explosion of the world of the printed book. While about 20 million copies of books were printed in total in the period before 1500, it is estimated that over 150 million deluged the sixteenth century.[16] This was an age of unprecedented literary and intellectual activity in Western Europe and as a result, the pineapple's early characteristics, real or imagined, were diligently chronicled.

While Europe was slow to appreciate the idea of the New World at first, by the 1550s many had become enthralled to news of it. Tales had been emerging about Africa and Asia for some time, but the New World was a total unknown: 'It is a striking fact', wrote the Parisian lawyer Etienne Pasquier in the early 1560s, that 'our classical authors had no

5. A drawing of the 'Indies' by Honorio Philopono, c.1621.

knowledge of all this America, what we call New Lands'.[17] The result was that most were prepared to believe just about every piece of information. In a drawing of 1621 by the Spanish missionary Honorio Philopono, it is depicted as a world not only of men gathering pineapples and playing the bagpipes, but also of sea monsters. So much was strange about the New World that the presence of sea monsters stretched contemporary incredulity very little.

It was at this moment in its history that it became an asset to the pineapple that it is not mentioned in the Bible or in the classical texts of Greek and Rome. That it was previously unknown in the Old World meant that it was free of the cultural resonances that engulfed other fruits. While the pomegranate, for example, was entangled in an elaborate web of myth around the goddess Persephone, the pineapple was a completely blank page on which to inscribe newly created meanings.

So how did those privileged enough to experience the pineapple first hand express their feelings about it? These must be treated with the import they deserve, for they were to inform perceptions of the pineapple for centuries to come – arguably, right up until the present day. In its first 150 years of celebrity, never has a food been so eulogised. 'I think it is the finest fruit in America,' proclaimed Jean de Léry in 1578.[18] 'There is not a nobler fruit in the universe,' marvelled the Dutch physician Jacob Bontius in 1629.[19] Others typically concurred.

The author of the first detailed account of the pineapple was Gonzalo Fernández de Oviedo y Valdes, known to most as Oviedo. Oviedo arrived in Panama in 1514 to help oversee the gold foundries for King Ferdinand. His knowledge of the New World was broad and perceptive, knowledge he shared with the rest of Europe with the publication in Seville in 1535 of the first part of his *Historia General y Natural de las Indias*. Many derived their sum knowledge of the New World from this one account; it even inspired Sir Walter Raleigh's attempt to establish a colony.[20]

When he comes to discuss the pineapple, Oviedo's generally sober analysis begins to collapse, with an account that amounts to six pages of hagiography.

[I do not think] there is any in the whole world to equal [the pineapple] in those things which I shall now tell and which are: Beauty of appearance, delicate fragrance, excellent flavour. So that of the five corporeal senses, the three which can be applied to fruits and even the fourth, that of touch, it shares these four things of senses excelling above all fruits.

6. The earliest known illustration of a pineapple. From Oviedo's *Historia General y Natural de las Indias*, 1535.

And so it goes on. It stretches even his vocabulary: 'My pen and my words cannot depict such exceptional qualities.' To compensate, Oviedo attempts the earliest illustration of the fruit. He also highlights the difficulty of even being graced by an appearance by the pineapple: he tried to ship some specimens of the fruit, which rotted, then the shoots, which also decayed, due to the lengthy journey they were forced to endure.

Oviedo raves about the way the pineapple tasted: 'To taste it is so appetising a thing, so delicate, that words fail to give it its true praise for this.' A sample of other sixteenth-century accounts demonstrates that he was by no means alone in his appreciation: 'In truth the most delicious fruit that can be found';[21] 'it is more delicious than any sweete apple sugred';[22] 'very excellent, as well for his sweetness as his relish, as pleasant as fine sugar and maze';[23] 'very pleasant and delightfull in taste, it is full of juyce, and of a sweete and sharpe taste'.[24] To be sure the taste of the pineapple is fairly wonderful, but with the sensation of sweetness so hard to track down in Europe, to experience it direct from the arms of Nature was all the more extraordinary – especially so to an explorer who had been living on biscuits for months on end. The only misgiving voiced by Oviedo was that it tastes horrible after wine.

Yet it was the appearance of the pineapple that most impressed those new to it. The irony is that while Nature had designed it thus in order to protect it from casual predators, it had not bargained with the peculiar demands of Man. According to the love-struck Oviedo,

When a man looks upon the beauty of this fruit he enjoys seeing its composition, the adornment with which nature painted it and made it so pleasant to the sight . . . [It is] the most beautiful of any of the fruits I have seen . . . Certainly as among the birds, Nature works with elaborate care on the feathers as seen in the birds of our Europe. In the same way, I have found equal care in the composition and beauty of this fruit, more than all I have seen, beyond comparison. I do not suppose there is in the whole world any other of so exquisite and lovely appearance.

Overflowing with hyperbole, the pineapple is here cast as a somewhat artificial beauty – 'painted' with 'adornment', buffed and scrubbed like a Hollywood starlet. It was by no means the last time that a strangely sexual quality was to be ascribed to this seemingly so unsexual of fruits.

Early accounts of the pineapple are strikingly concordant on this subject of beauty. Appearance has always been an important element in the way foods are received. Sugar, for example, was immediately popular in Europe in part because its pure, off-white crystals convinced people it was healthy. But in the case of the pineapple, it is a less easy reaction to comprehend. It is certainly no conventional beauty, and while the supposedly idyllic context in which it was first discovered helped its cause, the reaction its physical appearance elicited was far beyond that of any other foodstuff discovered in similar circumstances. How is this to be explained?

It is possible that it is here that the Divine Proportions of the pineapple – in Oviedo's words, its 'composition' – come into play. For centuries, philosophers have considered beauty to be all about proportion: to Aristotle, it was to be found in 'order and symmetry and definiteness', while St Augustine was convinced that the secret lay in geometric form and balance.[25] Whether a human, an insect or a plant, the theory goes that the source of beauty is the same, regardless. This is perhaps because, to the human eye, such qualities are an indicator of overall fitness – fitness to mate with, to eat or to plant.[26] Since few other foodstuffs boast Divine Proportions so visibly (while bananas have three sections and apples have five sections, both numbers in the Fibonacci series, this is only apparent once you cut them open), the pineapple already had a head-start.

In theory then, the pineapple's makeup is such that, to the human eye, its beauty is a given, a given that early explorers were powerless to resist, for it was hard-wired into their brain. In a sense they had been pre-programmed to collude with the pineapple. It is a hypothesis that suggests the existence of objective, rather than simply subjective, beauty. The twentieth-century architect Le Corbusier called it 'the axis which lies in man' – in other words, a universal code of beauty which resonates with our inner being. It is possible, therefore, that the way the pineapple actually tasted was a secondary consideration to the way it looked.

Such a conclusion belies the much more widely accepted hypothesis that beauty is subjective: it means different things to different people, rather than just being a function of mathematics. There may have been other explorers who did not perceive the pineapple to be beautiful in the slightest, but simply chose not to mention the fact. In the meantime, however, the likes of Oviedo are also to be blamed – caught up in the whirlwind of wonder that surrounded tales of the New World, they essentially wrote to sell copies and please their readership.

Clearly, that the pineapple was discovered in the context of the New World was much in its favour. The possibility that this might be Eden made real intoxicated explorers of the age. Rui Pereira wrote that, 'if there is a paradise on earth, I would say it exists presently in Brazil',[27] while Joseph de Acosta was convinced that if Europeans could only manage to conquer their financial greed, they too 'could no doubt live very well and happily in the Indies, for what poets sing of the Elysian Fields . . . or Plato recounts, or avers, of his Isle of Atlantis, men could in fact find in these lands'.[28] With all its fruits the fruits of Eden, no wonder they sought to embrace any element of the New World available to them.

Even though medical commentary is supposed to be scientific in its inspiration, the earliest analyses of the pineapple's qualities were in reality inevitably framed within a European cultural context. Nicholas Monardes believed that it was 'good for the Stomacke and likewise of the harte, and restore[s] the appetite lost': conceptualised here as a restorative, it is seen to be a means of recovering a 'paradisial' state of health.[29] Just as the New World was often characterised as a new Eden, so the pineapple played a part in this Christian myth: Eden is here translated into physical terms, with the pineapple at its centre. An antidote to the first apple, it is a means of curing the sick, fallen 'harte' of Mankind. Christopher de Rochefort echoed this assessment of its potency, developing associations of renewal: 'The juice does admirably recreate and exhilarate the Spirits . . . it gives present ease to such as are troubled with the Stone, or stoppage of Urine; nay it destroys the force of Poyson', the latter (apparent) effect suggesting the fruit's near-miraculous qualities.[30]

Within contemporary art and sculpture, the pineapple also slotted neatly into the prevailing European vision of Paradise. The Dutch artist Frans Post was not only the first artist of the Old World to paint the New World, but also the first to illustrate the pineapple within its natural setting. He features it far more than any other fruit, depicting it in no less than eight of his paintings of the Brazilian landscape.[31] I came across one of these in the Musea de Arte in São Paulo in Brazil (colour plate 1). Post positions a conspicuous bright yellow pineapple in the foreground of his enticingly exotic composition, alone but for luscious palm trees and verdant bushes. For a moment I thought that the museum had somehow misaligned the room's spotlight, but I soon realised that it was just the way the pineapple has been painted – it shines out of the darkness, with the result that the eye is drawn inexorably towards it. The pineapple has become a kind of shorthand: 'Paradise this way!'[32]

Evidently, the pineapple largely managed to avoid any associations with the more unsavoury elements of the New World. It had been discovered in a world where cannibalism was supposedly the norm, with one of its major functions the intoxication of the natives in preparation for them to indulge in dark, almost demonic rituals. But Europe chose to reject this aspect – wanting it to be precious treasure, this is precisely what it became.

The speed with which the pineapple scattered itself outside Europe in the course of the sixteenth century is truly remarkable. Little more than 100 years after being discovered by Europeans, it was being grown – and eaten – in tropical areas throughout the world, to such an extent that many believed it to be native to places like India. What was it that captured the hearts and minds of so many gentlemen explorers?

The pineapple rarely had a problem securing a place aboard a ship, partly because it was a useful antidote to scurvy but also because its high acid content meant that it could be used to scrub the deck. However, ships were slow and small and it is still impressive that the pineapple managed to stow away so successfully. While the fruit is short-lived, the plant itself is relatively hardy, able to live for many months even on board a ship. Because of its resistance to drought and tolerance of desiccation, it simply bides its time until conditions are right: 'without any trouble to the agriculturist it grows and sustains itself' was Oviedo's verdict.[33]

The pineapple was therefore able to take advantage of the fact that this was an era in which Europe was all but fixated on the prospect of global colonisation. Whether the purpose was trade, exploitation or the spread of Christianity, in the sixteenth and seventeenth centuries ships set sail day after day in search of unfamiliar lands. The English and the Spanish were among the most high-profile adventurers, but by far the most common sight at sea was the flag of the Portuguese.

The Portuguese were the most successful explorers of the age in terms of the complexity and variety of the conquests they made. Among the firsts they may claim are the opening to Europeans of the south-east passage around the Cape of Good Hope, the first voyage by sea from Europe to India, the first European trade mission by sea to China and the first European landing in Japan. No Europeans before them had set foot on Madeira, the Azores, Cape Verdes, St Helena, Nova Scotia, New Guinea or Korea; there is also evidence that they were the first outsiders to land in Australia, two and a half centuries before Captain Cook was to snatch this honour. The pineapple went along on many of these adventures. Its dependence on the Portuguese in part explains why it took so long to penetrate North America – one area of the globe that had thus far failed to capture their imagination.[34]

In the course of the sixteenth and seventeenth centuries, the Portuguese were responsible for introducing and diffusing the pineapple along the west and east coasts of Africa. Most of the native languages of Africa still know the fruit as *ananaz*, *nanasi*, *manasi* or some other derivation of the Portuguese word that had in turn been inherited from the Tupí-Guaranís. By 1602, it was commonly cultivated in Guinea – in Michael Hemmersam's account of a trip he later made to the coastal areas of the country, he tells how 'the Moors consume quantities of ananas, as they call this fruit, which is like an

artichoke; they also cook it, mixing it with palm oil which they use for
all their food in the place of fat; it belongs to the best fruit of this
country'.[35] In 1653 pineapples were planted by the Dutch at the Cape
of Good Hope,[36] while the following year some were spotted in
Madagascar.[37]

The Portuguese also introduced them to enclaves on the west coast
of India. In 1596 Jan Huygen Van Linschoten described them as 'one
of the best fruites, and of the best taste in all India . . . at the first it was
sold for a noveltie, at a Pardaw a piece, and sometimes more, but now
there are so many groweth in the country, that they are very good
cheape'.[38] The Indian climate really suits the pineapple and the
Mughal Emperor Jahangir related in his memoirs how, by the 1610s,
several thousand specimens of the 'extremely good-smelling and
tasting' fruit were grown every year in the gardens of the palace at
Agra;[39] while in Goa a few years later, the traveller Peter Mundy was
adamant that the pineapple 'deserves the first rank for its excellent
refreshing taste and smell, senting and tasting (but far transcending)
the daintiest melon apple with us'.[40] Most commonly consumed in its

7. *Farming Large Pineapples in China*, 1690.

fresh form, it was also fermented to make wine 'like our cider, but better, being stronger and more exhilarating' while its leaf fibre was used to make clothes 'which in fineness equal Silks'.[41] Since today it is one of the nation's most commonplace fruits, it is amazing to learn what a relative newcomer it is.

It was not long before the pineapple was under cultivation in China. By 1656 it was so common in the country's southern provinces that the Polish Jesuit priest Michael Boym mistakenly included it in his *Flora Sinensis*, the first Western work ever published on Chinese plants, in the section on native plants.[42] The following year, a clerk for the Dutch East India Company named John Nieuhof who was on a trade mission to see the Emperor of China in Peking was also impressed by it.[43] He was not the only one: according to the German Jesuit scholar Father Athanasius Kircher in 1667, 'it has such an excellent taste that the nobility of China and India prefer it to anything else'.[44]

All such triumphs lead to the conclusion that the evolution of the pineapple was an uncompromising success. By enticing first the tribes of South America, followed by European explorers, to transport it far beyond the Amazonian interior, this seemingly parochial plant managed to proliferate its genes far and wide. Its next major challenge, however, was to penetrate England – a country that, in the aftermath of the Civil War, already had rather a lot on its plate, so to speak. As a result, the pineapple had to exploit every trick available to it in order to make itself known.

3

'Let him try if any Words can give him the taste of a Pine-Apple'

John Locke (1689)

No one knows for certain the identity of the first person to bring a pineapple into England. The only surviving evidence is an entry in the diary of the writer, horticulturist and friend of Charles II, John Evelyn, on 9 August 1661: '. . . the first [pineapples] that were ever seene here in England were those sent to Cromwell, foure-yeares since'.[1] Under whose aegis, however, is very much up for discussion. A wide range of candidates has been proposed in the past – among them Admiral William Penn, Sir Joseph Jordan, Sir Robert Blake, Richard Ligon and the Dutch ambassador. But none of the dates when these men returned to England from overseas fits the date that Evelyn ascribes to the event (the accuracy of which there is no reason to doubt).* Instead, I have discovered a much more likely candidate. His name is William Goodson.

---

*Admiral Sir William Penn returned from the West Indies in August 1655 and was then imprisoned in the Tower of London until he moved to Ireland in 1659. Sir Joseph Jordan returned from the West Indies in 1655. Sir Robert Blake spent 1657 in the seas around Tenerife where pineapples did not yet grow. Richard Ligon was back from Barbados for good by 1650. The Dutch trade mission to China in 1655–7 about which John Nieuhoff wrote is one other contender. Nieuhof returned to Java in March 1657 and it is possible that from there he very speedily shipped a pineapple plant to the Netherlands in order for it to be presented to the King of England by the Dutch ambassador. That the first

William Goodson was a staunch Puritan originally from Yarmouth. He lived in Cartagena in Spain for a while, possibly as a prisoner, but in 1652 joined the Navy. Two years later he was appointed Vice-Admiral of a fleet about to leave for the West Indies under the command of Admiral William Penn on a mission to capture Hispaniola from the Spanish. It was a disaster. Two attempts were made on the capital, San Domingo, both of which failed dismally. Disease, combined with enemy attack, killed over 1,000 men. As a consolation prize, Jamaica was seized instead. Following Penn's shame-faced departure to England to seek Cromwell's forgiveness for his bungling, Goodson stayed behind to act as Commander-in-Chief of sea forces in Jamaica. He made a success of the remaining two years he spent there, plundering Spanish ships and keeping the population under some semblance of control.[2]

On 26 April 1657, Goodson docked back in London, presumably with considerable trepidation.[3] Penn and his side-kick Venables had both been unceremoniously imprisoned in the Tower of London immediately upon their return. Was Goodson to receive the same treatment? Apart from the Hispaniola débâcle, he had acquitted himself admirably during his stay of service, but it paid to be cautious. Despite his Puritan beliefs, he needed to do all he could to ingratiate himself with the Lord Protector, particularly as it was only a couple of months until Cromwell's Second Investiture. A locally produced present might also convince Cromwell of Jamaica's importance to the nation: at the time, the colony was desperately in need of supplies.

Taken together, it makes sense that Goodson may have made some attempt to bring a pineapple back with him, as far and away the most lauded fruit of the New World. Those trade ships that returned in 1657 may be all but discounted – their captains had

pineapple to be seen in England had come all the way from China is an intriguing proposition – but it is a little far-fetched and there is no further evidence to support it. In addition, the Leiden Hortus would surely have made every possible effort to keep such a rare specimen in the Netherlands.

little use for a pineapple at this stage, its value still symbolic rather than economic. Instead, its chosen vessel was almost certainly a ship of political consequence and Goodson's was one of only a small number of these to return from the West Indies that year. He was also the sole person with a really convincing reason to bother to nurture a pineapple on the long voyage home.[4] In the end, not only did Goodson manage to avoid a stint in the Tower, but a couple of months after his return he was recommended for a payment of £350 'as a gratuity for his extraordinary service and expense', according to the State Papers.[5] Did the pineapple help his cause? I think so.

Just as the background to Cromwell's first encounter with the pineapple is unclear, so his ensuing reaction is murky, and forces speculation. There are many reasons why the pineapple might appeal to Cromwell. Foremost amongst these was the fact that it originated in Jamaica: this demonstrated on a practical level the potential for trade. With impressive foresight, the Elizabethan adventurer Carew Reynell had cast Jamaica as the key to the West Indies because of its position 'lying in the very Belly of all Commerce'.[6] The pineapple was inextricably associated with its origins in the emerging empire that constituted Cromwell's so-called Western Design, a plan intended not only to expand England's power overseas but moreover to spread the (Puritan) word of God.[7] In July 1654 Cromwell publicly argued in favour of exporting the revolution he had helmed – 'because we thinke God has not brought us hither where wee are but to consider the worke that wee may doe in the world as well as at home'.[8] The pineapple was a highly charged visual symbol of the myriad benefits that the Western Design could bring.

Furthermore, on a personal level Cromwell evidently appreciated the pleasures of imports. Never had the court kitchen seen such uproar as when, in 1655, Lady Cromwell responded to the rising prices of quality oranges and lemons due to the raging war with Spain by instructing the cook no longer to prepare the Protector's favourite dish of loin of veal with orange sauce. When Cromwell protested, he was informed in no uncertain terms that he should have thought of that before causing such upheaval.[9]

On the other hand, Cromwell, the archetypal Puritan, was a man of simple tastes. Of his diet, one contemporary observed that it was 'spare not curious . . . at his private table very rarely, or never, were our French quelque choses suffered by him, or any such modern gustos'.[10] The pineapple must have seemed an insufferable luxury compared to, say, the humble pear. This, however, was of minor importance next to the other reasons why Cromwell and the pineapple could never be dinner companions.

First of all, it had Catholic overtones. It had been introduced to Europe by a crew from Spain, England's long-standing enemy in part due to its continuing loyalty to the Pope. Catholicism was based on a hierarchical and opulent culture of symbols and signs, into which the pineapple slotted very neatly. Puritanism, conversely, vehemently rejected all such supposed distractions from the word of God. While William Goodson clearly managed to overcome any such reservations, what the pineapple represented was the anathema of many of the ideals that Cromwell had fought for so passionately during nine long years of Civil War.

Even more damning was the fact that by the middle of the seventeenth century the pineapple had acquired an inescapable air of kingliness. The French priest Father Du Tertre seems to have been the first to call it 'the king of fruits', but his contemporaries and near-contemporaries concurred without exception.[11] The way it looked was perceived to be a sign that it was put on this earth to rule: 'that which gives it far greater lustre, and acquir'd it the supremacy among Fruit is, that it is crown'd with a great Posie', observed Christopher De Rochefort in a clear echo of the doctrine of the Divine Right of Kings.[12] For many years, royalty remained its most potent association and it is impossible to overstate just how important this fact was. In a society unquestioningly governed by the dictates of religion, it bestowed upon it the sense that this was a fruit chosen by God – not only thanks to the crown that it bore so proudly, but also to the chroniclers who pounced upon this feature to promote their own agenda with regards to the New World.*

Cast in this guise, what is also revealed is a propensity to anthropomorphise the fruit. More than any comparable foodstuff, it has always been approached in such a fashion. Yet while the King of Fruits was its most common moniker, some disputed this assignment of gender. Thus in 1596 Sir Walter Raleigh described one seen in Guinea as 'the princesse of fruits' – a term explained, perhaps, by the fact that pleasing the Virgin Princess (Elizabeth I) was the overriding aim of most of his utterances.[13]

The widespread dissemination of such accounts amongst England's ruling class meant that it is likely that it was the pineapple's incarnation as 'the king of fruits', more than the fruit itself, that guided Cromwell's reaction. In a country that remained deeply divided over the issue of governance, the pineapple was like a grenade – nothing could have been constructed to annoy him more. The only aspect of it he might have been able to enjoy was divesting it of its crown. For by rejecting the pineapple, he was making a powerful statement to the court. The Divine Right of Kings? Phooey. On 8 May, just a few days after he was presented with the pineapple, Cromwell finally refused the Crown of England, which was still being urged upon him, in favour of a more humble title – Lord Protector.

Elsewhere the pineapple had received an almost universally ecstatic reception; yet the way it was entirely ignored by Cromwellian chroniclers and not heard of again even once during the Protectorate suggests that at this crucial juncture, for all the reasons discussed, its

---

*This found its most potent expression amongst writers on the Continent – unsurprisingly in view of the absolutist monarchies that still reigned there. According to the French physician Pierre Pomet, 'It was thought a just Appellation . . . to call the Ananas the King of Fruits, because it is much the finest and best of all that are upon the Face of the Earth. It is for this Reason that the King of Kings has plac'd a Crown upon the Head of it, which is as an essential Mark of its Royalty; and at the Fall of the Father, it produces a young King, that succeeds in all his admirable Qualities . . .' Pierre Pomet, *A Compleat History of Drugs, Written in French by Monsieur Pomet from Messrs. Lemery and Tournefort* (1712) VII. 152. In evidence here is an overtly political comment in favour of the concept of the Divine Right of Kings.

charms failed it. Timing is all and, in this, the pineapple had undoubtedly got it wrong.

Fortunately, the fruit had already acquired enough of a reputation elsewhere to ensure that this was by no means the last to be heard of it. While word of mouth was undoubtedly important, numerous written accounts of the New World by early explorers also found their way across the Channel. Descriptions of the pineapple by Peter Martyr, Oviedo, de Léry and others were widely disseminated among a readership hungry for news of the New World.

Perceptions were further consolidated with every new work that appeared. In one example among many, John Parkinson wrote breathlessly in his widely read work *Theatrum Botanicum* (1640) of 'the Pines so much esteemed for the most excellent and pleasant sweete fruite in all the West Indies is the fruite of a kinde of Thistle . . . tasting like as if Wine, Rosewater and Sugar were mixed together . . . . This Pina as I said surpasseth all other fruites of the West Indies, for pleasantness and wholesomeness.'[14] It was becoming standard practice to qualify even a passing reference to the fruit with some obsequious adjective or other – 'most delicate' (Captain John Smith, 1624), 'delicious' (Edmund Waller, 1645) and so on.[15]

In 1657, the same year that the pineapple was offered up to Cromwell, Richard Ligon's *True and Exact History of Barbados* was published in which he provides one of the earliest extensive accounts of the pineapple to be written in English. Ligon had lived in the West Indies for three years, but wrote his book back in London incarcerated in the Upper Bench Prison, he claims due to the debt of another – a decidedly hellish environment in which to write about such a heavenly place.[16] The book gives an enthralling description of the state of Barbados in its earliest incarnation as a colony, at a time when it was flourishing and its only worry, revealed in the State Papers, appears to have been a chronic shortage of shoes and boots, for which application after application was granted to export out more and more pairs.

Ligon's account was to influence many writers to come, not least in its perpetuation of the pineapple as the acme of all fruit.

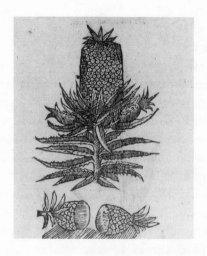

8. From *Theatrum Botanicum* by John Parkinson, 1640.

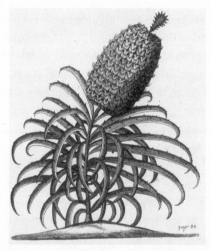

9. From *A True and Exact History of Barbados* by Richard Ligon, 1653.

I must name the Pine, for in that single name, all that is excellent in a superlative degree, for beauty and taste, is summarily included . . . when it comes to be eaten, nothing of rare taste can be thought on that is not there; nor is it imaginable, that so full a Harmony of tastes can be raised, out of so many parts, and all distinguishable.[17]

KING OF FRUITS 41

This is strikingly reverential language to use about what is, lest we forget, only a fruit. Also noteworthy, however, is the way that the passage swiftly takes a darker turn.

Following a lengthy description of the pineapple's appearance in the kind of language more commonly used about a beautiful woman, he then compares the sensation of penetrating its flesh to being 'like a Thiefe, that breaks a beautifull Cabinet, which he would forbear to do, but for the treasure he expects to find within'. In the (physical and conceptual) appropriation of the pineapple, Europeans were indeed like 'a Thiefe', taking and reshaping something other than their own. Ligon acknowledges the sense of guilt that this engenders, but implies that this is easily overridden by the profound pleasure he gets from the appropriation of this 'treasure', almost because of, rather than in spite of, the illicitness. For while in economic terms the pineapple may not have represented the 'treasure' that many had hoped the New World might yield, its golden riches offered other symbolic rewards.

Ligon's writing reveals a real and present thread of violence in his attitude towards the pineapple. Similarly, in 1666 the Dutch writer Christopher De Rochefort echoed Ligon's metaphor of the pineapple as a valuable cache: 'It is so delightful to the eyes, and of so sweet a scent, that Nature may be said to have been extremely prodigal of what was most rare and precious in her Treasury to this Plant.'[18] While associating the pineapple with the wealth of Nature certainly served to boost its cause, much of the source of his delight in eating the fruit seems to arise from the penetration of the female's 'Treasury'.

The presence of the pineapple in the poem 'Bermudas' (1653) by Andrew Marvell not only sealed the fruit's position within English cultural mythology, but also revealed a further level of complexity to the way writers were responding to this emotive fruit. Marvell never visited Bermuda, but based the poem on first-hand accounts gleaned from books and friends (it was composed while he was living with the Reverend John Oxenbridge, one of the commissioners responsible for the colony): these he cheerfully refashioned to form one of the earliest conscious reflections on the implications of what had been found in the New World. Marvell was, however, a deeply conflicted individual – an introspective writer who sought a career in public life, a civil servant for Oliver Cromwell who later became a flatterer of Charles II, a Puritan who loved all things sensuous. No wonder, then, that the poem itself is conflicted too.[19]

Marvell's interpretation of the island of Bermuda, a British colony since 1609, sees proof that the New World really is the paradise it is said to be in the form of the fruits nurtured in its soil. At the pinnacle is the pineapple (referred to here as the 'apple'):

> . . . He hangs in shades the orange bright,
> Like golden lamps in a green night,
> And does in the pom'granates close
> Jewels more rich than Ormus shows.
> He makes the figs our mouths to meet,
> And throws the melons at our feet,
> But apple plants of such a price,
> No tree could ever bear them twice . . .[20]

A vibrant evocation of the breathless excitement that surrounded the West Indies in this period, Bermuda is portrayed as the New Eden, created for Man by God with His bounty on display for all to see.

However, the poem also suggests a darker vision of the colony and, by association, of the pineapple. While the island's 'grassy Stage' and 'golden lamps' intimate a certain theatricality to be distrusted, the economic cost of the fruits is also emphasised with pomegranates 'jewels' and pineapples 'of such a price'. The long list of sensuous delights highlights the sinful indulgence it seems to encourage. In this way, just as the poem mythologises the New World, it also presents it realistically as a project with decidedly impious financial overtones – for there were indeed a variety of sinister interests behind its colonisation.

Marvell's Puritan instincts lead him to suggest that this is not the only reason to be cautious. Eden was where the Fall of Man occurred

– with the 'apple' its cause, it indeed had a huge 'price' for mankind. The pineapple is cast in the guise of temptation – a 'jewel' to be grabbed, but only in the knowledge that the consequences are potentially disastrous.

Such Puritan sentiments inform a further dimension of Marvell's thinking, too. The word *tree* in this period was often used to denote Jesus's Cross. With this in mind, the line 'No tree could ever bear them twice' becomes a crucial one. While on a literal level it is true that each pineapple plant gives up its own life to produce a single fruit, in this context it is a sacrifice that also recalls the one that Jesus made for Man when he died for his sins. Thus Marvell attempts to contextualise the pineapple within the canon of Christian mythology from which, until now, it had mostly been excluded.

Others in this period also referred to the pineapple as 'apple'. What to call it was an enduring source of confusion. Contenders included 'apple', 'ananas', 'pine' and, finally, 'pineapple', all further complicated by a multitude of creative spelling decisions. The source of the muddle may be traced back to the Middle Ages. The earliest known form of the word 'pineapple' is 'pynappel', a term originally used to denote what is today called a pinecone. The first written use of the word according to the *Oxford English Dictionary* was in 1398 in John Trevisa's translation of Bartholomew de Glanville's *De Proprietatibus Rerum*: 'Pynea, the pynappel, is the fruyt of the pyne tree . . . The pyneappel is most grete notte and conteyneth in itself in stede of fruyt many curnelles yclosed in ful harde schales.'[21] The term was also applied to the edible seeds of the pinecone, known as pine nuts.

With the arrival of the pineapple, however, both in effect had their name stolen from them, rudely forced to go in search of another. Almost every European language used some derivation of *ananas*, but the English took their lead from the rather contrary decision by the Spanish to call it *piña*. By bestowing upon it the name of an already familiar plant, they displayed their mistrust of the exotic, accompanied by a consequent need to reshape its meaning to fit their own setting. It was a typically colonial reaction. In addition, the 'apple' in 'pineapple' associated a markedly foreign commodity with the most quintessentially English of fruits. That not even a feeble attempt was made to dig up a new name (they managed it in the case of the tomato or the pumpkin, after all) is depressingly revealing of the reluctance of the English not only to expand the limits of their language but also, by inference, the limits of their mental world, despite the fact that, in geographical terms, their world was expanding at a faster rate than ever before.

The linguistic anomaly continues to cause confusion now that the original meaning of the word 'pineapple' has been lost to history. In September 2003 *The Times* excitedly reported the discovery that at a banquet thrown in 1560 at Longleat House by Robert Dudley, Earl of Leicester, Elizabeth I had been served pineapples, along with a feast of ten sheep, six herons and forty-one dozen loaves of bread.[22] Yes, Dudley was trying to impress the Queen, but he was no miracle-worker. The use of the word at this date refers to pine nuts, not pineapples.

It is not only in the medium of text that pine nuts, pinecones and pineapples came to be conflated. Since the latter two do not look dissimilar, especially as architectural decorations, hardly a Bank Holiday weekend goes by without a friend ringing me up to squeal about a sighting atop the gates of some stately home or other. More often than not, it turns out to be a pinecone. The way to tell it is a pineapple is to look for a crown of spikes coming out the top or a rosette of leaves around the bottom. Do not be fooled by just an oval shape with criss-crosses: it is almost certainly an impostor.

Not only the name but also the supposed attributes of the pinecone were transferred to the pineapple. The pinecone, a plant indigenous to Britain, has long been a traditional symbol of fertility, resurrection and immortality. Such depictions can be found in the Far East, in Assyrian art, in Roman architecture, in the Egyptian Isis cult and in the Greek Dionysius cult, while Christianity portrays the pine tree as the tree of life. Since it was often assumed that the pinecone and the pineapple were somehow related, this symbolism was gradually inherited by the pineapple. Yet still very few people had actually set eyes on a real one. Fortunately, it was soon to get another shot at stardom.

It was 9 August 1661 and John Evelyn had just returned home from a busy day typical of one of the founding members of the Royal Society: in the morning he indulged in some casual experiments with plants, while dinner was spent with a Mr Palmer of Gray's Inn who had recently invented a new type of clock that played a tune on its bells every hour. Tired though he was, he had promised himself that he would write in his diary. Settling down at his desk in the library of his house, Sayes Court in Deptford, having finally found a candlestick with enough wax left to provide light for his musings, he proceeded to scribble: 'I first saw the famous Queene-pine brought from Barbados presented to his Majestie.'[23] The prosaic style in which he reports this thrilling news is typical of Evelyn's carefully measured approach.

It was no coincidence that the King was presented with a pineapple from Barbados in the summer of 1661, a period when issues of huge significance to the future of the colony, by far the richest in English America, were the topic of prolonged discussion within the Privy Council. Again there is no record of the source of the fruit, but it is probable that it was intended to accompany a petition: the gesture was made four days after the Privy Council first discussed one petition submitted by a consortium of those with an interest in Barbados (planters, merchants and so on) asking Charles II to impose a minimum price on the sale of sugar.[24] If granted, this would incalculably boost the future economic prospects of English colonies overseas, the basis of much of the nation's power and influence at the time.

Petitions were a vital feature of Charles II's reign. For the merchants (among others) of the realm, they were a privilege that represented the sole means of direct access to the King through which they might transmit their concerns. Prevailing economic wisdom, as well as a desire to ensure their loyalty, greatly encouraged such a channel. While the well-connected were able to present petitions direct to the King themselves, most had to do it via the Privy Council or the Master of Request.[25] The deluge that ensued – one (conservative) estimate is that between 1661 and 1670, over 10,000 people submitted one – meant that it was imperative to find a way to get yours noticed.[26]

As a result, petitions were often accompanied by a lavish gift: one time, the East India Company offered up 10,000 ounces of silver plate, the result of which, not surprisingly, was a fair few royal decisions in its favour.[27] While a pineapple was by no means so financially impressive, it was a playful but powerful visual reminder of the importance of trade in the New World. Rarely had the politics of display been more blatant.

The petition submitted by the Barbados consortium was first discussed in the Privy Council on 5 August. On 9 August, a pineapple – the perfect symbol with which to make the case – was presented to the King. After further debate on 12 August, then again on 19 August, it was decided that the King would write to the petitioners 'expressing his Majesty's care of them, and putting them in mind to revise the laws for making sugars; also acquainting them with the overtures made by the merchants and trades here to take said sugars off their hands at such rates as may probably make the planter comfortably subsist and encourage the merchant to trade with them . . .'[28] Whoever the genius was who thought to present a pineapple to the King, it may well have helped the planters successfully achieve the outcome they had been lobbying for.

Annoyingly for Evelyn, seven years were to pass before he had a chance to taste the fruit. On 10 August 1668 it made another appearance at court. The only source for this is again an entry in Evelyn's diary.

Standing by his Majestie at dinner in the Presence, There was of that rare fruite called the King-Pine, (growing in Barbados & W. Indies), the first of them I had ever seen; His Majestie having cut it up, was pleased to give me a piece off his owne plate to tast of, but in my opinion it falls short of those ravishing varieties of deliciousnesse, describ'd in Cap: Liggons history & others; but possibly it might be, (& certainly was) much impaired in coming so farr: It had yet a gratefull acidity, but tasts more of the Quince and Melon, than of any other fruite he mentions.[29]

That the fruit described here had been grown by the King's gardener at St James's Palace, John Rose, is, sadly, another myth. At the time, Rose and Evelyn were in frequent contact: just two years earlier, Evelyn had written the preface to Rose's first book, *The English Vineyard Vindicated* (1666).[30] If Rose had grown it, Evelyn would without question have mentioned his achievement. In addition, the necessary technology simply did not exist. Instead, the provenance of this pineapple was again probably Barbados.[31]

What is interesting in this passage is the admission that Evelyn had already been guided in his response to the pineapple by reading Ligon's ('Liggons') version. When the text was confronted by the reality, the result was a discernible sense of disappointment. However, this may have a subtext. Whilst Evelyn was a royalist and a close confidant of Charles II, he also harboured many criticisms of the way the king conducted himself. Charles was the most indulgent King that England had seen in recent times, lavishing cash with abandon on his mistresses, his friends, even his horses. With the demands of the kingdom rarely his first priority, he frequently failed to live up to the expectations of Evelyn and others, an assessment echoed in Evelyn's assessment of the pineapple: they both 'fall[s] short' of their reputation. He was not the first or the last to conflate the two.

Evelyn's reaction, however, was all but irrelevant in comparison to that of the pineapple's intended recipient: Charles II. Since it was he who had the power to make or break it, it was fortunate that the two were an ideal match. The incendiary weapon that was the pineapple's crown was first in its arsenal to seduce the King. Following the tumult experienced by the institution of monarchy over the past twenty-five years, this was one piece of visual symbolism that Charles was whole-heartedly ready to embrace. Furthermore, here was a man with a passion for all things exotic, indulgent or somehow debauched (the contrast with Cromwell could not have been more pronounced). Not surprisingly, Charles II plucked the pineapple from the pages of books once and for all.

The dinner at which this happened was held in the Banqueting Hall in the Palace of Whitehall in honour of the French ambassador

Charles Colbert, Marquis de Croissy. The Restoration saw the revival of royal dining in the high public style – spectators were allowed to watch and marvel at power in action, a tactic that the absolutist courts of Europe had employed for some time. Service was *à la française*, the table laden with dishes, a fashion that had trickled over from France in the 1650s but one that, with the French ambassador himself present, put the kitchen under real pressure to perform. Based upon principles of order and balance, the meal culminated in the dessert course: an elaborate tableau of sugar sculptures, sorbets, ice-creams, cheeses and flowers, all arranged around a focal point most commonly made of fruit, balanced in a spectacular pyramid above a stemmed salver.

How better to impress the ambassador than with a fruit so rare, so novel, that Colbert would have no choice but to report to his master Louis XIV that this was a nation to be reckoned with? The pineapple's first specifically public outing in England was hijacked to provide a crucial public relations opportunity. The summer of 1668 saw tense negotiations between England and France over rights to the island of St Kitts and to this end, the pineapple functioned as an aggressive symbol of England's ascendancy in the West Indies.[32] The fact that Charles II had access to a fruit from so far away served to emphasise the strength of his position in the colonies – all the more so when he himself chose to 'cut it up'. In its role as a pawn between two bickering nations, ulterior motives infused the pineapple with a new power; a side-effect was that it was now a real talking point at court, in the coffee houses and even down the back stairs.

It was common knowledge at court that Evelyn was engaged in writing *Elysium Britannicum*, a monumental account of the nation's gardens and gardening practices. It is therefore no surprise that the King offered him, a close confidant, a taste of this unusual creation of Nature's. Written mostly in the early 1660s, the *Elysium* singled out the pineapple as a star of the horticultural world, 'reported by all that have tasted it, to resemble the gusto of whatsoever the most luxurious or distinguishing Epicure can summon to his wanton imagination'. The way the pineapple is 'reported' remains of paramount importance. Most of Evelyn's information is paraphrased from Richard Ligon's account, for example the assertion that 'It is so beautifull to the eye, so sweete of sent, that Nature seemes in favour of this fruite onely to have displaid whatsoever she had reserved for most rare and preciouse in all her Elysium.' But the more these hyperboles were repeated, the closer they came to being universally accepted.[33]

One additional crucial nugget of information in the *Elysium* has thus far gone unnoticed by historians. Scrawled in the margin of the manuscript of Evelyn's passage on pineapples is a tantalising comment in his own hand: 'his Majesty having had divers of these [pineapples] sent him over, & even ripening after they were here in his Garden at St James, we are not altogether to disparage propagating them'.[34] While it is impossible to put an accurate date on the comment, it is likely to have been added some time during the 1670s. This affirms that the pineapples mentioned by Evelyn in his diary were not the only ones to reach England in the 1660s; more importantly, however, it provides the first conclusive piece of evidence that attempts were made to ripen them in Charles II's garden.

One of the most unusual paintings of the Restoration era is often cited as further evidence for this. Some time before 1677, Charles II was painted being presented with a pineapple by the royal gardener, John Rose, in the grounds of an opulent stately home (colour plate III).[35] Though commonly attributed to the Dutch artist Hendrick Danckerts due to a tentative suggestion made by Horace Walpole in his *Description of Strawberry Hill* (1774), the house where the painting hung for some time, a letter he wrote in 1780 makes it clear that in fact he had no idea who was responsible for it.[36] While Danckerts was adept at landscapes, he was not a portrait painter, certainly not of the skill involved here. It is more likely to be by a painter of the English school of the 1670s, possibly John Michael Wright.[37]

The stately home featured in the painting is widely believed to be Dorney Court near Windsor. This has resulted in the claim that it was the location of the first pineapple grown in England: a carved stone pineapple is still displayed in the Great Hall of the house, while a pub

in the nearby village is named after the fruit.* However, it is again
Walpole who has led us astray: Dorney Court was a guess on his part
that he himself later contradicted, calling the house in the painting
merely 'a good private house, such as there are several at Sunbury and
about London'.[38] That it really does not look much like any of these
houses has not deterred people from presenting his guess as fact.
Others have suggested that it was in the Netherlands. It is, however,
much more likely to be simply a figment of the painter's imagination.

While the painting goes by the title *Mr Rose, the royal Gardener,
presenting to King Charles 2nd the first pineapple raised in England*, this
is almost certainly the final and most important misleading piece of
information. It all depends on how the term 'raised' is defined.

To propagate a pineapple in England – that is, to grow it from a
crown or suckers until a ripe fruit is produced – was undoubtedly
beyond the technology available. A pineapple needs a constant and
even air temperature of over 60°F, achieved without noxious fumes
from coal and the like, a constant and even soil temperature of not less
than 70°F, a plentiful supply of light and just the right amount of
water. Had this been achieved, it is unthinkable that it would have
gone unnoticed by the plethora of gardening writers around at the
time.

However, it is possible that by 'raised', what is really meant is
'ripened'. To raise a pineapple from an already-growing pineapple
plant – that is, just to ripen a fruit, a small withered fruit like the one
in the painting – was a feasible prospect. In the background of the
painting there are two pots that contain what look like young pineapple plants, while Evelyn's scribbled note in the *Elysium* manuscript
confirms that one had indeed been ripened at St James's in the past.
In my opinion, therefore, Rose may take the credit for being the first
to ripen a pineapple in England and it is this event that the painting

---

*It may have been the pineapple's mistaken association with Dorney Court that has led to
the story that Charles II's pet name for one of his most notorious mistresses, Barbara
Villiers, was 'my sweet pineapple': Villiers was wife of the owner of Dorney Court. If
true, this would have contributed to the sexual connotations of the fruit no end. However,
no proof for this story has been found.

commemorates.* Yet it tells us more than just the horticultural history. This is also a crucially important moment in the formation of the pineapple's public image. If the pineapple was good enough for Charles, it was certainly good enough for those who toiled beneath him. It was thereby established once and for all as a symbol of status.

The association also served Charles II well. While the fact that he is depicted in a private capacity, rather than in his king's robes, demonstrates that this was not intended to be an official portrait, it is still surprising, on the face of it, that he agreed to be immortalised alongside a fruit, of all things. Charles and his advisers, however, had their reasons. The image of the King with this piece of exotica is a powerful assertion of royal privilege. More specifically, it was a compelling physical statement of Charles II's commitment to the promotion of overseas trade. While the Dutch experience had demonstrated that there was a fortune to be made from trade, England had been slow to catch up until Charles II decided to address the matter. During his reign, the privileges of the older trading companies were confirmed and new companies established, and a series of Navigation Acts, passed from 1660 onwards, entirely reformulated the mercantile policies set out during the Protectorate. Because the pineapple was from the West Indies, its presence in the painting showed the value he placed on trade with the region. Although it had little economic value in comparison to sugar or tobacco, by dint of its origins it came under the same banner – it had been successfully transported from British dominions across the seas. Charles's motives were not entirely disinterested: that trade 'conduces more to a universal monarchy than either arms or territories' was also a factor,

---

*There has been speculation that the influential gardener John Tradescant the Younger attempted to grow pineapples as early as the 1640s. This is based on the discovery of the remains of pine pits in the foundations of Oatlands Palace in Weybridge, where he worked. However, these were in fact the remnants of later pineapple cultivation by the nurseryman Henry Scott in the 1750s. In any case, it was at this stage impossible to grow a pineapple in the cold and rainy climate of England. There is no doubt though that the pineapple is just the kind of curiosity that fascinated Tradescant: an inventory of 1656 of Tradescant's museum The Ark includes dried pineapple, for instance. See Mea Allan, *The Tradescants* (1964) 144 and Prudence Leith-Ross, *The John Tradescants* (1984) 193.

no doubt.[39]

An additional dimension is the way the artist seeks to depict his own interpretation of Eden in which the produce of Nature is seen as a work of art – a 'Cabinet', as Ligon put it. Evelyn's assertion in *Kalendarium Hortense* (1664) that we should try to make our gardens 'as near as we can contrive them' to resemble Eden was a commonplace one. Since fruit was the original food of mankind before the Fall, it was seen as one of the most crucial elements with which a garden might recapture the innocence of the human spirit.[40] The pineapple was one of the most potent visual expressions of this: in the frontispiece of John Parkinson's *Paradisi In Sole Paradisus Terrestris* (1649), a book about how to make your own garden resemble Paradise on earth, it is the most prominent of all the crops being gathered by Adam and Eve. It accordingly benefited Charles to associate himself thus – and, in fact, he had a genuine interest in gardening, spending long hours tending the palace gardens at Whitehall.

By the beginning of the 1670s, the pineapple had become a subject of such intense fascination among English men of letters that it is no wonder that one of its most notable written representations in this period comes in John Locke's enormously influential *Essay Concerning Human Understanding* (first drafted in 1671). Locke was fascinated by the idea of the New World. His library contained over 195 works of travel literature, including Jean de Léry's *History of a Voyage to the Land of Brazil*.[41] Just how significant a role did reverential reports of the pineapple, like de Léry's, play in the formation of Locke's philosophy of language, a philosophy that was to be a central tenet of Enlightenment thought?

> . . . let him try if any Words can give him the taste of a Pine-Apple, and make him have the true Idea of the Relish of that celebrated delicious Fruit. So far as he is told it has a resemblance with any Tastes, whereof he has the Ideas already in his Memory, imprinted there by sensible Objects not Strangers to his Palate, so far may he approach that resemblance in his Mind. But this is not giving us that Idea by a Definition, but exciting in us other simple Ideas, by their known Names; which will still be very different from the true taste of the Fruit it self.[42]

Because Locke had no first-hand experience of the pineapple, and neither did his readers, it illustrated his point perfectly. To Locke, taste was impossible truly to 'know' without direct sensory experience. The pineapple was the pre-eminent example of a fruit whose taste could never be understood without actually tasting it for oneself. Even then, taste was more about 'the Ideas already in his Memory' – that is, the associations it engenders. This helps to explain why so many rhapsodised about the taste – it was a metaphor for their passion for all that the New World represented, all of which was seen to be encapsulated within the shell of a pineapple. Locke did cling to the idea that such a thing as a 'true' taste exists – not everything is subjective. But he felt that elements of this 'true' taste had already been 'imprinted' by accounts of the pineapple that insistently compared it to, for example, all that is 'most delicate in the Peach, the Strawberry, the Muscadine-grape, and the Pippin'.[43] Forced to resort to inadequate comparisons in the attempt to be comprehended, a crisis of language is prompted. Words are simply not enough.*

While Locke was the first to spin a philosophical bent out of the pineapple, he was not the first to view it in this light. That it existed

---

*Though Locke's *Essay Concerning Human Understanding* was first published in its complete form in 1689, the point about the pineapple initially appears in 1671 in Draft B of the *Essay*: 'Those simple Ideas being to be conveyed to the minde noe other way but by the eyes them selves. Nor can all the words in the worlde which is very observable, produce in a mans minde one new simple Idea unless it be of the sound itself. For I demand whether after all the descriptions a traveller can give of the taste of that delicate fruit called a Pineapple a man who hath never had any of it in his mouth hath or can have any Idea of it or noe, or whether he thinkes he have, it be any new Idea but rather it be not some one old Idea or a composition of such severalle old Ideas which he is told hath some resemblance to the tast of a Pine apple which Ideas were before imprinted on his minde by other sensible objects.' Peter H. Nidditch and G. A. J. Rogers (eds), *Drafts for the 'Essay Concerning Human Understanding' and other philosophical writings* (1990) I. 170. The pineapple features in a similar context in a preparatory essay for the *Essay Concerning Human Understanding* entitled 'Pleasure, Pain, the Passions' (17 July 1676) in John Locke, *Political Essays by John Locke*, ed. Mark Goldie (1997) 242. It also appears in David Hume, *A Treatise of Human Nature* (1739): 'We cannot form to ourselves a just idea of the taste of a pine-apple, without actually having tasted it.' David Hume, *A Treatise of Human Nature*, ed. David Fate Norton and Mary J. Norton (2000) 9.

at the outermost limits of language was a common theme among those who had had first-hand experience of the fruit. When faced with its wonders, self-expression was often a problem: one lamented, '. . . and if it were here, to speak for it selfe, it would save me much labour, and do it selfe much right', while another sighed, '. . . I wish one of them in your hande with this paper, for nothing can express it but it selfe . . .'[44] Also in evidence here is the increasing anthropomorphisation of the fruit as it is extorted to 'speak for it self' and 'express . . . itself', among other expressions of frustration at its silence.

Yet for all that the pineapple featured in the most prestigious texts of the age, this was not enough. What use were words, even the most flattering of words, when what was really needed was for it to reproduce itself in all its glorious, golden reality? For the pineapple, the stakes were high. It had been an instant hit in the topics and subtropics, but northern Europe continued to elude it – for good reason. Delicate and unpredictable, it is entirely unsuited to the climate. It fulfils no essential dietary function. It is not addictive. In other words, it possesses few of the qualities that have tended to sustain other foodstuffs. Somehow the inhabitants of these nations had to be persuaded that the pineapple was indeed worth the effort. It was here that the escalating rivalry between the two most powerful nations of the age became an essential element of its story.

4

'I hope to see the Ananas flourish for the future in many
of our English Gardens, to the Honour of the Artist . . . the
greater Difficulties we have to encounter with, the greater
the Honour we gain by the Victory'

Richard Bradley (1721)

To attempt to grow a pineapple under England's cold, rainy skies is
clearly a preposterous project. But in about 1714, a Dutch gardener
named Henry Telende, with the support and investment of his
ambitious employer Sir Matthew Decker, succeeded in doing
precisely this in the grounds of the Deckers' opulent mansion in
Richmond in west London. Today there is not even a plaque on the
site to commemorate the achievement; and yet, to me, Telende is a
hero. At the beginning of the eighteenth century, to produce such a
curiosity from a sucker or crown, amid the prosaic realities of the
English garden, was a true manifestation of the wonders of Nature.
That Telende had managed this was thanks to years of investment of
time, money and even emotion. Most of all, it was the culmination of
a protracted and sometimes bitter tussle over the pineapple with
England's great rival, the Netherlands.

Human beings love a challenge, and to grow a pineapple in
northern Europe was certainly this. Even to get access to a crown or
sucker was a formidable task: because they had to be shipped all the
way from the West Indies, Africa or Asia, survival was a hit-and-miss

affair. If the plant did happen to survive the epic journey, it then had to be deluded into thinking it was in the tropics, even in the midst of the bitterest European winters when snow fell all around. It was only in the seventeenth century that the necessary technology to do this emerged. The race was on.

Europe's first greenhouses were designed to protect orange and lemon trees – as status symbols, the forerunners to the pineapple – from frost through the coldest months of the year. Based on designs developed by Louis XIV's brilliantly talented gardener, Jean de la Quintinie, these were unheated – made primarily of brick, the only wall constructed out of glass was on the side that faced south in order to capture the sun's warmth in winter. Since there was not much need for overhead light (during the winter the plants lay dormant, while in the summer they were moved outdoors), the roof tended to be made of wood. The pineapple, however, demanded heat and light *all* year round.

By 1650, most greenhouses were heated by freestanding iron stoves, fuelled first by coal then later by charcoal. But these were exceedingly unreliable: they prevented the plants from being destroyed by frost, only to poison them to death instead with the potent fumes they emitted. In *Kalendarium Hortense* (1664), John Evelyn proposed a radical new kind of stove that conducted heat into the greenhouse through pipes on the outside. This at least introduced some fresh air into the construction, but it seldom gave off uniform heat and was hard to control. It was also unable to provide sufficiently tropical temperatures. The fact that the first reliable thermometer was not invented until 1714 in any case made the regulation of heat a matter of guesswork on the part of the gardener. This combination of factors meant that the pineapple had little hope of finding a suitable environment in which to flourish. It might have been the end of the home-grown pineapple in northern Europe, but for one major factor.

'By God, I think the Devil shits Dutchmen,' exclaimed Sir William Batten while at dinner with Samuel Pepys in 1667.[1] Such deep-seated antipathy was not only a legacy of the three Anglo–Dutch wars of the second half of the seventeenth century, but was also rooted in fundamental differences over commerce, the colonies and shipping. As the two most powerful imperialist nations, there was a real conflict of interest, expressed most intensely in the East Indies, West Africa and the Caribbean. Yet, for the time being, the Netherlands was repeatedly coming out on top. The runaway success of Dutch merchants abroad meant that theirs was a sumptuous culture that flaunted the nation's newly acquired wealth at every possible opportunity, the garden included. It was a state of affairs of which the English disapproved, but which at the same time they desperately envied.[2]

The English and the Dutch had been engaged in a dialogue about matters of horticulture for some time. In 1611, John Tradescant the Elder had bought trees from a nurseryman in Delft, while John Parkinson recounted the plants that had reached England via Leiden. By the 1680s, horticultural enthusiasts such as William Gerard were regular visitors to the gardens of the Dutch aristocracy. The Bishop of London supplied the Amsterdam Hortus with rarities he had obtained from Virginia, while in 1682 Paul Hermann, the director of the Leiden Hortus, spent time in the gardens of the Oxford and Chelsea Physic Gardens (he brought back with him almost 200 living plants, including the first peach to be seen in Holland); a year later John Watts of the Chelsea Physic Garden made the return visit to Leiden.[3] Underlying this exchange of species, technology and ideas, however, was a rivalry that refused to dissipate.

Gardening was an ever more fashionable pastime of the English aristocracy: 'I doe believe I may modestly affirme that there is now, 1691, ten times as much gardening about London as there was Anno 1660.'[4] This was in part a reflection of contemporary political culture. In the period after the Civil War the bounty of Nature came to be viewed as in some way the reward of the English political system. If only a way could be found to grow the pineapple, the most exotic of all exotic fruits, surely this would serve to prove the fact once and for all?

Yet to the chagrin of the English, the Dutch aristocracy always seemed to remain one step ahead. Since the foundation of a botanical garden at Leiden in 1590, the nation had emerged as the undisputed master of gardening in Europe, spurred on by a new-found fascination with the wide range of new and unknown plants offered by returning Dutch ships that, with the decline of Portuguese power, dominated trade with the New World, as well as with West Africa and parts of Asia: by 1650, the Dutch had a merchant marine of over 2,000 vessels.[5] From ginger to chocolate and from nutmeg to coffee there was an eagerness to unlock not only the potentially very lucrative economic value of these exciting commodities, but the medicinal cures believed to be contained within them too.

As early as 1592, a Dutch doctor named Bernadus Paladanus attempted to cultivate pineapples in his garden in Enkhuizen: 'I have had some of the slips here in my garden that were brought mee out of Brasilia,' ran one of the annotations he supplied to his friend Jan Huygen Van Linschoten's book, 'but our cold country could not brooke them.'[6] Since the hothouse was a long way off, he was right to think that there was no way of maintaining a sufficiently high temperature. At least the project gave Paladanus something with which to occupy his mind: the previous year, he had been forced to decline a prestigious post at the University of Leiden to be curator of plants and herbs because, much to his frustration, his wife did not want to move away from her home town.[7]

For many years Dutch traders had shipped preserved pineapple back from the Dutch West Indies. But the pineapple only really found its nook in Europe some time between 1636 and 1641, when a pineapple plant featured for the first time in the catalogue of the Leiden Hortus.[8] The Leiden Hortus had by this time established itself as Europe's pre-eminent clearing house of plants from overseas and its influence was far-reaching. In 1652, just a few months after becoming the first European to land at the Cape of Good Hope in South Africa, Jan van Riebeeck put in a request for some pineapple plants to help boost the collection of the botanical garden he had established there.[9] It was rather a roundabout route for the pineapple – via the Netherlands in order to reach South Africa – but it worked. Pineapples soon spread well beyond the Cape peninsula to become a familiar feature of the markets of the African continent.

Keen to keep abreast of the competition in Leiden, the Amsterdam Hortus soon also had its own pineapple plants; and it was here that in 1680 a Dutch sea captain by the name of Tak attempted to cultivate some he had brought over from Surinam, at the time a Dutch colony.[10] While both Amsterdam and Leiden clearly managed to propagate pineapple plants even at this early stage, actually to ripen a fruit, let alone ripen fruits of quality and quantity, was proving to be an entirely different proposition.

Two separate developments were soon to make this possible.[11] In the past, the transportation of plants had not been viewed as a priority, despite the demand back home. But in 1675, William of Orange put in a request that he be honoured every year with 'all sorts of animals, birds, tissues, cabinets and other curiosities' from his new territories.[12] The result was a shift in policy by the Dutch trading companies, who were eager to comply, mindful of the potential favours to be gained from the Stadtholder in terms of customs and excise duties. The following year, the Governor of Malabar was instructed to employ botanists and draughtsmen to send serious quantities of plants back to Holland; the Governor of Ceylon received a similar request. The results mostly ended up at either the Leiden or the Amsterdam Hortus, to be experimented with for the purposes of trade, medicine or just pure and simple curiosity. In this way, plants found their way on to the national agenda.

Secondly, the latter part of the seventeenth century saw the invention of the hothouse. The world's first hothouses were the ones designed for the Amsterdam Hortus in 1682. Constructed out of glass, the larger one was eighty feet long and four and a half feet wide and rested against the garden's outer wall; the smaller one rested against the wall of the gardener's lodge and was thirty-six feet long and five feet wide. Heating was from below from ovens fed with peat, one for each ten to fifteen feet. An underground system of flues also led hot air through the hothouses. In architectural terms, they were eminently elegant creations.[13]

The Leiden Hortus built its own hothouse in 1685, while the few private gardens able to afford such an extravagance (Magdalena

Poulle's Gunterstein in Breukelen and William Bentinck's Zorgvliet near The Hague) swiftly acquired similar constructions. It was the catalyst that the pineapple needed. While the issue of soil temperature remained a conundrum, at least now the fruit was able to enjoy a relatively reliable, constant and non-noxious air temperature all year round.

Thus the race to grow pineapples intensified. With the help of specimens obtained from Leiden, Agnes Block had one in fruit by about 1685 at her estate, Vijverhof (colour plate IV). She is probably the first to have done so in the Netherlands (indeed, in all of Europe) and so proud was she of the achievement that she commissioned a silver medal to commemorate it. Its inscription reads 'Fert Arsque Laborque Quod Natura Negat' ('art and labour bring about what nature cannot'), a theme articulated in Jan van der Groen's *Den Nederlantsen Hovenier* (1669) and one that ran through much of the theoretical basis behind the Dutch passion for gardening: art functions to perfect nature, all to the glory of God, and it is Man's duty to assist in this. The pineapple was one of the most exalted expressions of this sentiment. In this way, the race to grow one in Europe was driven not only by a competitive instinct between individuals and between nations, but also by a competitive instinct with Nature itself.[14]

Around 1685, Casper Fagel, the Grand Pensionary of Holland and William of Orange's right-hand man, had some success with the pineapple at his estate De Leeuwenhorst in Noordwijkerhout.* There was no way that the Dutch botanist Jan Commelin was going to be left

---

*Fagel's was the most important private plant collection in the country. In 1684 it was visited by George London, Bishop Henry Compton's gardener, and the same year, Fagel obtained permission from the Dutch East India Company to send a representative to the Cape of Good Hope to collect plants. Whether this was the source of the pineapple plant he eventually fruited at De Leeuwenhorst, or whether it was Leiden, is not known. But by 1685 when William of Orange commissioned Stephanus Cousyns to draw the plants on Fagel's estate, pineapples were a major feature of the collection: they are prominently depicted in the frontispiece drawing of the house's terrace in the codex of Cousyns' work, *Hortus Regius Honselaerdicensis* (1688). Jacques and Arend Jan van der Horst, *The Gardens of William and Mary* (1988) 73.

behind. In 1686 he arranged to be sent pineapple plants from Surinam, with more arriving from Curaçao the following year. A few of Commelin's plants fruited in the Amsterdam Hortus, of which he was in charge, in around 1688–9. 'In winter this plant should be kept in a place that is warm enough to secure its continued growth; our glasshouses are perfectly suited for this,' Commelin boasted.[15] It is a testament to the pineapple that so many felt the urge to commemorate its successful subjugation, even when it was merely a one-off fluke. Possibly others were also successful in their efforts, but were a little more modest about their achievements.

Yet the man who really deserves our respect, for it was he who was the first to cultivate the pineapple on a grand scale in Europe, is a wealthy Dutch cloth merchant named Pieter de la Court, the son of the Dutch politician, economist and philosopher Pieter de la Court van der Voort.[16] One of the latter's most influential works was *The True Interest of Holland* (1662) in which he advocates not only the principle of free trade, but also, in a precursor to the writings of men

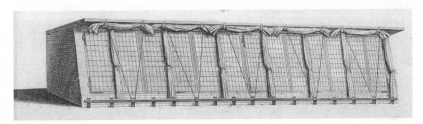

Fig.1: a long, low greenhouse

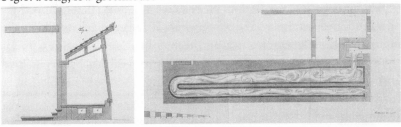

Fig 2: cross-section   Fig 3: the heating system

10. The first hothouses in Europe for pineapples, from *Byzondere Aaemerkingen* by Pieter de la Court, 1737.

like Adam Smith, the idea that the pursuit of pleasure is a prerequisite to the wealth of a nation. This soon found practical expression on the family estate Allemansgeest at Voorschoten, near Leiden, where his son oversaw the cultivation of many foreign fruits, including the pineapple, by his gardener, William de Vinck.

The one book published by the younger la Court, *Byzondere Aaemerkingen* (1737) bursts with details of how to cultivate his passion, the pineapple, plants of which he obtained from ships returning from the New World – probably Surinam or Curaçao.[17] Letters of thanks from the bishops of Mainz, Wurzburg and Munster show that he was so proud of these plants that he sent a few as presents.[18] He also sold some to the hordes who made the pilgrimage to his garden from all over Europe. Thirty years on, one horticultural writer had the chance to visit the scene of la Court's triumph: he enthused that he

> built Stoves of divers kinds, as I am inform'd, to a great Number, before he met with one that would answer his Design, and at length had the Happiness of producing and ripening several hundred Fruit a Year, and encreasing the Plants to that degree, that his Gardener told me he often bury'd or flung away some Hundreds of them.[19]

While la Court's gardener may have exaggerated, his achievement was extraordinary – and much of his success may be attributed to his innovative use of tanner's bark.

Tanner's bark is the bark of an oak tree which is then chopped up and ground down into a coarse powder. Its advantages over manure are manifold. It generates heat in the way manure does, but without the smell; more importantly, it maintains its heat for between three and six months, much longer than manure, then, once cooled, it is easily reactivated just by giving it a hefty stir with a pitchfork, with the result that it can be made to last for over a year. Thus a hotbed was created that not only maintained a temperature of about 80°F, but also heated evenly throughout and without having to be renewed all the time, thereby disturbing the plants. In addition, it created less of the steam that so easily damages plants kept under glass.

The Amsterdam Hortus was one of the first places to try out tanner's bark, but la Court's garden was where the technique was really perfected. The amount of input la Court himself actually had in comparison to his gardener William de Vinck is impossible to ascertain. While he was later described by a visitor to his garden as 'a Gentleman of extraordinary Skill in the Affair of Gardening', this was often conventional parlance when what was really meant was that he employed a gardener with these attributes.[20] Either way, there is no doubt that tanner's bark was the making of the pineapple: it made it possible to produce not just a single lucky pineapple once every few years, but instead a steady and relatively reliable supply.

La Court's success was galling for the upper echelon of gardeners in England. By mastering the cultivation of a fruit so 'dazling to the Eye . . . one can never be tire'd with looking on it', the Dutch had made an emphatic statement of supremacy in the symbolic battle-ground that the garden had become.[21] It may seem like a trivial victory (compared with, say, disputes over the Caribbean territories), but, at the time, it genuinely seemed important: the Dutch had claimed possession of 'the king of fruits' in a period when all such victories were interpreted in the light of God's favour. Pride demanded that the English at least attempt to reclaim the sense that He was on their side.

Like many areas of English life, the garden was increasingly taking its lead from the Netherlands. One of the first noticeable effects was the proliferation of the number of exotic plants brought into the country. While the Leiden Hortus had engaged seriously in the practice from the 1630s, it was not until 1673 when the Society of Apothecaries founded the Chelsea Physic Garden that a comparable botanical establishment existed in England. Even then, Chelsea only began to acquire its international links with the appointment in 1680 of the merchant apothecary John Watts to manage the garden – Watts started to stock it partly with imports from Virginia, but also with many species that came via the Netherlands. There was a real sense of optimism in the air about what the future held.[22]

Yet Chelsea still lagged way behind its counterparts in the Netherlands. It did not possess its own greenhouse until 1680, and even then it was unheated, despite the fact that it cost £138 (today about £15,000) to build. The following year, however, a stove was added; and by the end of 1684, just a few months after the Amsterdam Hortus, it had erected the first greenhouse with underfloor heating to be seen in England. On 11 November, Hans Sloane wrote admiringly that Watts

> has a new contrivance, at least in this country; viz. he makes under the floor of his greenhouse a great fire plate, with grate, ash-hole, etc., and conveys the warmth through the whole house, by tunnels; so that he hopes, by the help of weather-glasses within, to bring or keep the air at what degree of warmth he pleases, letting in upon occasion the outward air by the windows. He thinks to make, by this means, an artificial spring, summer and winter.[23]

The design was almost certainly based on the one developed by the Dutch with know-how gained by Watts during his jaunt to Leiden the year before – given the rate of cross-pollination between the two nations in this period, the introduction of the hothouse to England was inevitable. Yet the methods employed in it were still not ideally suited to the pineapple: the structure emitted very irregular heat and was difficult to control.

The intimate though fraught relationship between England and the Netherlands was soon to intensify further. In the wake of mounting discontent over the rule of James II, the Whig aristocracy conspired to invite William of Orange and his wife Mary to make an attempt to seize the throne from Mary's father, the King. On 5 November 1688, William landed with great audacity at Torbay in Dorset with a force of nearly 15,000 soldiers. Two days before Christmas, James II fled to France. The crisis was resolved with the Declaration of Rights, followed by the triumphant accession to the English throne of William III and Mary II.

Yet by 1689, Anglo–Dutch rivalry, in particular commercial rivalry, had become a deeply entrenched feature of the mental landscape of these two nations. It was not magically going to evaporate in the wake of William and Mary's coronation, as Daniel Defoe made clear in his spot-on satire *A True-Born Englishman* (1701). It simply shifted in emphasis from the military and naval sphere to more subtle manifestations. However much William used propaganda to convince his newly acquired subjects that France was the real enemy, suspicions were to remain.

There was a widespread sense that it was the freedom of the Dutch from 'the popish yoke' of Catholicism that had in large part facilitated the newly Protestant nation's extraordinary rise to prominence as not only a major political and economic power, but also as the epicentre of European scholarship. Dutch intellect had reigned supreme through-out much of the seventeenth century, with the brilliant analytical minds of men like Joseph Scaliger, Hugo Grotius and Daniel Heinsius; but the end of the century saw the resurgence of England in its ability to yield scholars of the calibre of John Locke and Isaac Newton, both of whose most famous works, *Essay Concerning Human Understanding* and the *Principia*, were published in the year that William and Mary ensconced themselves on the throne. Now that England had been similarly released into religious liberty, it seemed to many that it was also her turn to take over the reins of cultural advance and the garden was one area in which this was seen to manifest itself. In a variety of ways, therefore, the Glorious Revolution provided the pineapple with the impetus it needed to persuade the British aristocracy to pursue the goal of a home-grown specimen, a statement if ever there was one of significant scientific advance.[24]

William and Mary infused Britain not only with the sensibilities of the Dutch, but also with the botanical and horticultural expertise developed in the gardens of Leiden, Amsterdam and Utrecht over many decades. It was in this period that 'the practical Part of Gardening began to rouze out of the long Lethargy it had lain in, and especially on the coming of King William III and his Royal Consort, whose Genius and Inclination to the innocent and delightful Divertisements of a Garden, animated others to imitate their Examples', as the author of a gardening manual of 1730 put it.[25] It was truly a timely piece of luck for the pineapple. With England emerging as the world's greatest military and naval power, the royal gardens were a potentially powerful assertion of confidence in the nation's ability to subject to its will everyone and everything in its path.

Keen to establish their ascendancy in the aftermath of the Glorious Revolution, William and Mary set about the renovation of Hampton Court palace, in particular of the gardens. The project was personally supervised by the Queen – it gave her something to do other than her somewhat eccentric hobby of knotting, a primitive form of crochet that she pursued 'with so constant diligence as if she been to earn her Bread by it', as one contemporary was moved to comment. In 1689 Mary had three glass cases built in the Pond Yard at Hampton Court by Hendrik Floris, a specialist Dutch carpenter; designed to shelter exotic plants, they were based on a Dutch design probably similar to those depicted in Pieter de la Court's 1737 book. A devoutly religious young woman (she went to church three times a day), the amount of money spent on the gardens racked Mary with guilt. She was only able to ease her conscience with the thought that 'since this employed many hands, she was pleased to say that she hoped it wd be forgiven her'.[26]

It is also in 1689 that pineapples are first listed in the gardens' plant collection, probably donated by the Dutch nobleman Hans William Bentinck. Bentinck had first earned William of Orange's approval by 'Showing' him a comely innkeeper's daughter when they were both young men.[27] In years to come, he was given the somewhat more respectable responsibility of overseeing the Netherlands' royal gardens and was also the owner of Zorglievt, one of the first places to have a hothouse. Following his employer to England, he was appointed Superintendent of the Royal Gardens, as well as honoured with the title of the Earl of Portland. Many at court failed to warm to him – he was an incredibly extravagant individual, as warrants a man with a passion for pineapples come rain or shine. To quell resentment of the foreign influence, an English deputy was appointed, George London.

There was still room in the collections for improvement, however.

On the death of Caspar Fagel, one of the first to grow the pineapple in the Netherlands, William arranged to buy his plant collection: on 3 March 1692, a sum of 435 florins was paid to Fagel's heirs to have the collection shipped to England by a nurseryman based in Harlem.[28]

This was just the boost the Hampton Court hothouses needed. A letter written home on 14 October 1693 by Tilleman Bobart recounts that, 'Here is at this time a very fine Ananas near ripe in the stove which is to be presented to ye Queen in a few days.'[29] Tilleman Bobart was the brother of the keeper of the Oxford Physic Garden, Jacob Bobart, but he had been employed by George London to work not only at Brompton Oratory but also at Hampton Court. It was from the latter, the 'Royall garden', that he wrote his missive. Queen Mary was of course the only suitable recipient for such a prize; yet because it appears to have been ripened successfully just the once and from a plant rather than from a crown or a sucker, its impact was insignificant. Still no reliable method had been discovered. This was not only because tanner's bark had not yet been adopted in England, but also because the design of the hothouses was all wrong, with all but one side still made out of brick. The first design for a partially glazed roof did not appear until 1718 in Richard Bradley's *Gentlemen and Gardener's Kalendar*.

In part, the intent was to take possession of a fruit that was still very much seen as an exotic. In October 1692 William and Mary endorsed a new Great Seal for Jamaica on which it featured prominently, cast as the most potent symbol available of the newly conquered land.[30] Yet at the same time, attempts to naturalise it continued apace. In a move typical of English colonial policy, while the exotic is glorified by its visual inclusion in the Great Seal, it is at the same time incorporated into the political and cultural discourse of government.

Once again the pineapple had been given the stamp of royal approval. The race to grow one intensified. Hothouses sprang up all over the place. Mary Somerset, Duchess of Beaufort, was especially swift to commission one of her own in the grounds of her estate at Badminton, and by 1694 her gardener Mr Adams was attempting to

68 THE PINEAPPLE

grow pineapples in it.* The Glorious Revolution ushered in a new confidence amongst the landed classes, expressed in the development of England's great gardens. In power was a monarchy – but a parliamentary monarchy, one that basically supported the property rights of the aristocracy. It was they who had extended an invitation to William and Mary in the first place. The ability to control Nature symbolised their ability to manipulate the nation's government, and powerfully demonstrated that the Whig aristocracy were a force to be reckoned with.

By the time Queen Anne acceded to the throne in 1702, England was not the only country in Europe showing an interest in the cultivation of the pineapple. The same year, one was ripened in Germany for the first time by a Dr Kaltschmidt in Breslau, also rumoured to have learned his tricks from the Dutch. The fruit was of course presented to the Habsburg court at once.[31]

It is no wonder that mainland Europe also showed an interest in the pineapple, exposed as it was to a plethora of accounts that, with more and more zealousness, continued to portray it as the acme of all fruits, representative of God, King and everything else thus worshipped. Take *Fruits of Brazil*, an account by a Franciscan monk named Antonio do Rosario published in Lisbon in 1702.

> The pineapple is born with a crown like the King: within its skin, which resembles a brocade of pinecones, lies the Royal opal, guarded by its thorns, like soldiers, with its Royal insignia, created so uniquely by nature, with its great and beautiful stature . . .[32]

It was commonly believed that the physical appearance of Nature's creations was a clue to the secret symbolism contained within them.

*The papers of Mary Somerset's gardener, Mr Adams, reveal that a pineapple plant was sent over to the estate by a Mr Southwell (probably Sir Robert Southwell, Secretary of State for Ireland but also President of the Royal Society and a friend of John Evelyn's) on 21 April 1694. Though Mary Somerset was the first to succeed in ripening a guava fruit in England, she apparently had less luck with the pineapple, for there is no record of one being kind enough to fruit for her. Another of the earliest to try was the gardener to Lady Cotton (the wife of Sir John Cotton, also a friend of Evelyn's): in a letter written by him in 1696, he also offers 'Pines a ffrut' to Mr Adams. *British Library Sloane MSS* 3343, Folio 52.

To this end, Rosario casts the pineapple as a direct representation of God on earth: 'in her colour the mysterious wonders, in her thorns the pains and in her formal dress the glories'.

More specifically, however, to Rosario the pineapple signifies the Virgin Mary. His evidence for this lies in its name, *ananas*. For it was not only appearance that was believed to reveal its symbolism, but also its name: 'if names are symbols of the nature of their owners, the pineapple is the fruit that best signifies our Lady of the Rosary'. Accordingly, *ananas*, a Tupí-Guaraní word, was to be interpreted as *Anna nascitur*, translated as *born of Anna*, referring to Anna, the mother of the Virgin Mary. In other words, the pineapple is the representative in the New World of Our Lady of the Rosary, the Virgin Mary, in the same way that the rose was in the Old World. It led Rosario to conclude that 'Against the poisoned apple of Paradise, God, with the assistance of his mother, created the pineapple of Brazil in the form of the rosary, in which are to be found the mysteries of our redemption.' To equate the pineapple so directly with the Virgin Mary was to put an extraordinary spin on it but one that, once again, was only to the pineapple's advantage.

Similar religious responses abound, but it is more difficult to say how women perceived the fruit in this period. On holiday in Germany in 1716, Lady Mary Wortley Montagu had the privilege of viewing two ripe pineapples while at dinner with the Elector of Hanover (who was by this time also George I). She wrote with amazement, 'You know they are naturally the growth of Brazil, and I could not imagine how they came to be here but by enchantment.'[33] To see and smell the pineapple for the first time outside the context of the tropics or the subtropics must indeed have been a bizarre sensation. Yet the suggestion of the miraculous allowed Montagu to erase the (financial) conditions necessary for the appearance of the pineapples at the dinner table, attributing it more to divinity than to economics. In fact, they were a present from a local nobleman.

Since Columbus, many had celebrated the perceived medicinal properties of the fruit. Oviedo was the first to assert that 'It restores a healthy appetite and stimulates them to endeavour to eat, restoring enjoyment,' an assessment echoed by the Spanish doctor Francisco Hernandez in 1651.[34] Paladanus heard tell that they are 'holden for a most certaine remedie against the heate of the liver and the kidneys',[35] while Louis Lemery, a doctor at the Royal Academy of Science in Paris, was confident that they 'are very nourishing, allay the sharp Humours in the Breast, and are good for phtisical and consumptive People; they qualify the heat of the Urine occasioned by sharp and pricking Humours, and they increase Milk and Seed'.[36] Perhaps bolstered by the perception of the New World as a place of infinite abundance, repeated here is the misguided association of the pineapple with notions of fertility – one, however, that Louis XIV is said to have taken to heart.

Such notions were endorsed by the well-respected English botanist and physician Hans Sloane in his *Natural History of Jamaica* (1707). Written following a fifteen-month sojourn on the island working as physician to the governor, the Duke of Albemarle, it contains an extensive commentary on the pineapple. He too was of the opinion that 'It is a great Cordial to fainting spirits, and helps a squeamish stomach. Its Juice and Wine is good for the suppression of Urine, and Fits of the Stone, as also against Poysons, especially Cassada.'[37] Though much of this repeated what he picked up from the natives and previous writers, he seems to accept the fruit can perform minor miracles. Sloane does not submit to received opinion in every respect, however. While he alludes to the oft-repeated judgement that pineapples are the most delicious fruit ever discovered, he goes on to say that 'they seem to me not so extremely plesant, but too sower, setting the Teeth in edge very speedily'.[38] But then Sloane was a man with a naturally questioning temperament.

At the same time, however, the fruit had become shrouded by an air of danger. Charles V, Holy Roman Emperor, King of Spain and grandson of Ferdinand and Isabella, had an early opportunity to taste the pineapple but refused due to a terror of being poisoned.[39] It is not an entirely unreasonable reaction – the pineapple does look more like a decorative plant than a foodstuff. To this end, Oviedo warned that even to touch it was a potential hazard: 'To the feel it is not actually so smooth and manageable, because it seems that it wishes to be handled with circumspection, by means of a cloth or kerchief but, placed in the hand no other offers such satisfaction.'[40]

Many asserted that it caused cholera, while others were influenced by botanist Willem Piso's verdict that it over-heated the blood.[41] In 1705 the Dutch slave trader William Bosman conjured up the gory image that 'this sharp hot Juice forces Blood from the Throat and Gumms'; John Nieuhof agreed with him but added that actually, 'the main hazard is produced by its pleasantness, which is such, that it will melt in the mouth like Sugar'.[42] This very ambiguity recalls the Forbidden Fruit itself: though it tastes so delicious that it is nigh on impossible to resist, to succumb is to risk getting hurt.

Many of these were irrational fears translated into the minds of supposedly rational men – men of science fell victim to the myths that surrounded the New World just like everyone else. Yet several of these hunches, many of them gleaned from the New World's natives, have turned out to be true – for example, that it is good for the digestion.

One other (rather Freudian) myth that is dutifully repeated in almost every late seventeenth- and early eighteenth-century work on the subject is that if you stick a knife in a pineapple for more than about half an hour, the knife dissolves. One of the first to assert this was Christopher de Acosta, brother of Joseph de Acosta, in his influential work of 1578 on the medicinal properties of the flora found in the Americas.[43] It is not true, of course, but the fact that writers felt driven to exaggerate the pineapple's dangers demonstrates its capacity to engender extraordinary hostility.

Despite this, the turn of the eighteenth century in England saw the gardeners of the rich pick up their spades to attempt the challenge of growing a pineapple, a fruit that most of them had never even seen in real life, let alone tasted or smelt. Few records survive because, reasonably enough, most of us do not want to allow history to remember our failures. But in about 1714, after what must have been years and years of dedicated and patient experimentation (since a pineapple takes two to three years to fruit, any mistakes take quite some time to manifest themselves), Henry Telende, gardener to Sir Matthew Decker at his home on Richmond Green in west London, finally succeeded. While others before him had managed to grow the occasional pineapple here and there, Telende was the first to establish a working and reliable method of growing pineapples in England of a consistently high quality and quantity, rather than just as a one-off curiosity.[44]

Born in Amsterdam in 1679, Matthew Decker arrived in London at the age of twenty-one to set himself up as a merchant. His real passion, however, was his garden, and his speedy success in the City allowed him to bankroll this to his heart's content. His gardener was also originally from the Netherlands, the country that then boasted the most talented gardeners in the world. Telende obtained his pineapple plants and many elements of his technique from Pieter de la Court. Everything we know of Telende relates to what contemporary writers tell us about his efforts to grow the fruit: like la Court's gardener and many others to come, no documents survive to tell us what kind of a man he really was. It was not the last time that the pineapple's true benefactors, the gardeners, were ignored in favour of the men or women who provided the funds. In the aristocratic age that this unashamedly was, this was inevitable.

By 1724, the stove Telende had painstakingly constructed housed over forty fruiting pineapples, in addition to others in various stages of growth, some as large as those seen in the West Indies. For Telende, it was the triumphant culmination of what must have been many hundreds of hours spent in tropical temperatures early in the morning, crouched over to tend his tiny charges – do they have enough food? water? shelter? – as the sweat dripped down his brow, the ache up his back worsened (the bark had to be shovelled anew every day) and his worries intensified about whether his master would keep up the endless flow of funds the project seemed to demand. But for Decker this unparalleled success in the garden served as a powerful assertion of Dutch superiority: his investment (both financial and temporal) soon paid dividends when, the following year, he was elected a Director of the East India Company. His proven commitment to the championship of the emerging empire in his own back garden surely helped his cause.*

What were the secrets of Telende's method? Each pineapple sucker or crown was planted in a six-inch pot in around July or August. These were then plunged into a specially constructed hotbed about 5 feet deep, 11 feet long and 7½ feet wide. In order to retain heat, its sides were lined with brick, while the bottom was strewn with pebbles. Layered on top were about 300 bushels of horse dung, then about the same amount of tanner's bark. Telende was the first to use tanner's bark in England, despite the fact that the Dutch had realised its potential some years back. One side-effect of the innovation was that, even though tanning is hardly odour-free, the smell inside the hothouse was no longer quite as offensive as it used to be – all the more welcoming for (aristocratic) visitors, in other words.

The plants were covered by a sloping frame made of glass and wood designed to allow in as much light as possible, just like the one built by la Court: they remained here until October when the pots were transferred to the hothouse for the winter, then, once the season had ended, returned to the hotbeds for the next six months. So the complicated cycle continued. Telende made certain not to over-water the plants, and to ensure that the water was a suitable temperature. The other crucial factor was the regulation of the heat to make sure it remained constant. Much of Telende's success may be attributed to the fact that he was the first to appreciate the importance of this: he invented the first standardised spirit thermometers, marked in inches – cold, temperate, warm, pineapple heat, hot and sultry. These soon became readily available from Mr Thomas Fairchild's shop in Hoxton in London.[45]

Having brought into play all the horticultural technology and ingenuity of the late seventeenth and early eighteenth centuries, the pineapple was thus claimed as a product of England at last – albeit

---

*This was only the beginning of what was to be a very successful career for Decker: by the time he died in 1749, he had been the Governor of the East India Company, as well as a Tory MP for Bishops Castle and, for a time, the Sheriff of Surrey. He also wrote two influential tracts on the promotion of free trade, appropriately enough.

with the assistance of a native of the Netherlands. The basic technique Telende introduced was to remain in use for many years to come, albeit with an enormous number and range of modifications. He had appreciated one crucial factor: the pineapple needed attention. Who doesn't? By getting to know it, he was able to bring it under his control – although from another perspective, he himself had been brought under the pineapple's control in order to service its needs.

Henceforth, the context in which the pineapple was cultivated contributed to the way it was perceived, creating a physical frame in the same way that the early literature created a verbal one. The enclosure of the plants within a hothouse mostly made of glass demonstrated the expense of the enterprise: deceptive in its transparency, the glass not only kept the pineapples in but also kept others out of the exclusive microcosm it protected. Look, but don't touch. Inside, the tropical temperatures of up to 80°F intensified the sensory experience of the master's daily inspections, often accompanied by guests, reminding them of the exotic origin of the produce. For men and women clothed in the various trappings of Georgian fashion, the humidity surely heightened the experience to make it even more memorable. It may even have encouraged the sexual connotations that later came to envelop it.

So proud was Decker that he commissioned a painting to commemorate Telende's achievement (colour plate v). He is also said to have served a pineapple to George I at a banquet to celebrate his induction as a baronet in 1716.[46] True or not, the story illustrates the kind of hype that the pineapple had a knack of surrounding itself with. It also did Decker's public image no harm at all, with his obituary notice in the *Gentleman's Magazine* singling out one attribute in particular: 'By an orderly and well-understood hospitality, the great who frequented his house were properly received.'[47] For the presence at dinner of the pineapple, 'Fruits of all fruits the first, / Which are, which were, which will be, / Pineapple, most eminent of fruits!', was the act of only the most generous of hosts, whichever country in Europe you had chosen to put down roots.[48]

In 1721, Telende's technique was described in print by the prolific and popular horticultural writer Richard Bradley. No stranger to pineapples, on a working holiday to the Netherlands Bradley had visited not only the Amsterdam Hortus but also the garden of Pieter de la Court. In 1720 he was elected a Fellow of the Royal Society, then three years later became Professor of Botany at Cambridge University. It was not long, however, before it was discovered that he had secured the appointment on the basis of a fabricated recommendation. This, combined with the fact that he was – shockingly – utterly ignorant of a single phrase of Greek or Latin, caused quite a scandal. In his writings, however, he proved himself to be a little more diligent.

The account of the pineapple in Bradley's *General Treatise of Husbandry and Gardening* opens with all the usual praise: 'The Fruit of the Ananas is soft, tender and delicate, and excels all the Fruits in the World in Flavour, and Richness of Taste.' He then gives a detailed and practical account of Telende's methods, followed by a plea: 'I hope to see the Ananas flourish for the future in many of our English Gardens,

11. From Richard Bradley's *Treatise of Husbandry and Gardening*, 1721.

to the Honour of the Artist.' By 'Artist' he means the gardener, a
sentiment that (perhaps consciously) echoes the inscription on Agnes
Block's medal. The passage concludes with the maxim that 'the greater
Difficulties we have to encounter with, the greater the Honour we gain
by the Victory'.[49] It was indeed a victory: over the neighbours, over the
Dutch and over the foreign in a more general sense, now assimilated
into the most English of worlds, the garden. In this way, it was also a
victory over Nature.

Bradley's account had a dramatic effect. Until 1721, the pineapple's
future in England was unsure. However much the master of the house
shouted, cursed and stomped around his garden to demand it yield the
fruit, how was a gardener to oblige when advice was generally
unavailable? Word-of-mouth among the higher echelons of gardeners
proved a help in dealing with new plant arrivals, but with published
work scarce, most erred on the side of caution when faced with a plant
as tricky and expensive to obtain as the pineapple. Bradley effectively
liberated gardeners from these shackles.

By the mid-1720s every self-respecting aristocrat in England
aspired to owning a pinery. A deeply eccentric ambition, really, in a
country well known for its wind and rain, nevertheless the pineapple
had somehow managed to convince them that it was worth the time,
effort and expense. This was not simply because the home-grown
kind tasted better than those shipped from abroad: as Bradley put it,
'tho' every Year the Traders to those Countries, where this Fruit is
natural, bring home the Pine Apples growing, to be ripen'd here, yet
that Fruit has not the high Flavour which is found in those which are
cut full ripe in the Place of their Education'.[50] The pineapple had
come to mean far more to the English. Therein lay the beginnings of
a frenzied fashion that was to engulf the country for the next 150
years.

5

'A Single Seed thrown into the hot Bed of Fashion will produce an immeasurable crop – All must have their Fooleries as well as their Pinaries; and the only struggle seems to be, whose Fruit shall be the largest and most talk'd of'

James Ralph (1758)

Dinner was reaching its conclusion at a lively affair hosted by the eighth Lord Petre at his imposing Essex estate, Thorndon Hall, in the summer of 1741. At the age of just twenty-five, Petre was one of the richest and most well-connected men in the country and he had managed to assemble a sparkling array of guests. Glasses chinked. Candles flickered. Ladies' eyelashes fluttered. The talk was mainly of the hanging of the highwayman Dick Turpin. What a terrible business! What was to be done about crime in this country? Opinions differed, but just as the discussion was becoming rather uncomfortably heated, a distraction presented itself. The door gently opened and through it appeared to float an astonishing apparition. Atop an ornate silver tray, beneath which a spindly pair of legs dressed in the white breeches of a footman peeped out, were precariously balanced a huge pile of pineapples, direct from the Thorndon Hall hothouses, in the fog only just visible through the dining room window and past the stables. The smell alone was quite overwhelming. Mesmerised for more than a few seconds, spontaneous applause eventually erupted at the magnificent spectacle that had come to rest in the centre of Petre's dinner table. As Peter Collinson, a Quaker merchant and one of the illustrious dinner guests, wrote, extremely impressed, 'to be at his table, one would think South America were really there, to see a servant come in every day with ten or a dozen pine apples, as much as he can carry'.[1]

Following the first published account of a workable method of producing pineapples in England's temperate climes, within just a decade the pineapple found itself cultivated in hothouses the length and breadth of the country. Not only was this an entirely new development, it also introduced the fruit for the first time to the guarded world that lay within the four walls of the English country house. A real-life, home-grown pineapple was the ultimate status symbol – the one essential guest to feature at all the society parties of the age.

An unwonted combination of social and political factors conspired to make the period between 1720 and 1770 so conducive to the steady social progress of the pineapple. With the trauma of the Civil War a memory of sixty years past, the nation was currently experiencing a period of (relative) domestic tranquillity. The Glorious Revolution had established a system of rule that emphatically supported the interests of the propertied classes, while the Toleration Act of 1689 promoted intellectual and spiritual freedom; in 1707 the Act of Union with Scotland quelled some of the unrest north of the border; and the Treaty of Utrecht in 1713 made peace with France. The cumulative result was that the British aristocracy were at last liberated to concentrate on matters other than just the political stability of the realm.

It was the British aristocracy who steered the fortunes of most of the population. While the nation was on the brink of what we now know as the 'modern' age, for the moment it remained an overwhelmingly hierarchical, hereditary and privileged society, essentially still agrarian in its makeup and dominated by the country estate and all associated with it. The possession of a pineapple asserted this. As Karl Marx was later to articulate, in every era it is the members of the dominant class who produce the dominant representations. Once they had adopted the pineapple, therefore, its position within society was secured.

Fortunately for our fruit, the mid-eighteenth century also ushered in a brief interlude in which the pursuit of pleasure at last became respectable.[2] As Alexander Pope rhapsodised in 1734,

> Oh happiness! Our being's end and aim!
> Good, pleasure, ease, content! Whate'er thy name;
> That something still which prompts th'eternal sigh,
> For which we bear to live, or dare to die.[3]

Happiness had become a right, rather than a privilege. Such thinking was a rebellion against the increasingly passé Calvinist taboo on all kinds of indulgent behaviour; suddenly, such an attitude seemed a bit . . . well, dull. The Georgian world was one of liberal sexual mores, a penchant for whist and a talent for spending money. In part, this was a response to the increasing wealth of the peerage. While around 1700 their wealth averaged about £7,000 (£800,000 today) a year, some were soon to rejoice in annual incomes reaching £20,000, and the diffusion of Enlightenment ideals encouraged them to spend it however they wished. As the Earl of Chesterfield advised his son, 'Pleasure is now, and ought to be, your business.'[4] Applying this mantra to his own life, Chesterfield himself acquired an affection for pineapples entirely appropriate to a man of his stature: 'The growth, the education and the perfection of these vegetable children,' he wrote in a letter of 1752, 'engages my care and attention, next to my corporal one, who is now going to Hanover, and who I hope will reward all my care, as well as my ananas have done.'[5]

By 1730 such was the demand that 'Stoves and Glass cases for the culture of the Pine-Apple . . . are now found in almost every curious Garden.'[6] In the period after the Civil War, political power had shifted away from the Crown and into the hands of the landed aristocracy: their estates became the gauge of fashion. As transport methods improved, life in the country was no longer nearly as remote as it used to be, with the result that it was important to maintain appearances everywhere and at all times. The country estate was a dramatic expression of an aristocrat's wealth, power and status in a society where image was increasingly of concern. One manifestation of this was the race to produce the most admired pineapple crop – a challenge that the aristocracy soon assumed with an admirable seriousness of intent.

One of the primary functions of the country estate was to entertain guests. Balls, assemblies and the rest were arranged in order to entice and impress one's peers: generous hospitality was widely admired, a legacy of the medieval ideal of offering an open house to all who came. Unfortunately for whoever paid the bills, it now began to coincide with the newer demands of conspicuous consumption emanating from the capital. Such expectations created a major headache for the host. The French natural historian Faujas de Saint-Fond described a typical day in 1784 at home with the Duke of Argyll. At ten o'clock the bell was rung for breakfast.

> We then repair to a large room ornamented with historical pictures of the family; here we find . . . in the midst of all bouquets of flowers, newspapers and books. There are besides, in this room a billiard-table, pianos and other musical instruments . . . After breakfast, some walk in the parks, others employ themselves in reading or in music, or return to their rooms until half-past four, when the bell makes itself heard to announce that dinner is ready.

After dinner,

> . . . those who wish retire to their rooms, those who prefer conversation or music remain in the drawing-room; others go out for a walk. At ten o'clock supper is served and those who please attend it. I find that as a rule people eat a great deal more in England than in France.[7]

Keeping guests occupied and stimulated was a constant struggle. Once they arrived, they tended to stay for days, even weeks: travel by coach was quite an ordeal, for while main roads were gradually improving, minor roads remained bumpy and uncomfortable. As a result, the art of leisure time was regarded more as a career than a hobby.

The state of the garden was as crucial as the state of the house. Such was the enthusiasm for outdoor exercise that foreigners blamed it for the notoriously large size of English women's feet. An excursion featured prominently in the day's timetable of events: to commune with Nature was considered chic, and many had their enormous gardens redesigned to indulge this trend. Straight avenues, canals or walks were replaced by a more circular layout. Parties of people might stop at a temple to take tea or at a rotunda to admire the view through a telescope. At Stourhead trips were made to the fishing pavilion on the lake, which was equipped with its own kitchen to cook the catch of the day, as well as a mini-dining room in which to eat it. The spectacle of a pineapple was an additional such enticement to ensure the host had the highest calibre of person possible present at dinner.

Indeed, once the London season finished in June, there was little else with which to occupy oneself. Everyone who was anyone went to the country, a tradition peculiar to the English according to traveller Arthur Young: 'Banishment alone', he wrote in 1787, 'will force the French to execute what the English do from pleasure – reside upon and adorn their estates.'[8] One contemporary horticulturist had his own theory on the attraction of a pinery,

> especially to those who reside much in the country: For as many months intervene between the first formation of fruits, and the time of their perfection, there is an almost daily variety; which occupies, and at the same time relieves, the speculative mind when oppressed by long attention to objects of business or study.[9]

The typical English aristocrat revelled in his estate, not only to consolidate his stature, but also for personal pleasure. How else was he to dispose of his ever-increasing wealth but with the kind of overt ostentation demonstrated herein? The state demanded no inheritance tax, no income tax, only five shillings in the pound on income from land and various taxes on status symbols such as footmen, carriages and the use of glass. Consequently, it was common to invest spare cash in the country estate, an essential and intrinsic feature of any aristocrat's public image.

The cultivation of pineapples demanded not only cash, but also expertise. Most followed the instructions lovingly detailed by Philip Miller in his best-selling book, *The Gardener's Dictionary*. Miller had built a pineapple stove in Chelsea Physic Garden (of which he was by this time Director) as early as 1723. It took him a while to establish his own working method – his *Gardener's and Florist's Dictionary* (1724) slavishly follows Richard Bradley – but by the time Miller's *magnum opus* was published in 1731, it was apparent that he had had the chance to pursue his own experiments in order to supply his readers with a comprehensive account of the cultivation of a fruit 'Justly esteem'd for the Richness of its Flavour, as it surpasses all the known Fruits in the World'.[10]

Miller was soon one of the greatest authorities in Europe on the subject: following a visit to Pieter de la Court's garden in the Netherlands, he consistently managed to produce pineapples of such a high standard that some were presented to the King. Modesty, however, was a virtue less valued than most: Miller has a couple of swipes at the small size of la Court's pineapples, relative to his own, an interesting indication of continuing rivalry with the Dutch. The 400 subscribers listed at the beginning of the *Dictionary* comprise a 'who's who' of the most prominent horticulturists in the land. They include the Earl of Carlisle's gardener at Castle Howard, the Earl of Burlington's gardener at Chiswick House and Lord Petre's gardener at Thorndon Hall, in addition to a copy designated for Lord Petre himself. All of these went on to become well-known for their pineapples. The *Dictionary* was the best starting-point available.[11]

The costs involved in managing a pinery were astronomical. First came the construction. It was estimated in 1764 that to build a pineapple stove 40 feet long and 12 feet wide cost about £80 (nearly £5,000 today) near London, even more outside the capital because of the problem of access to materials.[12] This varied tremendously,

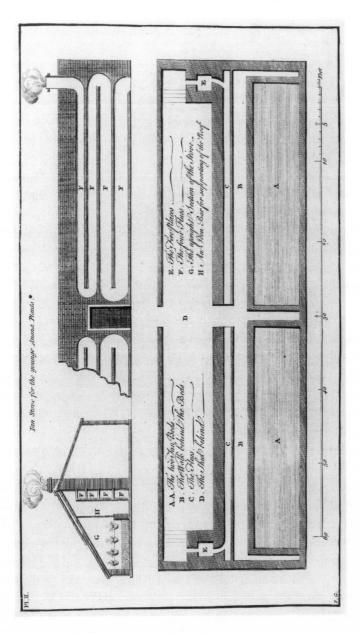

12. A diagram of a pinery from Philip Miller's *The Gardener's Dictionary*, 1731.

however: one built in Hillington in Norfolk cost nearly four times this.[13]

About £30 (£2,000 today) should have sufficed to stock a stove with plants.[14] In the early days, these had to be specially ordered and shipped from the West Indies: the Duke of Chandos, for example, obtained his from his friend Mr Ashley in Barbados.[15] It was a delicate and complicated process, and in 1750 Peter Collinson told his friend Arthur Dobbs (later the Governor of North Carolina) that 'The best Way of Transporting them is to pack them in Very Dry Moss heads and tails in a Box Bored with Small Holes on all sides. Thus I had them come from Barbadoes in fine order.'[16]

Alternatively, it was increasingly possible to obtain plants from a neighbouring estate: in 1781 Lord Harcourt's gardener wrote to the Duke of Portland's gardener to ask him about the 'good clean Queen pine plants' that he had heard were available.[17] For estates with well-known pineries like Castle Howard, Londesborough and Sledmere, this was a familiar request. Either way, it was not cheap. In 1760, Sir William Lee of Hartwell in Buckinghamshire had a pinery designed, constructed and stocked for him by the esteemed gardener Richard Woods. One bill charges him £7 10s. 6d. for fifty succession pineapple plants at 2s. 6d. each and £15 for forty fruiting pineapple plants at 7s. 6d. each.[18] Clearly, just to get the project off the ground demanded a significant financial outlay.

Maintenance costs were also a consideration – about £21 a year. One writer's attempt to break this down provides a vivid expression of the hard work the enterprise necessitated. Eighteen pence a week was required to pay a garden boy solely to 'attend' the stove for fifty-two weeks a year to ensure that it did not burst into flames at an inopportune moment; it was not uncommon for this to extend to night-time duty too, as at a Mr Frederick's of Burwood.[19] This was in addition to the many arduous days of labour required to fill the pit with tan, plant the pots, stir up the tan occasionally and so on – those responsible for this were on the higher but still not exactly princely rate of two shillings a day. With all this in mind, over the two to three years it took to grow, the average total cost of the cultivation of just one pineapple was about £80 (nearly £5,000 today), all things considered – about the same as the cost of a new coach.[20]

Yet despite the huge expense, almost all the greatest estates of the age chose to succumb. This was evident to contemporaries: as the eminent gardener Thomas Knowleton wrote to a friend in October 1738, 'Mr Baine at Raby Castle is Building a stove for pine apples & likewise another at Chatsworth & one more in Lincolnshire where my man Jono is gone to Live so that ye pine apples will gain very much in this island in a few years time.'[21] He was not wrong. A visitor to the Oxford Physic Garden in 1744 marvelled that its pineapples 'have nearly the same Flavour as those raised in warmer Climates', while by 1748 the fruit was in evidence in the garden of the Vice-Master of Trinity College, Cambridge, Richard Walker.[22] Like other crazes of the age – melons, for instance – countless more examples soon cropped up in every corner of England.

It was not only those born with money who indulged themselves in the tussle to raise a pineapple, but also those who had scrabbled their way into upper-class society. For example, Alexander Pope, author of *The Rape of the Lock* among other works, developed a passion for pineapples as soon as he was able to afford it. Pope was the first to command contemporary garden enthusiasts to 'consult the genius of the place'. This was one of the mantras of the landscape garden movement which sought to shift the emphasis from ultra-formal gardens to a more 'natural', wild look. It released gardeners from the toil and expense of maintaining formal gardens, with the result that there was more time and money to spend on exotics.

Pope was also a chronic social climber. In 1718, at the age of thirty-one and England's most distinguished living poet following the success of his translations of Homer, he moved to a villa in Twickenham with a garden of four to five acres. The Richmond-to-Twickenham section of the Thames had acquired a reputation as *the* venue of the fashionable English garden. A common Sunday afternoon excursion for the moneyed Londoner in the eighteenth century was a stroll along the river to admire the sights on offer. Pope soon began to tinker with pineapples and in the spring of 1735, he wrote to his friend William Fortescue that he was improving and expanding his garden, 'making two new ovens and stoves, and a hot-house for anana's, of which I hope you will taste this year'.[23] Pope was clearly keen to share the experience with others, but it did not prove to be an easy one. In August 1738, he was forced to 'borrow' Henry Scott, the Earl of Burlington's gardener at Chiswick House and an expert on growing pineapples, to advise him and his resident gardener, John Serle, on the matter.[24] Sure enough, by the following year, a number fruited in Pope's hothouse, some of which he sent as presents to friends like Ralph Allen.[25] The poet's position in polite society had truly been secured.

The first English recipe appeared in 1732 in Richard Bradley's *The Country Housewife*:

> To make a Tart of the Ananas, or Pine-Apple. From Barbadoes. Take a Pine-Apple, and twist off its Crown: then pare it free from the Knots, and cut it in Slices about half an inch thick; then stew it with a little Canary Wine, or Madera Wine, and some Sugar, till it is thoroughly hot, and it will distribute its Flavour to the Wine much better than any thing we can add to it. When it is as one would have it, take it from the Fire; and when it is cool, put it into a sweet Paste, with its Liquor, and bake it gently, a little while, and when it comes from the Oven, pour Cream over it, (if you have it) and serve it either hot or cold.[26]

This is followed by a recipe for how to dress the giblets of a sea-turtle, another great delicacy at the time but a somewhat less useful piece of advice today.

Yet a pineapple grown on an English country estate was only occasionally actually eaten. Due to its expense, this was perceived to be a waste. Instead, it became the most desired of all ornaments for the dinner table. Dinner was the major event of the day, requiring studious planning on the part of the hostess. The menu had to be debated with the cook, supplies checked, special items ordered from the grandest London shops like the Ham Warehouse off the Strand or Thomas Twining at the sign of the Golden Lion, and seating arrangements fretted over. A formal dinner in a large household consisted of two main courses plus a dessert course, of twelve to twenty-five covers each. In this enduringly agrarian society, handsome eating, both in the way the food tasted and looked, was a token of success. Decorations could be as simple as a sprinkling of rose petals across the tablecloth, but at other times, those in the kitchens worked long hours to produce elaborate confections out of sugar (what a nightmare it must then have been, transporting such delicate works of art above stairs). The dinner table was, quite simply, one of the most eloquent means of expression for the lady of the house. It was a chance to display her prodigious wealth, her impeccable taste and her extensive contacts – in town, a pineapple was still a considerable challenge to obtain. For the first time, here was a distinctly female context for the fruit.

Served with dessert, the pineapple was placed at the peak of a pyramid of fruit (grapes, strawberries, oranges and the like), arranged on a silver platter and placed in the middle of the table for everyone gathered to ooh and to aah. As a centrepiece, it was often made to last for quite some time, passed on from party to party until it began to rot so much it smelt out the whole household (quite a feat in view of the terrible stink that smothered much of Britain in this period). One of the challenges that faced a scullery maid was its transportation through the streets without being accosted by thieves. A pineapple featured prominently at all the most fashionable gatherings; indeed, right up until the 1920s, a dinner party was only deemed really grand if there was in attendance both 'a pineapple and Lady Curzon', as one society hostess commented.[27]

As the eighteenth century progressed, however, it became more acceptable for a pineapple to be eaten rather than just admired. This was a reflection of the fact that it was now marginally easier to obtain the fruit. No longer would it have been such a total disaster to chop it in the wrong direction or to bruise it on the way up the backstairs. Anyway, such seemingly reckless behaviour acted as an even more aggressive assertion of wealth. Yet caution was still practised. The Georgian pineapple was served raw to ensure that it was not unnecessarily spoiled in the preparation. Once its shell had been cut off, it was chopped into slices by the (no doubt rather nervous) cook, arranged on a plate then eaten with a fork. This was almost certainly William Stukeley's experience of it in 1741: 'I visited Sir Robert Walpole at Houghton. We ate a pine apple, a delicious mixture of . . . fruits.'[28]

Walpole's presentation of the pineapple at the dinner table is typical of its symbolic role. The Walpole family had been minor gentry in the country of Norfolk for many centuries until Sir Robert, through a combination of connections and ability, rapidly raised himself to a dominant position. As a young and ambitious politician, it was essential that he played the part. To this end, in 1706 he threw a lavish ball, even though he was unable to pay his creditors at the end of the evening. He was later elected to the Kit-Kat Club, the most fashionable of all the Whig gentlemen's clubs. It was a Kit-Kat tradition for each member to take it in turns to be the host, vying with one another to produce exotic food and fine wines. Walpole's bills reveal that he spent over £1,000 a year on food, including a regular order for 100 lbs of chocolate at a cost of £17 – more than he paid his housekeeper or his cook in a year.[29] This seduction of his peers bore fruit in 1721 when he was not only made First Lord of the Treasury, but invested with such extensive powers that he became in effect the first modern equivalent of what we now call the Prime Minister.

The following year, Walpole embarked upon the reconstruction of his family house at Houghton; he spent £1,219 3s. 11d. (about £135,000 in today's money) on the trimmings alone of his magnificent green velvet state bed. Like the pineapple served to Stukeley, it functioned as an assertion of Walpole's new-found power and wealth. In a letter to the Prince of Wales in 1731, Lord Hervey described a typical dinner there:

> Our company at Houghton swelled at last into so numerous a body that we used to sit down to dinner a little snug party of about thirty odd, up to the chin in beef, venison, geese, turkeys, etc.; and generally over the chin in claret, strong beer and punch. We had the Lords spiritual and temporal, besides commoners, parsons and freeholders innumerable.

In public we drank loyal healths, talked of the times and cultivated popularity; in private we drew plans and cultivated the country.[30]

It is no wonder the phrase 'drunk as a lord' was coined in this period. The dinner table was one of the most effective social arenas in which to communicate status, and the pineapple was an invaluable pawn in the intimate world of politics where as much could be achieved at dinner as at a formal committee meeting.

The demand for pineapples was soon such that the quality of the fruit became almost irrelevant. In January 1750, the Earl of Chesterfield sent three out-of-season and unripe pineapples to the great French beauty and courtier the Marquise de Monconseil with the excuse that 'As the longings of women with child are satisfied rather with the name than by the merit of the thing, I hope these pine-apples will do for the dauphiness as well as good ones, but it is fact that they are bad.'[31] Whether the recipient appreciated the green, unripe, cannon-ball-like fruit delivered to her by a breathless courier, history does not relate.

The French had first been privy to a pineapple in 1733 when Louis XV was presented with one grown by Monsieur le Normand in the gardens of Versailles from a plant imported by Jesuit missionaries: according to one onlooker, the King was so 'charm'd with its delicious flavour' that he dispatched a piece of it to every nobleman in the land so that they could try it for themselves.[32] In 1738, a dedicated hothouse was built for the fruit that soon housed over 800 plants. Others followed the King's lead, often to an exceedingly lavish extent: in 1782, Louis-Sébastien Mercier reported that 'I have seen 4000 pots of Ananas at the home of the Duke of Bouillon, at Navarre, near Evreux; the Duke has eight or ten on his table every day. Their cultivation is managed by an Englishman.'[33] It was typical of the kind of blatant extravagance that was to precipitate the French Revolution just seven years later. Similarly, Catherine the Great of Russia ate pineapples from her own gardens by the time of her death in 1796. In view of the fruit's continued association with royalty in the literature of the period, this comes as no surprise.[34] Germany was also in the vanguard. Clearly, the dream of home-grown pineapples was being pursued all over Europe.[35]

Castle Howard in Yorkshire provides an illuminating case study of the attention lavished on the cultivation of the pineapple in the Georgian period. It was the seat of one of the most powerful families in British history, the Howards, and in 1758 Frederick Howard succeeded to the title of the fifth Earl of Carlisle at the age of just ten. Though he grew up to occupy a series of influential government positions, including Treasurer of the Royal Household, Privy Councillor and Lord Lieutenant of Ireland, he was far more renowned for his extravagant lifestyle. Wickedly encouraged by his best friend from Eton, Charles James Fox, Carlisle was a social butterfly, a gambler and, above all, a hit with the ladies. He lamented in his diary many years later, 'I can enumerate from memory, and limited to a period of a few years, 37 Ladies who presided over the Town who would all have been affronted had you supposed there had been a grain of conjugal fidelity between them.'[36] Carlisle prided himself on being the best-dressed man in town, with a penchant for the ultra-fashionable Macaroni style of dress – three-inch heels and wigs over a metre high. In the words of one contemporary, 'Possessing a small but elegant figure, in which symmetry was happily blended with agility and strength, he shone one of the meteors of fashion.'[37] This was a man devoted to spectacle.

Despite continual money difficulties, Carlisle loved to throw parties. On 26 February 1770 all of fashionable society descended upon a fabulous fancy dress ball he gave for 800 guests at what had once been the Howard family house in Soho Square in London. Many had spent weeks and weeks worrying about what to wear. According to a journalist from the *Gentleman's Magazine*, who recorded the evening with glee, outfits included a Hungarian Hussar, a Cherokee Chief, a Political Bedlamite, a Druid, a Quaker, a Vestal Virgin and an Indian Sultana. The host disguised himself as 'A Running Footman; the prettiest imagined dress at the ball; and showed the universal opinion of the wearer's superior taste of any kind has its foundation in truth.' One reveller caused a particularly scandalous kerfuffle when he turned up dressed as Adam: 'The unavoidable indelicacy of the dress (flesh-colored silk with an apron of fig leaves worked in it, fitting the body with the utmost nicety), rendered it the contempt of the company.' I imagine most of the other guests rather enjoyed the display; it certainly put Carlisle in an excellent mood – the same night, he proposed to his future wife, Lady Margaret Caroline Leveson-Gower.[38]

Fortunately for the pineapple, such a hedonistic attitude to life was typical of Georgian high society. With Carlisle's encouragement, Castle Howard soon became famous nationwide for its pineries, producing an average crop of forty a year. The head gardener was the legendary Robert Teesdale. A man dour in demeanour but passionate in intent, Teesdale was a founder member of the Linnean Society, still the foremost botanical society in Britain today; his salary was an astonishing £50 a quarter (the men under him received a shilling a day, the women just sixpence). He was certainly worth it. In 1771 Sir John Cullum, an eminent horticulturist from Suffolk, wrote of Castle Howard:

The Pine Apples are cultivated to such a degree of luxury almost beyond belief. Some of their leaves were much above 6 feet high; and the fruit, I was told, frequently weighted between 4 and 5 pounds. This much Art may do, but the Climate is very unfriendly.[39]

Sir John here attributes the gardener's success to 'Art' rather than to Nature, in much the same way that Agnes Block had done nearly 100 years before.

This belief that Man was able to use art to dupe the natural world into submission (in the case of the pineapple, through the use of hothouses, flues and tanner's bark) was typical of the Enlightenment. In response to a trip to see the 'hundreds of pineapples of unusual size' in the hothouses at Osterley Park in Middlesex (the home of the Child family of bankers) in September 1786, the charming young Austrian diarist Sophie von la Roche was moved to comment, 'I always loved the plant world for its charitable actions; entrancing, curative, it yields up sustenance and support, offers itself ungrudgingly and unremittingly for our service and pleasure.'[40] La Roche casts Nature, in the form of the pineapple, as the servant of Man; but the multitude of sightings of the pineapple in this period in the unlikeliest of places suggests that the real power in the relationship was quite the reverse.

Carlisle frequently dispatched some of his precious crop (most of which was no doubt destined to be displayed at parties) to distinguished neighbours such as the Reverend Sydney Smith.[41] Smith was certainly a fan of the wonders of exotic fruit: on his appointment as vicar of Foxton in 1806, he lamented that it amounted to an effective exile to a place 'so out of the way that it was actually twelve miles from a lemon'.[42] It was common for the gift to be accompanied by a request that the pineapple's crown be wrapped up and returned by the next coach in order to renew the crop.

For the upper classes, the gift of a pineapple was more than just an act of generosity, but a habit used to assert the status of the 'lord of the manor' in relation to those around him. This is implicit in the letters of Henry Simpson, private secretary to the third Earl of Burlington, to the Earl's distinguished gardener at his country estate Londesborough, Thomas Knowleton. Having built a pinery at Londesborough in 1738, it was just months before Knowleton was able to boast that 'I have abundance of fine frut still wch is a grat Pleasure to his LdShipe & creaditt to me . . . I am apt to belive my new pineapple fram[e] or Bead beats all that ever I see yet for that.'[43] In July 1743 Simpson wrote from Chiswick House in London especially to ask Knowleton 'to send up hither six Pine Apples to his Lord and if you have more, to send to the Archbishop of York and if you have any spare, He woud have 'em given to his friends, as you have usually given to'.[44] After all, what was the point of extensive investment in a pinery unless you showed off the results to as wide a circle of acquaintances as possible? Knowleton wanted to be kept informed of the progress of every single precious specimen he produced: from whether they had arrived safely, to the fact that Burlington's mother very much enjoyed them at dinner, to how to dispose of the crowns. Reams and reams of letters from Simpson detail it all.[45]

But Burlington was not Carlisle's most determined rival when it came to pineapples. This honour fell to the third Duke of Portland. A passionate interest in exotic fruit seems to have been a family trait: he was the grandson of Hans William Bentinck, William of Orange's trusted aide and one of the earliest champions of pineapples in both Holland and England. Portland inherited the dukedom in 1762; four years later he married Lady Dorothy Cavendish, a union that produced four sons in total, all of whom were named William (dinnertime must have been a rather confusing affair). Once described as 'reserved, ungraceful and apparently unpolished. But he was thoroughly sincere', he was a very different character to Carlisle in almost every respect.[46]

What he did share with Carlisle, however, was not only an enthusiasm for pineapples but also money problems; by 1770 he was so in debt that even the servants were owed a year's worth of wages. A few years later, Carlisle received a letter from his friend George Selwyn with the latest gossip on the subject: 'the Duke of Portland pays his debts, to the last *obole*, as Lord E. has told me, and they amount to £27,000; and what is as extraordinary he pays his own, which amount, I suppose, to an enormous sum'.[47] Gambling was a fashionable weakness: it was the main debauchery at London clubs like White's and Boodle's, the state ran its own national lottery (funding institutions from the British Museum to Westminster Bridge), and when George III led his troops to battle in 1743 the odds were four to one against him being killed. No wonder Portland succumbed.

Regardless of ongoing financial straits, the Duke spent thousands of pounds a year on the improvement and maintenance of his estate at Welbeck Abbey in Nottinghamshire.[48] It was important to him to keep up appearances. From 1767 until 1804 the gardens were managed by one of the most eminent practical horticulturists of the day, William Speechly. It is evident from his regular correspondence with his employer that Speechly was diligent, conscientious and obsessive about pineapples. His very first letter from Welbeck, written on 17 March 1767, passes brief comment on the general state of the garden, then proceeds to give a very detailed analysis of the pine stove:

> The prospect in the Stove is still worse [than the rest of the garden], for the Pines have been heated in such a Manner, that they will be all over by the Month of May, or June farthest, and will be good for little or Nothing when they are in Season; the condition of the Succession Plants is equally as bad as the Fruiting Plants; nor do I think that Your Graces Pines has been good for little for several years past . . . In short if I were to make every just complaint, Your Grace wou'd perhaps think that I were prejudis'd against the late Gardener.[49]

What is amusing is the way he criticises his predecessor, just like a plumber or a hairdresser unfailingly criticises the handiwork of whoever came before them.

Speechly kept the Duke informed of every minute detail of garden affairs, even in matters of personnel – in one letter, he comically comments on his new assistant:

> A good gardener, uncommonly sober (I believe he *dares* not to drink anything stronger than water), writes well, has much to say for himself, and a great turn for Religion, I believe a tincture of Methodism.[50]

Yet the pineapples remained the main focus of his energies. Even the scratchy black ink he uses to set down the word 'pine' on the page, in a distinctly swirlier hand than any of the other words and pressing down more firmly on the page, suggests he is trying further to imbue it with a sense of majesty. Almost every letter contains some form of update on the progress of his charges – be it that they have been infected by insects, that he is worried that the prolonged cold spell may affect the taste, that he wants to repair the woodwork in the hothouse or that the plants have started to show their fruit 'bold and strong'. Speechly appreciated the importance of his exertions.[51] Much of his employer's social credibility depended upon them.

With more and more pineapples produced each year, it was important that every single one found a home. Since each took an average of three years to raise, Speechly's letters reveal a continuing concern about how Portland wanted to distribute them. The biggest and best pineapples from the estate took pride of place at his lordship's table. If he did not happen to be staying at Welbeck at the time a fruit ripened, however, it was sent by coach up to Burlington House, Portland's main London residence. In this respect, the pineapple's hard shell gave it a discernible advantage over both grapes and melons, 'a fruit that will not bear Carriage to Town', as Speechly lamented.[52] A pineapple created even more of a splash in London than on the country estate because its origin was even more inscrutable: it was as if this fruit from the West Indies had appeared by magic, so alien did it seem amongst the soot and stench of life in the capital.

The state of the pineries was a matter of real rivalry between Castle Howard and Welbeck Abbey. Between 1767 and 1770 Speechly periodically used to order batches of £30 (about £2,500 today) worth of pineapple suckers from his counterpart Teesdale at Castle Howard, to be sent round by coach. The implication was that Welbeck Abbey was unable to supply its own needs. Some of the bills still survive.

1767 May 11

To 100 Best pick'd Pine plants to fruit the next Year	20.0.0
19 Sugar Loaf Pine Plants	2.0.0.
1 King Do.	2.0.0.
Hamper, Basket & package	0.4.2.
Aug. 19th 100 Strong Pine Suckers	5.0.0.
Hamper and Package	0.3.0.
Dec. 3rd Best Red Beet Seed	
Bag	0.0.3.
	£29.7.5.

Received the 18th of Feby. 1768 of Mr Speechly by the Hands of Mr Wm. Mason the Contents of the above p. me (signed) Robt. Teesdale[53]

It is notable that it took nearly a year for the account to be settled. For Portland, 'a proud though bashful man' according to Horace Walpole, this would have been a humiliating state of affairs.[54] Pineapples had become an essential weapon in every country estate's battle for status, but it was a battle that he was at risk of losing.

In 1758, polemicist James Ralph attempted to explain the enthusiasm with which men like Carlisle, Portland and their peers vied with each other over the pineapple.

A Single Seed thrown into the hot Bed of Fashion will produce an immeasurable crop – All must have their Fooleries as well as their Pinaries; and the only struggle seems to be, whose Fruit shall be the largest and most talk'd of.[55]

The dominant metaphor is one of Nature's 'Single Seed'; and yet, Ralph suggests, all that results is ultimately artificial and trivial. Once again, the pineapple is accused of being a fake – the crop not of Nature, but of fashion. The emphasis is on the way the pineapple had been popularised by being gossiped about ('most talk'd of') during a day at the Derby or a visit to the Drury Lane Theatre, rather than the display of the real thing. The deployment of the pineapple within the competitive struggle of the upper classes made it an eminently suitable symbol of the pitfalls of fashion that Ralph seeks to condemn. To many, however, it was precisely its pointlessness, its wastefulness, its frivolity, that made it so appealing in the first place.

It was imperative that Portland find a way to challenge Castle Howard's horticultural pre-eminence. A solution soon emerged. In 1771 (the same year that Sir John Cullum was so effusive about the Castle Howard pineapples), he dispatched Speechly to Holland to study techniques and acquire new plants. The pineapple was once again to be the beneficiary of Man's innate competitive spirit.

On his return Speechly embarked on writing the seminal work of the century dedicated to pineapple cultivation, *A Treatise on the Culture of the Pineapple*. Its publication in 1779 must have been a proud moment for his employer. Subscribers included 200 of the most distinguished men in the country: the Duke of Athol, the Earl of Bathurst, the Earl of Portsmouth, the Earl of Exeter, the Archbishop of Dublin, Sir Hans Sloane and even John Abel, assistant gardener to the Earl of Carlisle. All these men were known to indulge themselves in the cultivation of the pineapple – it was at the Duke of Athol's house in 1745 that Bonnie Prince Charlie had his first ever taste of the fruit[56] – reiterating Speechly's claim in the preface that 'Our Nobility and Gentry, with a spirit for gardening not equalled by any other nation, have of late been at great expense in building large and elegant Hot-houses, in order to have the Pine Apple in as great perfection as this climate will admit.' As an assertion of the depth of Speechly's knowledge, the treatise is a mightily impressive work, covering every aspect of cold weather cultivation. Innovative improvements he suggests include placing a large tank in the centre of the pinery to collect rainwater from the roof in order to increase humidity levels.[57]

By the 1770s, anyone who was anyone among the upper echelons of society grew their own pineapples: 'no garden is now thought to be complete, without a stove for raising of pine-apples'.[58] Within a phenomenally short space of time, they had acquired a central role within English high society. Now at the peak of their power, the phrase 'a pineapple of the finest flavour' came into common usage as a metaphor to evoke the very splendid: used, for example, by James Boswell to describe a letter he received from David Garrick while he and Samuel Johnson were staying at an isolated inn in the Hebrides in 1774.[59] An entire industry soon sprang up. From the nurserymen who supplied the plants, to the builders who constructed the pineries, to the writers who published treatises at a couple of guineas a go, it was clear to many that there was real money to be made from this exotic ostentation.

6

'How many depend for their share of the guinea paid for the pine-apple? The fruiterer, the gardener, the glazier, the carpenter, the brick-layer, the smith, the coal-merchant, the mariner, the miner . . .'

George Walker (1799)

Few gardeners were more in demand in the eighteenth century than Henry Scott. Originally from Scotland (hence the name), Scott's employment by the Earl of Burlington at Chiswick House in London made him well known. Where he really excelled, however, was in the cultivation of pineapples. The more the Earl loaned him out to advise his friends and neighbours, the more the ingenious Scott was alerted to a previously untapped but potentially highly lucrative opportunity. For the pineapple in the eighteenth century was not just the plaything of the aristocracy. It was also an object of commerce.

Having accumulated both capital and expertise, in the early 1750s Scott took the brave decision to set up on his own. As a tradecard intended to advertise his services read, 'Pine apples raised and sold by Henry Scott, gardener, at Weybridge, Surrey. Where persons may be supplied with ripe fruit during their season, and plants of all sizes are sold at the lowest price. And as the Chertsey coach goes every day from thence to London, so ripe fruit may be easily sent by that conveyance and plants may be safely sent by the Weybridge boats. To London, twice a week . . .' It must have been a strange sight indeed.

13. A tradecard for Henry Scott's nursery in Weybridge, 1754.

One such tradecard was sent to Thomas Knowleton, who was both an acquaintance (he too was once in the service of the Earl of Burlington) and also a prospective customer. In Knowleton's view, it was 'extreemly well done . . . the neatest thing of the Kind I have ever seen'.[1] It is clear from Scott's activities that the cultivation of pineapples had become an unashamedly commercial enterprise.

From about the 1720s, Britain began to emerge as the world's first consumer society. This was in part because, like never before, the intellectual climate existed for such a society to flourish. In the sixteenth century, exotics were seen as a threat to the balance of trade and, therefore, to the wealth of the nation. 'Mere consumption' was an unequivocally pejorative term. But around the turn of the century, an alternative point of view gained ground. One of the earliest to articulate this was Dudley North: 'The main spur to Trade, or rather to Industry and Ingenuity, is the exorbitant Appetites of Men, which they will take great pains to gratifie, and so be disposed to work, when nothing else will incline them to it; for did Men content themselves with bare Necessaries, we should have a poor World.'[2] While this rather radical analysis did not gain widespread acceptance until the 1770s, the seed of the idea had at least been sown. It came to be appreciated that the appetite to consume, consume and consume was also a route to unprecedented levels of national prosperity. In some influential quarters, luxury came to be seen as a primarily positive force.[3]

This was bolstered by the publication of Bernard Mandeville's *Fable of the Bees* (1714). In essence this sought to uphold the production and consumption of certain types of luxury as a prerequisite of economic growth: 'The Prodigal is a Blessing to the whole Society', whereas 'Frugality is, like Honesty, a mean starving Virtue . . . 'Tis an idling dreaming Virtue that employs no Hands.'[4] For what use was a man with an income of £100,000 a year if he refused to spend any of it? It is not surprising then that the second volume of *Fable of the Bees* (1729) featured the pineapple in a starring role. One example of luxury, 'Their darling Folly', is described in by-now very familiar terms: 'It excels everything; it is extremely rich without being luscious, and I know nothing, to which I can compare the taste of it: to me it seems to be a collection of different fine Flavours, that puts me in mind of several delicious Fruits, which are yet all outdone by it.' An elaborate toast to Sir Matthew Decker ensues.[5] While Mandeville is rarely read today, at the time his book was a best-seller, with far-reaching influence among the aristocracy.

Some sought to challenge Mandeville's controversial argument that luxury was an inherently positive force: 'Amongst the many reigning vices of the present age none have risen to a greater height than that fashionable one of luxury, and few require more immediate suppression, as it not only enervates the people, and debauches their morals, but also destroys their substance.'[6] The pineapple was seen to be the ultimate in such behaviour. It was extortionately expensive. It was extraordinarily time-consuming to grow and prepare. It had little nutritional value that was not available in the common apple or pear. It looked like God had designed it for a joke. It encouraged envy, extravagance and more.

But this was a money-driven, trade-orientated economy. Entrepreneurs became more and more prolific, always on the look-out for new ways to make a profit. From steam power to umbrellas to goldfish, novelty was all. Even bread was not safe. To the wonder of Pastor Moritz, 'there is a way of roasting slices of buttered bread before the fire which is incomparable. One slice after another is taken and held to the fire with a fork till the butter soaks through the whole pile of slices. This is called *toast*.'[7] All kinds of schemes were invented to make money and according to Samuel Johnson, 'There was never from the earliest ages a time in which trade so much engaged the attention of mankind.'[8] While on the Continent, such activity was seen to be beneath the aristocracy, it was a trait peculiar to the English peerage to engage so shamelessly in trade directly alongside the merchant class. The Duke of Chandos invested in mineral-prospecting in New York, pearl-fishing off Anglesey and building projects in Bath; he had shares in the playhouse at Covent Garden, was a leading figure in the York Building Company and funded his very own orchestra and laboratory. Not surprisingly, he also sold pineapples.

From the 1730s at Shaw Hall in Berkshire, one of Chandos's minor estates, pineapples were grown for sale at half a guinea each – about half the price of a new wig.[9] The more impressive specimens were even sold on to shops: Chandos's steward was instructed to take a sample 'to the topping fruiterers in Town'.[10] Throughout the century people still attempted to maintain the illusion that this was not a pre-eminently commercial venture: in 1790 Philip Saxe of Newark in Nottinghamshire advertised that he 'will be glad to serve any Ladies or Gentlemen with Pine-Apples, or Pine-Plants', an enterprising money-making scheme since he had just taken over the running of Robert Wilson-Cracroft's garden at Hackthorn Hall in Lincolnshire.[11]

There is a crucial distinction to be made here. On the one hand is the aristocrat with a canny gardener keen to sell off a few pineapples to raise cash; on the other are men like Henry Scott for whom this was a way to earn a regular and excellent living. By the 1750s, there was the additional encouragement of intensified class competition. Unlike France, Britain had always been a society in which it was possible to leap the fences dividing social ranks, at least in theory. Yet as real incomes increased in the midst of an economic boom, the rise of the middle classes suddenly made this a dramatically more feasible option, terrifying those already at the top. The conundrum was, how to respond to the threat?

Increasing mass consumption of previously exotic commodities forced the upper classes to seek out ever more luxurious ones to assert their dominance. Sugar got cheaper: 200,000 lbs were consumed in 1690, 5,000,000 lbs in 1760, while tea halved in price over the same period. A commentator in mid-century Nottingham marvelled at the refinement of habits right down the social scale:

> People here are not without their Tea, Coffee and Chocolate, especially, the first, the use of which is spread to that Degree, that not only Gentry and Wealthy Travellers drink it constantly, but almost every Seamer, Sizer and Winder will have her Tea in a morning.

Little remained the exclusive domain of the aristocracy; but those indulgences that did were determinedly defended.

The result was the emergence in the 1760s and 1770s of a thrusting luxury industry. Furniture from Chippendale, mirrors from Linnell and china from Wedgwood all fuelled the first stirrings of the kind of ostentatious consumerism that still dominates the posher shopping streets today. A German visitor marvelled at the way 'England surpasses all the other nations of Europe in . . . luxury . . . and the luxury is increasing daily!'[12] Commodities like the pineapple became a genuine source of revenue. According to one commentator in 1769, 'if [a pineapple stove] be intended for profit, there is scarce any branch of gardening more lucrative'. Prices varied according to the time of year. Ripe pineapples were sold at an average price of eight shillings per pound; but 'for what can be ripened as to come in at the end of May, to be ready against the 4th of June, the king's birthday, almost any price may be procured; such is the demand for forced fruit, on account of the many entertainments, which the ambassadors and nobility give on that occasion'.[13] Here was the emergence of a commercial sector that had simply not existed at the start of the century.

The recent demand for exotics in general had resulted in the phenomenal proliferation of professional nurserymen. One of these was Henry Scott's brother, James Scott of Turnham Green near London, who advertised that his pineapple plants 'may be convey'd in health and ripe fruit in perfection, any journey of sixteen days'.[14] It was from James Scott that James Justice (in 1732 the first to cultivate pineapples in Scotland) recommended readers of his *Scots Gardiners Director* to get their pineapple plants.[15] Potentially, this was big business – by the standards of the age, at least. Others that did a lively trade by specialising in this much sought-after but still exclusive commodity included, from about the 1760s onwards, the Pine Apple at 66 New Exchange Building on the Strand and the Pine Apple on Arlington Street off Piccadilly.[16]

Some nurserymen used seed catalogues to advertise their services. Complete with illustrations and fixed prices, these were a relatively new phenomenon, just one example of the emerging forms of advertising being used to lure consumers in this period.[17] A catalogue issued by James Gordon advertises seven kinds of pineapple plant, including the 'hard to be got' striped leaf variety.[18] Gordon had been gardener to Lord Petre (whose pineapples had been so admired by Peter Collinson), but in about 1738 he established his own nursery in Mile End in East London, followed by a shop at 25 Fenchurch Street in the City.[19] The source of the pineapple plants he sold there so profitably is revealed in a letter that Thomas Knowleton wrote to a friend: 'I have by ye same post a Lettr from my Ld pettra gardr Gordon who is about Leaveing him & settling some where about Mile End . . . he wrot to me if I could part with a few pine apples plants wch he intends to Lawnce out with.'[20] By the final decades of the eighteenth century, Gordon's firm was London's pre-eminent horticultural supplier.

The pineapple had been in cultivation in Ireland since the 1730s under the aegis of a man named Daniel Bullen at his nursery on Dublin's New Street, but by the 1740s such was the demand for plants that at a shop called The Sign of the Pineapple on nearby Christchurch Lane, it became necessary for the owner John Phelan to employ watchmen, two of whom were stabbed by intruders keen to get hold of the precious stock.[21] This instance is one of the first to break the resounding silence that surrounds the response of the working class to the pineapple in this period. Regardless of whether they intended them for themselves or, more likely, for resale, the implication is that those lower down the social ladder were affected by the increasingly noisy clamour for them, alert to the values they had come to represent.

There was yet more money to be made from building structures in which to nurture the fruit. Back in 1724 Richard Bradley had provided a useful list of recommended London suppliers: he suggests Mr Rogers of Shoe Lane, 'a very ingenious Architect', to design the stove and the aptly named Mr Eden, 'a Workman of extraordinary Capacity in these Affairs', at the Bricklayers Arms in Miles Lane near Monument to construct it.[22] In view of Bradley's propensity to spot financial possibilities, the suspicion is that this was not an entirely independent judgement. There were, however, many others to choose from.

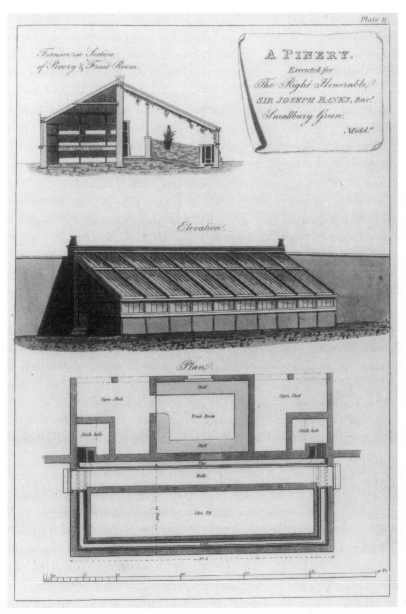

14. Sir Joseph Banks's pinery. From *Tod's Plans of Hot Houses* by George Tod, 1807.

By the end of the century, a wealth of expertise existed. In 1807 a book of hothouse designs by George Tod was published. In essence simply an extended advertisement for his work, most were based on ones that had been commissioned by such luminaries as Lord Heathfield and Sir Lionel Darell specifically for the cultivation of pineapples.[23] One of those featured is a pinery built for Sir Joseph Banks, since 1778 the President of the Royal Society, at Spring Grove in Middlesex. It certainly fulfilled its function splendidly: in 1784, Faujas de Saint-Fond commented upon the 'abundance of pineapples' displayed at a dinner Banks threw.[24] Another book of this kind published in 1798 by the architect William Robertson featured a design for a pinery that even incorporated a sitting room and a bedroom for the gardener, presumably to enable him to keep an eye on his cherished crop day and night.[25]

More than any other fruit, the pineapple had come to dominate the development of the science of horticulture, acting as the greatest challenge to which the gardeners of the upper classes could rise. For this reason, some head gardeners supplemented Bradley, Miller and the like by issuing their own instructive literature. The first dedicated practical work on the subject was written by John Giles, gardener to Lady Boyd, in 1767.[26] This was followed a couple of years later by a similar publication by Adam Taylor: 'in Deliciousness of Taste and exquisite Flavour, [the pineapple] so far exceeds all Fruits, that the Production of it in any tolerable Degree of Excellence, is becoming the fashionable Test of good Gardening'.[27] Taylor's claim to fame was that he was the first to ripen a pineapple using just the heat emitted by tanner's bark, with no stove to help it along; however, the small, withered fruit featured in the accompanying illustrations suggests it is an achievement that deserves only the very briefest round of applause.

Taking his lead from Giles and Taylor, William Speechly published his seminal work in 1779, while shorter articles and presentations to the Royal Society on the subject also abounded.[28] It was alleged, however, that certain authors, according to Thomas Hale in 1767, 'while they affect to disclose, apparently wish to conceal the Art for their private Advantage'.[29] This 'private Advantage' no longer consisted merely of personal prestige, but was also increasingly a major financial consideration.

The emergence of a modern consumer culture, especially in London, resulted in a whole crop of garden shops, fruit shops and confectionery shops.[30] This provided the pineapple with more opportunities than ever before to flaunt its charms. 'The magnificence of the shops', wrote the Prussian visitor Von Archenholz, 'is the most striking thing about London.'[31] By the late eighteenth century, Oxford Street alone had 153 shops to cater to 'the whim-whams and fribble-frabble of fashion'.[32] A number of these were luxury fruit-sellers, the most famous of which was Owen and Bentley's, just off the north end of Bond Street. In 1786, Sophie von la Roche described her awe at the range of desirable goods on display: 'Alluring are the confectioners and fruiterers, where, behind the handsome glass windows, pyramids of pineapples and all manners of fruits are on show . . . We inquired the price of a fine pineapple and did not think it too dear at 6s' (about the same amount as a junior garden boy might earn in a week).[33]

In an attempt to entice the casual passer-by, the rare and the exotic were prominently exhibited. Stylish carriages jostled for space with eager onlookers on the pavement outside. For the first time, the pineapple was on display to the masses but with one major caveat – 'look, but don't touch' was what the thick glass windows communicated. With its exclusive aura yet further enhanced by the glitz and the glamour of London's most à la mode streets, the pineapple really was a million miles away from its Amazonian origins. 'The age is running mad after innovation,' fumed Dr Johnson in 1783. 'All the business of the world is to be done in a new way.'[34] Sometimes the introduction of new products was stage-managed to enhance the sense of excitement: the fuchsia was at first priced exceptionally high to make it appear ultra exclusive and it was not until later that it was successfully popularised through auctions, lotteries and promotional campaigns. The pineapple, however, needed no such manipulation of its image in order to sustain its position as 'the king of fruits'.

15. A tradecard for Dominic Negri's confectionary shop on Berkeley Square, c.1785.

It was not only nurserymen and fruit-sellers that basked in the tropical lustre that emanated from the pineapple's core. All kinds of shopkeepers were aware of its power to flog a product to the upper classes. Most notably, it became the emblem of the confectionery trade. The Italian entrepreneur Dominic Negri was foremost among London's confectioners, supplying all the most glamorous households, making it entirely appropriate that he named his Berkeley Square shop The Pineapple. In a tradecard of c.1785, the premises are pictured surrounded by drawings of expressions of luxury, all presided over by a pineapple, the pinnacle of this.

This logic is cleverly echoed in Richard Brinsley Sheridan's popular play *The Rivals* (1775). Mrs Malaprop appositely confuses the two terms 'pinnacle' and 'pineapple', exclaiming in response to a flattering remark of Captain Absolute's, 'He is the very pineapple of politeness.' The pineapple had penetrated the public imagination to such an extent that the allusion would have been extremely familiar to contemporary theatre audiences.[35]

The pleasures of the pineapple could, however, be fatal. Rose Aylmer was the first love of the popular poet Walter Savage Landor. They fell for each other in the romantic setting of the Swansea Circulating Library; but almost before the relationship had a chance to splutter into life, Rose was sent away to India to join her uncle Sir Henry Russell, a judge at the High Court in Calcutta, leaving Landor in Wales with a broken heart.[36] She never returned. According to the well-known gossip William Hickey, then a member of the Indian Civil Service, on 2 March 1800 at the age of just twenty, Rose 'was attacked by a most severe bowel complaint brought on entirely by indulging too much with that mischievous and dangerous fruit, the pine-apple', despite the fact that he had in the past cautioned her against it, he claimed.[37] She died just a few days later and was buried in Calcutta in a tomb shaped like a pineapple (it is still possible to visit it). On hearing the news Landor composed a tribute entitled 'Rose Aylmer', I believe the only poem ever to recount a love affair thwarted by a pineapple.

Can this tale of death by pineapple possibly be true? It was not the only rumour. One of the most potent ones to resurface in this period was that it caused pregnant women to miscarry. A theory still commonly accepted in many Asian countries, it had first been mooted in the West by Father Du Tertre and later picked up on by Piso and many others. Despite the fact that it has no accepted scientific basis, it was given further credence by a surge in medical tracts concerned with childbirth, in particular cases of extraordinary childbirth. The *Gentleman's Magazine* contained a total of ninety-two articles on the subject in the 1740s alone. Around the same time aspersions were increasingly cast on the pineapple's harmful effects: '. . . 'tis subject to cause a Miscarriage, for which Reason Women with Child should abstain from it', Dr Robert James confidently asserted in 1747.[38] There also existed a long-standing theory, first propounded in Aristotle's *De Generatione et Corruptione*, that it was not only what you ate, but also what you saw, imagined or even thought about during pregnancy that somehow transferred itself to the baby when it was born. This line of thinking was dramatised to highly comic effect in Tobias Smollett's *Adventures of Peregrine Pickle* (1751).

Smollett was a physician, albeit not a very successful one, and he used his professional knowledge wittily in his books. Mrs Pickle is pregnant with the eponymous hero; and in order to get rid of her irritating sister-in-law, Mrs Grizzle, she pretends that she craves pineapples. She tells her that she 'had eaten a most delicious pine-apple in her sleep. This declaration was attended with an immediate scream uttered by Mrs Grizzle . . . [because if the] longing was baulked, the child might be affected with some disagreeable mark, or deplorable disease.' Mrs Grizzle is so worried that she searches the country for three days and three nights to find one. Contemporary readers, familiar with prevailing theories of the effect of the pineapple on pregnant women, would no doubt have appreciated the allusion. Smollett exploits the satirical possibilities in the legends that had grown up around the fruit to unmask – what? Society's deep-seated fear of female indulgence? An uneasiness about rampant consumerism?[39]

Most people, however, were more than happy to embrace that rampant consumerism. As the frenzy that surrounded the pineapple escalated, increasing efforts were made to sell the dream to the upper classes in all shapes, forms and materials. Here was a vessel through which the aristocracy was able to express a complicated but commonly understood cohort of contemporary values and mores within an arena that extended far beyond the garden or the dinner table. A pineapple in china or stone may not have been as impressive as the edible kind, but it did the job. Naturally decorative – symmetrical, simple, easy to stylise and recognise – to incorporate it into one's home was a form of self-expression. This trend had begun to emerge during the reign of William and Mary, for example in the form of a finial on the base of a silver pier table (1698), currently in the Queen's Ballroom at Windsor Castle, that was commissioned by the King himself.[40] But it was in Georgian furniture that it really became visible: among the multitude of examples that may still be seen today are ones on the state bed at Stowe House (c.1752) and on a gilt mirror at Castle Howard (c.1755). Once you begin to attune to the sight of an eighteenth-century pineapple, in England at least they seem to pop up almost wherever you go.

One of the pineapple's most memorable appearances was on chinaware designs manufactured by the great businessman Josiah Wedgwood. Wedgwood was among the first to appreciate the commercial importance of the endorsement of the upper classes, and in the early days of the business he targeted them shamelessly. The early 1760s saw the appearance of his earliest pineapple designs – glazed in green and gold, these epergnes, teapots, bowls, sauceboats, sugar dishes and tea caddies were made out of the cream-coloured earthenware he invented known as Queen's ware (colour plate VI). Exorbitantly expensive by the standards of the day, this was fashion at its most unabashed. Other designs also inspired by the fruit and vegetable world were offered – even the humble cauliflower featured occasionally – but it is no surprise that it was the motif of the pineapple that was one of his most popular products. The simple fact of associating oneself with it, in whatever form, had become imbued with meaning.[41]

16. A Coade stone pineapple on a gatepost outside Ham House.

More popular than any other form of representation was a stone pineapple atop a gatepost. This was the most public display possible – there was no danger that the neighbours might miss it. Many can still be seen today, for instance the ones made by Eleanor Coade in her patent stone in 1799 that are outside Ham House in west London.[42] However, eighteenth-century literature in Britain makes no allusion at all to this being a symbol of hospitality in the way it is often thought to have been in North America. Stone pineapples at the front gates of eighteenth- or nineteenth-century houses in Britain were instead erected to signify a certain lifestyle. Situated in such a way that they served to mark out the limits of property, these were a way of differentiating between those who could afford the pineapple, whether in reality or in replica, and those who could not. It is ironic that what we now think of as something of an archetypal symbol of Georgian gentility was in reality a vulgar, showy ploy.

One of the earliest examples is described in the diaries of Nicholas Blundell, a country squire from Lancashire in the lower ranks of the upper classes. He was a keen gardener, keeping a record of all the details of daily life outdoors, whether it is that his gardener has just planted a row of thirty-five trees or that the weather is unusually frosty for the time of year. Pineapple plants are not mentioned, seemingly out of his price range, but in 1722 he found a way of surmounting this problem to some degree, such was his desire to have the fruit somehow represented on his estate.

February 8 –
John Vose [has] now fixed the second Pine Apple upon the Pillers at the higher end of the Gravell Walk.

The job continued over the next two days.

February 9 –
John Vose, &c.: Plaistered the Pine Apples over with very fine Lime and Hear and almost finish'd all the Plaistering as it to be under them upon the Necks and Cornish.

February 10 –
The Punsh Bowl being fixed in the Middle of the Arch over my Coat
of Armes and it and the two Pine Apples being Plaistered I gave the
Brick-men a Drink upon the Scaffold.[43]

Blundell's younger brother Richard had died in 1704 in Virginia,
having ventured there as an apprentice to a Liverpudlian merchant.
Perhaps the pineapples on his gateposts were a way for Blundell to pay
private tribute to this close-to-home casualty of the New World.[44]

The decision by Admiral Thomas Mathews, Commissioner of the
Navy, to install stone pineapples in his garden in Chatham in 1736
may have been influenced by similar motives: he had spent years on
the high seas in command of a squadron against pirates in the East
Indies.[45] The 'long' eighteenth century (the period between the
Glorious Revolution in 1688 and the Battle of Waterloo in 1815) saw
imperialism evolve into a central tenet of British identity. At the same
time, Britain established its dominant position within the many
trading empires of Europe. As a result, as the century progressed the
pineapple's role as a symbol of status became increasingly intertwined
with its role as a compelling and high-profile expression of the
emerging British empire.[46]

A poem of 1766 by James Grainger recounts how on the island of
St Christopher's, 'the Sun's child, the mail'd anana, yields / His regal
apple to the ravish'd taste . . .', a metaphor for the way that the
'mail'd' native Americans had been forced to 'yield' themselves to
those who 'ravish'd', that is the British.[47] The exotic is a construct:
any entity only becomes exotic when it is different to what we know
already. As Peter Mason writes, 'It is not the "original" geographic or
cultural contexts which are valued, but the suitability of the objects in
question to assume new meanings.'[48] The new meaning attached to
the pineapple was that it was a physical manifestation of Britain's
spectacularly successful appropriation of the New World.[49] The
chapter on 'Trade' in the 1718 edition of *The Present State of Great
Britain* (read at the time by everyone who mattered) opens with the

proud assertion that 'Next to the purity of our religion we are the most considerable of any nation in the world for the vastness and extensiveness of our trade.'[50] Every time a pineapple appeared at the dinner table or in representation, those present were reminded of this fact.

Since the acquisition of Barbados in 1625, Britain had established a thriving network of colonies in the West Indies, the nation's primary supplier of pineapple plants. The next century saw British trade increase to an unprecedented level: between 1700 and 1798, total imports increased from a value of £5,819,000 to £23,903,000, while total exports increased from £4,461,000 to £18,298,000. In addition, in 1700 most foreign commerce, in volume and value, was still conducted with Europe; yet between 1700 and 1798, imports from the West Indies (mostly sugar, tobacco, rice, coffee and also, of course, pineapples) increased from 14 per cent to 25 per cent of total trade, while exports to the West Indies (mostly textiles, metalware and glassware) increased from 5 per cent to 25 per cent of total trade. Surviving records of shopkeepers, such as Abraham Dent of the village of Kirkby Stephen near Manchester, show that even in the depths of the countryside customers had access to produce from all over the world – ginger, quinine, cinnamon and the like. Evidently, Britain was becoming more and more dependent on trade with its colonies, a state of affairs upheld by Adam Smith's influential opinion piece *The Wealth of Nations* (1776) in which he put forward the proposition that 'Consumption is the sole end and purpose of all production; and the interest of the producer ought to be attended to, only so far as it may be necessary for promoting that of the consumer.'[51]

As the force of British imperialism penetrated territories to the West, the potency of the pineapple as a symbol of the power of the empire increased accordingly. The presence of a pineapple (whether at the dinner table or in the form of a decorative motif) served to emphasise the fruits of British victory overseas. This contributes a specifically political dimension, for example, to Sir Robert Walpole's presentation of a pineapple to his dinner guests at Houghton. Having been a keen advocate of free trade with the empire throughout his parliamentary career, his choice of dessert asserted the fact in a much more spectacular manner than the powdery crystals of sugar or the withered leaves of tea ever could.

Moreover, the aristocracy indulged in the exotic in order to remind and reassure itself of the role of Britain on the world stage. As Linda Colley argues, this was a period in which its people embarked upon a major re-evaluation of British identity; within this process the pineapple fulfilled an important function, by expressing a multitude of values in just a single fountain of yellow and green.[52] This explains the presence of the pineapple in the 1788 coat of arms of the Benson family of Lutwyche, Shropshire, alongside the family motto, 'Leges arma tenant sanctas commercia leges' ('Arms keep laws sacred both commerce and laws').[53] In 1785 Lutwyche Hall had been purchased by Moses Benson; at the time he was the Governor of Bermuda and therefore very much aware of the centrality of trade, a theme embodied and paraded in his newly designed crest.

Yet nowhere does the symbolic power of this fruit impress more than at the Pineapple at Dunmore Park in Stirlingshire, a garden folly looming fifty-three feet high inside the estate's walled apple orchard (colour plate VII). The architect is not recorded in official records, but tradition ascribes it to Sir William Chambers – its eccentric design is not dissimilar to the spirit of his contemporary work at Kew Gardens. The structure's classical base was built in 1761, but the stone sculpture on the top was probably a later addition commissioned by John Murray, the fourth Lord Dunmore.[54]

The fourth Lord Dunmore was the eldest son of William, the third Lord Dunmore, by his wife the Honourable Catherine Nairn. In 1770, at the age of thirty-eight, he was appointed governor of the colony of New York, to which was subsequently added that of Virginia. From the beginning of his tenure, however, he was deeply unpopular. Hindered by his Scottish ancestry that led him to appear boorish to the Virginian gentry, he did not do himself any favours with his impatient and abrupt manner. He was also rather a coward: with the onset of the mass unrest that was to culminate in the American Revolution, his immediate instinct was to retreat from the Governor's Palace to the safety of naval vessels moored offshore.

What was deemed even more unforgivable was that he became the only British commander ever to free slaves. Having failed utterly to establish his dominance, he went on to suffer a series of humiliating losses in battle that culminated in defeat on Gwynn's Island in the Chesapeake on 8 July 1776. It is likely that he commissioned the Pineapple on his return from the New World the same year.

No records survive to explain Lord Dunmore's reasons for choosing a pineapple of such spectacularly enormous proportions to decorate his garden retreat. The fruit's aesthetically satisfying appearance may have played a role, but surely there was more to it? By the 1760s Dunmore Park possessed a productive pinery of its own: perhaps the sculpture was a means to commemorate the first successful fruiting, as well as acting as a constant reminder to his neighbours of the extent of his wealth. Dunmore also owned an apartment at Holyrood in Edinburgh and must have enjoyed impressing his dinner guests in town with fresh pineapples from his country estate.

The Pineapple may also have been built for the associations it

17. A design for a garden temple, from *Grotesque Architecture* by William Wrighte, 1767.

inspired in the viewer's imagination. The theory of architectural association originated in Thomas Hobbes's *Human Nature* but in 1805 it was summarised by Richard Payne Knight: 'To a mind richly stored, almost every object of nature or art, that presents itself to the senses, either excites fresh trains and combination of ideas, or vivifies and strengthens those which existed before: so that recollection enhances enjoyment, and enjoyment brightens recollection.'[55] Applied to the architectural role of the pineapple, one aspect becomes clear: its most immediate and appealing associations are the other-worldly antithesis of the dull greys and greens of rainy Britain. This is a manifestation of a yearning for the escapist 'other' that was identified by James (now Jan) Morris as a kind of alter ego – 'as though the British had another people inside themselves . . . who yearned to break out of their sad or prosaic realities, and live more brilliant lives in Xanadu'.[56] For this reason it featured frequently in contemporary design manuals, for example at the top of a temple in William Wrighte's 1767 best-seller *Grotesque Architecture*.

In addition, the Pineapple reflects a subversive streak in the British aristocracy, bursting out of the rigid repression of the classical form of the Pineapple's base, as extravagant in its way as Horace Walpole's Strawberry Hill or William Beckford's Fonthill. The triumph of the whim of the individual over the rule of authority was a trend typical of Enlightenment thought, and the juxtaposition of European classicism and the New World influence in the form of the pineapple was relatively common in eighteenth-century architecture – though rarely in such an extreme form. For example, an *umbrello* built by the banker Henry Hoare in the 1740s at Stourhead in Wiltshire was supported on a Roman Doric column and topped by a pineapple.[57]

However, it is surely Dunmore's experiences in the New World that hold the key. It was there that he had proved so incapable of asserting his authority over the foreign. While it may therefore seem odd that on his return he chose to erect such a potent reminder, perhaps – by representing the pineapple in classical, Western terms – he sought to translate a foreign, somewhat threatening entity into the familiar cultural setting of his apple orchard, a setting in which he felt able to control it in a way he had failed to do with the reality. An attempt to contextualise the exotic, it was a reaction not dissimilar to the way that two centuries earlier, the 'ananas' had been renamed the 'pineapple'.

Yet the ambiguous nature of the fruit meant it continued to become entangled within the web of controversy over the rights and wrongs of luxury that had in fact changed little since the likes of Andrew Marvell. In the literature of the later eighteenth century, no other commodity is used more often to evoke the privileges of the upper classes. 'What right has one man to eat a pine-apple, for which he gave a guinea, when another is starving for want of a half-penny worth of bread?' cries the narrator of George Walker's radical and popular novel, *The Vagabond* (1799). His adversary has a convincing argument at the ready, however, in an implicit criticism of this kind of Jacobite, pro-revolutionary sentiment:

> How many depend for their share of the guinea paid for the pine-apple? The fruiterer, the gardener, the glazier, the carpenter, the brick-layer, the smith, the coal-merchant, the mariner, the miner . . .; and when you shall have divided the guinea between all these, I think the gentleman may eat his pine-apple with a good conscience . . .[58]

But the accusation was a common one. In the uncertain aftermath of the French Revolution, the world of extreme privilege was an uncomfortable place to be.

For this reason, the pineapple also became a regular element of satirical cartoons, in particular at the beginning of the Napoleonic Wars. One gorgeous example is *The Cabinet Dinner or a Political Meeting* by C. Williams (1804) (colour plate VIII). It depicts eight members of an opposition Cabinet – Fox, Buckingham, Carlisle and Grenville amongst others – that was formed by the Prince of Wales in response to the King's illness. They are asleep around the dinner table, red-faced and drunk, surrounded by the remnants of a lavish dinner. Strewn among the emptied glasses are two pineapples, one only half-eaten – an instant visual expression of the decadence of the ruling classes.

For the puritanical, further provocation was at hand. The lusty overtones of Georgian art and society gave an even more sexually charged symbolism to the pineapple than ever before. In the midst of an essay of 1761 about what makes a woman truly beautiful comes the unusual metaphor that 'a Woman is like a Pine-apple; yet the Similitude would hold much farther, and in more Particulars, than any one would first imagine. She has her Season of growing to her greatest State of Beauty, of Continuance in it, and of a Decay from it, as well as that; and the highest Season of their Beauty is just as properly timed in the one Case, as in the other.' Whoever the obnoxious author was then goes on to rate various well-known London society beauties of the age with an elaborate points system, based on marks out of twenty-five to be awarded in four different categories: colour, shape, expression and grace.[59] It was enough to make even Queen Charlotte retreat to her water-closet.

This anonymous author was one of the more restrained in the comparisons he made. In *The Seasons* (1730) the poet James Thomson lingers over the luscious fruit, 'the pride of vegetable life': 'Quick let me strip thee of thy tufty coat, / Spread thy ambrosial stores, and feed with Jove!'[60] The pineapple's association with a beautiful woman was not a new one – Christopher De Rochefort, Richard Ligon and many others had previously drawn on this theme – but it was one that in this period was to damage its reputation more than ever before.

Another constant was the linking of the temptation of the pineapple to the temptation of women. One to articulate this was the convivial actor John Henderson in a letter he wrote to a friend on New Year's Day 1770: 'I eat pine-apple the other day, and if that be the fruit the Devil offered Eve, I don't see how she could resist it.'[61] Perhaps in this era of lax morals, the suggestion that the pineapple was responsible for the Fall of Man simply enhanced its image as the bad boy of the fruit world. The more retro-Puritanical, however, did not see it this way. As the poet Christopher Smart put it in 1763:

> For Adoration from the down,
> Of dam'sins to th'ananas crown,

God sends to tempt the taste;
And while the luscious zest invites,
The sense, that in the scene delights,
Commands desire to be chaste.[62]

The emphasis on the theatrical nature of the pineapple ('the scene delights') perhaps knowingly recalls the way Andrew Marvell depicted it on a 'grassy Stage'.

The pineapple was born a performer: 'painted' was how Oviedo had put it. When raised in cold climes, its essentially artificial nature provided even more ammunition for the god-fearing. While today, for a fruit to be so violently denounced seems rather humorous, at the time it was genuinely a matter of debate. Mrs Grizzle in *Peregrine Pickle* attacks pineapples for being 'altogether unnatural productions, extorted by the force of artificial fire, out of filthy manure'. By recalling the fires of hell, she suggests that this is the destination to which eating the pineapple ultimately brings us. In a society dominated by the teachings of the Bible, straying into such conjury was sure to be criticised.

William Cowper's poem 'The Bee and the Pineapple', written in 1779 when the fruit was at the height of its power to seduce, encapsulates much contemporary thinking on the subject.

A Bee allur'd by the Perfume
Of a rich Pine Apple in bloom,
Found it within a frame inclosed,
And lick'd the Glass that interposed,
Blossoms of Apricot and Peach,
The Flow'rs that Blow'd within his Reach,
Were arrant Drugs compar'd with That
He strove so vainly to get at.
No Rose could yield so rare a Treat,
Nor Jessamine was half as Sweet.
The Gard'ner saw this Much Ado,
(The Gard'ner was the Master too)
And thus he said – Poor restless Bee!

I Learn Philosophy from Thee –
I Learn how Just it is and Wise,
To Use what Providence supplies,
To leave fine Titles, Lordships, Graces,
Rich Pensions, Dignities and Places,
Those Gifts of a Superior kind,
To those for who they were design'd . . .[63]

In Cowper's poem, the 'rich' pineapple is a symbol of the privileges of the upper classes, of 'Titles, Lordships, Graces'. An early draft had gone even further: 'Methinks, I said, in thee I find / The sin and madness of mankind.'[64] Yet much as he damns this social aspiration, Cowper's interpretation remains conservative, even snobbish – the pineapple should be left to 'those for who they were design'd' rather than be appropriated by all who had the cash. This is thrown into new light with the revelation that Cowper himself owned a pinery, for all his criticisms apparently unable to resist the fruit's charms.

Cowper was one of the foremost poets of his generation. His musings on the wonders of nature were well known; his depressive turns, however, were less so. In the course of one year he attempted suicide three times. His garden at Orchard Side in Olney in Buckinghamshire no doubt proved a welcome distraction. Here he was able to participate in the mania for pineapples not just imaginatively but in a practical sense as well. In May 1776 in a letter to Joseph Hill, Cowper's lawyer and close friend, he expressed his mortification that Hill's gardener had got a head start on him – 'but let him be upon his guard, or I shall be too nimble for him another year'.[65] And too nimble he was. In October 1779, in a letter to Hill in which he also enclosed an early draft of *The Bee and the Pineapple*, he wrote, 'The newspaper informs me of the arrival of the Jamaica fleet. I hope it imports some pine-apple plants for me. I have a good frame and a good bed prepared to receive them. I send you annexed a fable, in which the pine-apple makes a figure, and shall be glad if you like the taste of it.'[66]

Cowper's ambiguous stance – replete with denigration at the same time as he forks out yet more cash to ensure that pineapples flourish in his own back garden – is typical of the sentiments of the time. And the pineapple's aristocratic links were even more of a problem in efforts to popularise the fruit on the other side of the Atlantic. In the recently founded colonies of North America, where positions of rank were newly established and wholly unstable, there was all the more need to assert one's status. These colonies were also enslaved to all things English: the fashion for pineapples soon found its way there, to be replanted, recast and reinterpreted in America's own inimitable style.

7

'None pleases my taste as do's the pine'

George Washington (1751)

It was May 1774 and George Washington had a dinner party to plan. It was an opportunity to wine, dine and opine amongst his fellow Virginian plantation owners during a crucial month for the burgeoning Independence movement, and although it was scheduled for some weeks off, provisions had to be ordered right away – the very limited transport network meant that there was simply no knowing how long they would take to arrive. Washington's wife Martha was already under instruction to deal with most of the food – reams of beef, mountains of sea-turtle, half a sheep and enough oysters to keep the scullery maid busy from dawn 'til dusk – but it remained up to Washington to ensure that county gossip the morning after was left in no doubt whatsoever that his dinner table represented the epitome of what it meant to be genteel in colonial America. He thought he had found the answer: pineapples.

Washington had had a predilection for pineapples ever since he first tried one, aged just nineteen, on the only trip he ever made abroad – to Barbados with his half-brother Lawrence. 'None pleases my taste as do's the pine,' he confided to his diary.[1] It was a judgement no doubt influenced by his choice of holiday reading, a copy of Griffith Hughes's *Natural History of Barbados* (1750) that he had borrowed from a neighbour: 'If the general, or at least if the Judgment of the

18. From *Natural History of Barbados* by Griffith Hughes, 1750.

most numerous Part of Mankind, who have tasted of this Fruit, may be relied upon, it deserves the Preference of all other Fruits; the agreeable Variety, and the delicate quick Poignancy of its Juice is justly esteemed to excel every other.'[2] Who was Washington to disagree?

Following a typically sociable week (various dinners, a boat race and a barbecue), on 10 May Washington had a free day at home at Mount Vernon. Much of it was spent, pipe in hand, catching up on the mountain of correspondence he had to deal with before he left for Williamsburg to attend the May session of the House of Burgesses.[3] Among the notes promptly dispatched was one to an acquaintance, Captain Robert McMickan, placing an order, in exchange for a parcel of herrings and a hundred barrels of flour, for (among other things) three dozen West Indian pineapples.[4]

Washington knew that it might be five, six or even seven weeks before the pineapples arrived. He had recently heard tell that it was possible to circumvent the wait by growing your own, a friend of his near Baltimore, Charles Carroll, having done precisely this – an extraordinary feat in this unpredictable environment where finances were precarious, time and labour at a premium and horticultural knowledge scarce. Washington was also reluctant to buy the necessary equipment from London since it would have meant flouting the Non-Importation Agreements introduced in the colonies from 1767 onwards that prohibited the import of British goods. Nonetheless, he must have felt somewhat despondent at being left out of this fascinating new phenomenon. No stranger to the elevated habits of the English aristocracy (the kin of Lord Thomas Fairfax had been an influence in his life for some years), in the years that preceded the American Revolution few things served to cast Washington in the guise of a wealthy and cultured gentleman more effectively than a home-grown pineapple. For all his admirable qualities, Washington was, like most of us, not above the occasional chance to show off.[5]

In the same way that, for thousands of men and women, the recently discovered continent of North America presented a whole new world of near-limitless opportunities, so it did for the pineapple. Found in abundance in the Caribbean, it was a rare treat for crews, weary and weather-beaten by the epic voyage across the Atlantic, who stopped off on one of the islands to stock up on supplies from the last bastion of (relative) civilisation until they had to face the vagaries of the colony. It lasts well in the hold, after all. For this reason, the first decade of the seventeenth century onwards saw a fair few of the fruit successfully wend their way northwards.

The earliest known reference to the presence of a pineapple in North America comes from William Strachey. One of hundreds of brave or deluded men willing to sail into the all but unknown where the climate was harsh, the resources limited and the natives unfriendly, Strachey arrived in Jamestown in 1609 and was soon appointed secretary of Virginia. He had heard tell of a 'dainty' and 'nice' fruit that looked a little like a pinecone, yet the reality of it was a little less forthcoming, unfortunately:

the Rootes of the delitious Indian-Pina, sett in a sandy place, thrived and continued life, without respect had of yt, until the cold winter and the weeds choaked yt . . .[6]

The pineapple 'choaked' by the harsh and unfamiliar environment presents the reader with a powerfully anthropomorphic image. It perhaps echoes Strachey's sentiments about the effect of the miserable conditions experienced in the colony on himself too. He was not alone in harbouring some bitterness once he realised how misled he had been by the propaganda pumped out by the Virginia Company, who insisted that this was a land of infinite fecundity – 'Earth's only Paradise'.[7]

As more and more ships arrived, there were undoubtedly repeated attempts to naturalise the pineapple. In December 1621, settler Henry Earle noted that a ship arriving in Virginia from Bermuda brought with it 'Vines of all sorts, Oranges and Lemon trees, Sugar Canes, Cassado Roots (that make bread), Pines, Plantans, Potatoes,

19. A watercolour of *The Pyne Frute* painted by John White during the expedition of 1585 to establish a colony on Roanoke Island, Virginia, an expedition that took him via Dominica, Santa Cruz and Puerto Rico where pineapples grew prolifically by this date.

and sundry other fruits and plants, not formerly seene in Virginia'.[8] While he claims that all these began to flourish, it seems likely that he simply failed to single out the 'Pine' as the one disappointing exception.

The truth was that Virginia and the surrounding area simply did not suit it. To consent to grow outside its natural habitat, the pineapple demands time, attention and a finely tuned climate and soil. In the American colonies it experienced none of these. The winters were freezing, the soil was mineral-poor and the settlers were all but stranded in an environment where the daily strictures of finding food, keeping warm and fighting off the natives were quite enough to keep most occupied day to day. Non-staple foodstuffs like the pineapple were the least of their worries. As a result, its progress through the remainder of the seventeenth century is a little murky, and in 1672 it was still the case that 'this rare fruit is altogether a stranger to this Northern part of the World'.[9]

Nonetheless, it managed to maintain an imaginative presence through the many reports of what it was 'said to be', as William Strachey put it. De Rochefort, Ligon and others all produced texts with which many of the gentlemen colonists would have been familiar. Glowing accounts also came from people they actually knew. Captain John Smith, one of the founders of the Jamestown settlement, sampled a pineapple in Bermuda and proclaimed it 'most delicate',[10] while in 1634 Father Andrew White, a Jesuit priest aboard the first expedition to settle Maryland under Lord Baltimore, raved about a fruit he had come across in Barbados that was 'of the colour of gould . . . perfect . . . for sure it is the queene of all meat fruits without exception'. Also enticing is his description of the taste as a cross between wine and strawberries.[11] By casting the pineapple in these by-now familiar guises, these early chroniclers of North America did their bit to ensure the pineapple maintained its public profile.

It was not long before the struggle for survival in the American colonies receded to such a degree that the great planters could at last, with sufficient time and funds, concentrate on attaining the stylish living so exalted in England. From about the 1720s, whether you were a merchant from Rhode Island, a lawyer from Maryland or a plantation owner from Virginia, the common factor was the desire to create a home in conscious emulation of the English country house. There was a frenzy of spending on furniture, clothes, books and all the other accoutrements that somehow gave life to this proposition. Most were garnered from a select few London establishments through which the élite class, especially those south of Philadelphia, did almost all their shopping for luxury goods – either directly by placing orders through agents based in London or indirectly by patronising the numerous stores that sprang up locally to sell imported luxury goods.

As one of the most prevalent decorative forms of the age in England, it is no wonder that the first pineapples to find a role within American cultural life were those made of stone, silver, wood or porcelain. Particularly common were stone pineapples atop gateposts like those that adorned William Byrd's house, Westover, in Virginia from about 1730. If you had the cash, these were widely available: in 1769, Alexander Bartram's shop 'next door to the sign of the Indian king, in Market Street' in Philadelphia advertised pineapple stoneware 'Just imported in the last vessels from England'.[12] Representations of the pineapple also appeared resplendent in a variety of other locations, among them the Shirley Plantation on the James river in Virginia from 1725 and at the Poynton House in Salem in Massachusetts from 1750 – above the doorway, on the wood panelling or as a finial on the roof or the staircase, perhaps. Churches were no exception. In 1760, Charleston's showpiece church, St Michael's, acquired '1 Pine Apple at the top of the Pulpit' at a cost of £12, according to the labourer's bill – thereby exacerbating the conflation of the godly pinecone and the decidedly ungodly pineapple.[13]

But it was the craze for pineappleware at the dinner table that really captured people's imagination. Some of this took the form of silverware, like the 1763 silver epergne made by Thomas Pitts of London, now in the collection of the Colonial Williamsburg Foundation.[14]

20. Westover's front door.

21. A stone pineapple on a gatepost outside Westover.

Most popular of all was English Staffordshire pineappleware: available to buy in London from the early 1760s, it was only a matter of months before it found its way across the Atlantic. A riffle through the *Pennsylvania Gazette* from this decade throws up regular advertisements like that for Joseph Stansbury's shop on Second Street near Arch Street in Philadelphia where in December 1769 he had a range of pineapple teapots to offer his customers. Pineapple-shaped snuff boxes were also popular.[15] And it was not only in the major ports that such goods were available. In June 1766, Francis Wade publicised a new shop he had just opened in Wilmington in Delaware selling pineapple teapots, bowls, sugar dishes, mugs, cups and saucers, 'Imported in the last vessels from London, Liverpool, and Ireland' and offered for sale 'at the Philadelphia prices'.[16] Evidence of English Staffordshire pineappleware has been recovered in Colonial Williamsburg, at Thomas Jefferson's home, Monticello, in Virginia and throughout colonial America.[17]

Right now, somewhere on America's eastern seaboard, a hapless tour guide is pointing to one of these colonial-era representations of a pineapple as he or she relates the story of how the pineapple supposedly became a universal symbol of hospitality. It tends to go something like this: when sea captains returned from trade missions with the West Indies, they also brought with them a custom picked up from the natives. This was to place a fresh pineapple at the entrance to their home to signify to the neighbours that visitors would be welcome. The theory is that colonial gentlemen then sought to echo this custom in a more permanent form.

Contemporary sources, however, make no reference to this story. In fact, it only gained currency in the 1930s as historic house museums sought to recreate an idealised colonial past. While these admirable attempts to drum up interest in the history of colonial America – efforts now termed the Colonial Revival – have had a far-reaching influence on perceptions of the period, much of the early research upon which this was based has since turned out to be unreliable. The pineapple was no exception. Since it appears in many locations traditionally associated with hospitality – gateposts, teapots, dinnerware – it was given this association retrospectively. In the eighteenth and nineteenth centuries, it signified something else altogether.

All the associations that surrounded an artistic representation of a pineapple in this period were inherited wholesale from England, particularly status. On a gatepost, for example, it served to differentiate between the haves and the have-nots. In the frenzy to establish this kind of social differentiation in the colonies from the 1730s, the pineapple – rare, strange and expensive – was a useful and distinctive marker. A less democratic response to the fruit than previously thought, it was nonetheless the one recognised at the time.

Such resonance meant that the fashion for the real thing also found its way across the Atlantic before long. Preserved pineapple eaten as a sweetmeat had been available in the colonies for some time: it was a particular favourite, for example, of William Burnet, Governor first of New York and New Jersey and then of Massachusetts until his death in 1728.[18] However, it was not long before fresh pineapple in all its luscious and exotic reality also became an option for those so long starved of treats – albeit only for the very richest.

Pineapples had featured in cargoes coming north from the Caribbean (in particular the Bahamas) since the beginning of the century, but it was not until the 1750s that they began arriving all through the summer months at ports along the east coast from New York to Charleston and everywhere in between. One day in the summer of 1752, for instance, the *Virginia Gazette* announced the arrival in Williamsburg port of seven dozen pineapples from New Providence in the Bahamas.[19] Young scallions who scrimped a living by offering themselves up for casual labour at the dockside clamoured just for a peek at this strange fruit.

Local grocers stocked imported fruit – if you had the ready cash. For a small quantity, this was your best bet, though for more, for instance for a party, it was best to go directly to the dockside. Supply was still very limited. There were rumours that some colonial confectioners hired them out by the day (the same fruit were later sold on to more affluent clients). Within a decade, the size of a typical cargo of pineapples had increased more than tenfold: 11 August 1768 saw the announcement in the *Virginia Gazette* of a cargo of 100 dozen pineapples aboard the *Sally* from New Providence.[20]

Here, as in Britain, the pineapple had become one of the features of the dinner party to which everyone aspired. It helped maintain the sense that this was a society on the up, where social decorum, as in all civilised societies, really mattered. Because of this, proceedings tended to be as elegant and elaborate as resources allowed. The genteel hour for dinner was the early afternoon – about three o'clock. A description of a sitting at Robert Carter's country seat Nomini Hall in Virginia regales the reader with the ritual involved. Conversation strained to be the most cultured around – one night saw 'a conversation on Philosophy, on Eclipses; the manner of viewing them; Thence to Telescopes, & the information wich they afforded us of the Solar System; Whether the planets be actually inhabited &c.' Once grace had been said, the food was served: 'Sir – This is a fine Sheeps-Head, Mr Stadly shall I help you? – Or would you prefer a Bass or Perch? – Or perhaps you will rather help yourself to some picked Crab.'[21] While high-quality meat and fish was one way of impressing the guests, the pineapple was infinitely more spectacular. Served during the dessert course in the same way that it was in England, it topped a pyramid of fruit, surrounded by sweetmeats upon a porcelain platter. Thus the novelty of it existed for all to see.

One of the pineapple's best customers in the thriving colonial town of Williamsburg was the Governor of Virginia, the Baron de Botetourt. His grave demeanour was undermined not only by a double chin so gigantic that it looked like it might entirely engulf his tiny mouth, but also by bags under his eyes that suggested far too many late nights – this was a man for whom entertaining was a serious business. The accounts of William Sparrow, the palace cook from July 1769, support this. In Sparrow's first five months in the job, the average monthly cost of running the kitchen increased to nearly £70 – a staggering 40 per cent of the Governor's basic salary.[22] Pineapples were no small element of this. They were purchased on his behalf by the palace cook, either at the local town market, in a local store or from a hawker who brought them to the kitchen direct. The cost varied between 1s. 3d. and 2s. each, usually purchased in quantities of between six and twelve – in a period when 2s. represented a day's wages for the average tradesman. In July 1770, at the height of the pineapple season, a total of £1 14s. was spent on buying twenty pineapples, a little over half of what the cook spent on meat in the same period and the equivalent today of about £100.[23]

While this may seem like unforgivable extravagance in view of the hardships being faced by other colonists, it was accepted as entirely fitting for a man of de Botetourt's position. Originally from the West Country and a Tory Member of Parliament for Gloucestershire for over twenty years, in 1760 he had been appointed to the prestigious position of groom of the King's bedchamber. Eight years later, he was sent to the colonies to be the King's representative in Virginia – an emissary not only of the might of the King, but also, crucially, of the foibles and fads that upheld the innermost machinery of the English court. For those desperate for news from the mother country, he became the undisputed arbiter of what was and what was not 'polite' within the rigours of Virginian high society.

For de Botetourt, entertaining on a grandiose scale also provided a crucial validation of his position. It is impossible to over-estimate the central place that this took in colonial life and customs. A previous Governor, Francis Nicholson, had almost been unseated when he failed to live up to the standards that the gentry expected: as one writer spluttered, it was 'most scandalously penurious, no way suiting the dignity of her Ma'ties Governour, having but one Dish of meat at his table'.[24] Such a complaint may seem excessive, but it was seen as a genuine slight. The Governor's public image, of which the dinner table played no small part, was an essential element of his claim to power – and, by extension, the King's. Since de Botetourt was not married – his dinner guests tended to be mostly local gentry or businessmen from out of town – it was common for no women at all to be present, further encouraging the conversation not to stray too far from matters of politics, petitioning and patronage. That de Botetourt took his duties in this arena seriously was one reason why he became so highly respected: 'he is universally esteemed here, for his great Assiduity in his Office, Condescension, good Nature and true Politeness'.[25] On his death on 15 October 1770, he was succeeded as Governor by John Murray, the fourth Earl of Dunmore, who later built his famous Pineapple at Dunmore Park. In view of the premium that the Virginia gentry placed on the appearance of gentility, it is no surprise that the grumpy Dunmore was widely disliked.

Not surprisingly for someone in his position, June 1768 saw Thomas Jefferson make a purchase of pineapples and oranges at a total cost of 12s. 6d.[26] These were usually displayed at dinner whole, but pineapple pudding was also a popular recipe in the Jefferson household – it appears in a recipe book treasured by Virginia Randolph, Martha Jefferson Randolph's fifth daughter.[27] As an ambitious young lawyer in only his second year of professional practice at the Bar, this kind of expenditure was an investment. He had a reputation to uphold. In 1769 he began his political career when he was elected to the House of Burgesses by the freeholders of Albermarle. I do not propose that it was due to pineapples – but certainly, their presence helped him present to the world the kind of image that he wanted all to see.

In mansion houses up and down the country, men of the status of George Washington and Thomas Jefferson, amid delightfully gracious and measured chat flattered by flickering candlelight, were displaying a pineapple at dinner as one of a variety of means of asserting their place within this newly formed and deeply fragile social structure. It showed they had the hard cash necessary to purchase such a luxury. It also hinted at close contacts with the burgeoning trade network with the West Indies, a situation to be much envied. If it was possible to get hold of a pineapple, was there no limit to the novelties which this gentleman had the clout to conjure up? This is why, from early on, it was often given as a present: in 1734, Judge Benjamin Lynde (at the time the Chief Justice of the Supreme Judicial Court) noted happily in his diary that his brother-in-law had sent the household in Boston 'a fine pineapple' that he had bought off a Captain just back from the West Indies.[28]

The most common context for the pineapple in this period, then, was within the rituals of entertaining. To offer a slice of pineapple to a visitor was eloquently to express real respect or affection for them, and if the pineapple had connotations of hospitality (a vital tenet of colonial society), this is where they came from. They also served to justify and legitimise what everyone knew was really just an ostentatious display of wealth.

With imported pineapple winning more and more approbation, it was inevitable that the cultivation of home-grown specimens would soon become something to aspire to in order to ensure the estate kitchen had a fresh, reliable and plentiful supply available even at short notice. Some attempts had already been successful in the more southerly, warmer colonies where it did not require such extensive technical know-how: by 1728 pineapples grew extensively in the area around New Orleans, experiments were made in Georgia in 1763, and Florida had followed suit by 1770.[29] It was not long before the areas further north tried to emulate this. A revealing snapshot of the values and mores upon which this society was based, it is a story told here for the first time.

The colonies were able to pick and choose their way through the field of meanings that emanated from the pineapple by this time, depending on those which met their needs. Most potent was the need to connect with England, a world that many had only recently left behind. 'Every fashion in Virginia appeared to be imperfect unless it bore a resemblance to some precedent in England' was Edmund Randolph's view in his *History of Virginia* (1809) – he also remarked upon 'an almost idolatrous deference to the mother country'.[30] Those with the resources to do so sent their sons to Oxford or Cambridge, scoured newspapers for the latest fashions and built up houses, gardens and social circles all in conscious emulation of the prevailing whims of the English aristocracy. The fact that the cultivation of pineapples was a pastime indulged in by England's grandest families was alone enough to recommend it. Its appropriation signified that this was a society of increasing refinement, a fact many were keen to underline to English merchants and officials.

In a society as newly formed as this one, the battle for status was constant and hard-fought. Steady economic growth meant that one particularly powerful weapon was material culture, a notion wittily mocked in the 1726 novel *Gulliver's Travels* by Jonathan Swift.

> The other [project] was a Scheme for entirely abolishing all Words whatsoever . . . Many of the most Learned and Wise adhere to the new Scheme of expressing themselves by Things; which hath only this Inconvenience attending to it; that if a Man's Business be very great, and of various kinds, he must be obliged in Proportion to carry a greater Bundle of Things upon his Back, unless he can afford one or two strong servants to attend him.[31]

Many of the colonists had left England just at the moment when the pineapple was beginning to gain momentum as the 'Thing' to beat all 'Things'.

The American garden was emerging as a recognised way to define and maintain one's position within the hierarchy. 'As is the Gardener, so is the Garden,' wrote Thomas Fuller in 1732.[32] Like in England, the cultivation of the pineapple represented a significant ability to subject Nature to Man's will. However, this instinct had an added dimension in the colonies due to the uniquely American relationship with the land. If the will to dominate the land was evident in England, it was a far more pressing matter across the Atlantic. There it was a matter of life and death, since it demonstrated that you had prevailed over a harsh and unpredictable environment and won the struggle to survive.

While the pineapple had pretty much managed to shed its early Catholic overtones, the Puritan ethic still disparaged excessive flamboyance, whatever its form. London was said to be filled with scenes of 'Wantonness, Pleasure and Extravagance' and nobody wanted to be accused of aspiring to the same.[33] This contributed some uniquely American advantages to the use of the pineapple within the struggle for status, in contrast to fripperies like clothes or coaches. For in cultivating the pineapple, it was possible at least to pretend that it was for use, rather than merely for ornament. Here was 'the king of fruits' with all the Edenic connotations bestowed upon it by the early chroniclers of its attributes and a testament to the pious purity of its financier. It just so happened, of course, that it was a testament to his prosperity, too.

The first glasshouse in North America is thought to have been built by a French Huguenot merchant named Andrew Faneuil in Boston, some time between 1710 and 1738, but the fashion for these ensured that they soon dotted the landscape.[34] For the very highest echelons of society, there was a need to up the stakes. This was made possible by a dramatic increase in government spending as a result of the various military scuffles of the 1750s and 1760s, coupled with an increase in trade within and between the colonies, that resulted in a surplus of cash. Spending on consumer goods reached levels never seen before, as fashion reached the colonies in the blink of an eye. In 1771 William Eddis wrote from Annapolis, 'The quick importation of fashions from the mother country is really astonishing. I am almost inclined to believe that a new fashion is adopted earlier by the polished and affluent American than by many opulent persons in the great metropolis . . . In short, very little difference is, in reality, observable in the manners of the wealthy colonist and the wealthy Briton.'[35] One such fashion was the cultivation of the pineapple.

The first point of reference for almost everyone was Philip Miller's *Dictionary*, found on the shelves of the libraries of colonial gentlemen more commonly than any other gardening book. The Governor of South Carolina, H. E. James Johnson, was a subscriber to the first edition, as was a Mr John James of Boston. Most followed it to the letter regarding all matters of horticulture, and the pineapple was no exception. Others were educated about the fruit by first-hand experience of the wonders contained within its shell. The scholar and plantation owner William Byrd II was lucky enough to see one while on a visit to John Warner's celebrated garden in Rotherhithe, east of London:

I never saw nature better assisted by art than I did there. You had corrected the rigour of that northern climate, and reconciled it to the productions of the south . . . You gave us an instance of it by treating us with a pine-apple very perfect in its kind, of your own growth.[36]

Because the colonial garden tended to be two or three decades behind in terms of both the theory and the practice of horticulture, many an American gentleman took his inspiration from a visit to an English garden. Some arrived already armed with knowledge: in 1750, Arthur Dobbs wrote to Peter Collinson to ask for advice about the best way to transport and grow pineapple plants – advice that went with him when he departed three years later to be Governor of North Carolina.[37] Others picked up tips from a stint in the Caribbean.

It is not possible to ascertain the first person in North America to attempt to cultivate pineapples under glass. So many colonial houses and gardens have disappeared from view, along with their records. The evidence that does exist, however, points to Abraham Redwood. The son of a plantation owner from Antigua, the family moved to Newport, Rhode Island, when he was just three years old. On his marriage to Martha Coggeshall in 1727, the newly-weds moved into a townhouse they had built for themselves on Thames Street. Redwood made his money from trade with the West Indies, mostly New England timber and fish in return for sugar, but sometimes also slaves. He also retained ownership of the family's plantation. Despite the underlying Quaker ethic of Rhode Island society, life was a never-ending whirl of enjoyable activity for gentlemen like Redwood who could afford it. There were lavish entertainments almost every night of the week – horse races on Easton's Beach or frolics with the turtles on Goat Island – while many kept sailboats for pleasure and there were taverns a-plenty.[38]

Redwood had shown an interest in the potent symbolism of pineapples early on, with the receipt in 1729 of two carved pineapples from his agent back in Bristol, soon resplendent atop the gateposts of his townhouse.[39] But it was in the garden of his country estate just north of Newport in Portsmouth that Redwood most indulged himself. One June day in 1767 a fourteen-year-old boy by the wonderfully Dickensian name of Solomon Drown paid a visit.

Awestruck, he confided in his diary that it was 'one of the finest gardens I have ever seen in my life. In it grows all sorts of West Indian fruits, viz: Oranges, Lemons, Limes, Pineapples, and Tamarinds and other sorts.'[40] Drown grew up to be one of the greatest botanists of his day. Perhaps it was this very garden, chock-a-block with wonders, that inspired him.

The garden, including the hothouses, was overseen by an Englishman named Charles Dunbar, 'a sober solid and industrious young man'.[41] His salary of $100 a year is testament to his talents, though no doubt he also made considerable use of the copy of Philip Miller's *Dictionary* that was in his master's library. The connection with Antigua meant that access to pineapple plants was not a problem: around 1760 Abraham asked his plantation manager to send him 'one Dozen root of pineapples with the young fruit upon them'.[42]

For Redwood, the pineapple was more than a nod to fashion. It acted as a constant and daily reminder of his birthplace, Antigua, where pineapples were a common sight. It also functioned as a daily declaration of the fact to his Rhode Island neighbours, since trade with the area was the source of his enormous wealth.

It is possible that Redwood was something of an anomaly in Rhode Island in his cultivation of pineapples, since I have come across no further evidence that his neighbours followed suit. Was he just an eccentric, growing pineapples as a novelty in the same way that he grew limes and lemons? His Caribbean origins, in addition to his tendency towards ostentation, meant that he did exist somewhat outside the Quaker circle that dominated Rhode Island. Alternatively, however, perhaps he was a visionary, ahead of his time in the way he asserted his position. The pineapple required so much more time, effort and expense than any of the other fruits he attempted, after all.

However, the place where there was real money to burn in the furnaces of a pinery was the southern colonies. While Maryland was not the wealthiest colony in terms of goods shipped and received, it was generally prosperous – tobacco exports rose from about £30 million in the 1720s to about £100 million in the 1770s – with far more disposable income available than, say, in Virginia, still an over-whelmingly agricultural society and heavily in debt. A French visitor in 1765 felt that 'On my arrival in Maryland, I thought there was something pleasanter in the Country than in Virginia', perceiving that the land was 'beter Cultivated and settled'.[43] Baltimore and the surrounding area were especially opulent. The French and Indian War had increased demand for products from the Chesapeake, while the area boomed after the Maryland Non-Importation Agreement of 1769 that stimulated the market for American staples by banning a variety of British imports. At the same time, however, the political situation appeared increasingly unstable. The escalating unruliness of the masses intent on having a say in the way the state was governed – for example, a dispute with the Governor over officers' fees – meant that positions of power and influence could not be taken for granted.

One Maryland tycoon who succumbed to the tyranny of English fashion was Charles Carroll. Born in 1723, the eldest son of an Irish Catholic doctor, Carroll was sent to be educated in England at the age of ten. After Eton and Cambridge he sailed back to Maryland where the family had set up home just west of Baltimore, only to be sent back to England five years later to study law at the Inns of Court. This time he enjoyed it so much that he considered staying there: his father was forced to write to persuade him that 'as to any notion of settleing there I fear it will not answer for Ladies of ffortune will scarce give it to fforeigners whose Estates they deem in England very precarrious. Therefore you must fix your Eye for future Life in Maryland.'[44] When he did eventually return in triumph as a fully qualified barrister-at-law, he had spent sixteen of the first thirty-two years of his life in the world capital of all things fashionable and polite. Following the death of his father in 1755, he inherited the family estate and a fortune that made him one of the wealthiest members of the entire Maryland aristocracy: one year later he began building the estate south-west of Baltimore for which he was to become famous, Mount Clare.[45]

With spectacular views across the Patapsco river, Mount Clare was an imposing Georgian mansion built out of soft pink brick. The interior was filled with the most fashionable and lavish modes of decoration available, mostly ordered from England: one list of 1764 includes a request for 'One Turkey Carpet', '1 Good English Carpet with Lively Colours', '12 Mahogony Chairs', 'One four Wheeled post Chariot', as well as 'An Arabian horse'.[46] But such luxury was apparently not enough. As an active lawyer, businessman and politician, it was imperative that the garden too fitted in with Carroll's vision of himself. How to do it? A sight he had no doubt been familiar with during his time in England must have seemed like the perfect solution – home-grown pineapples.[47]

In September 1760, Carroll sent to London for a copy of Miller's *Dictionary* for his library, as well as a thermometer.[48] Coming from England, the thermometer would certainly have had 'pineapple heat' as one of its markers. Getting hold of the plants was not too much of a problem: he had a close relationship with Messrs. Lux and Potts, merchants in Barbados from whom he frequently ordered supplies of sugar, coffee and rum.[49] He also owned a copy of Thomas Hale's *Eden: or a compleat body of gardening* (1757). Hale rhapsodises:

No Plant is more regarded, or deserves it more than [the pineapple]. The Singularity of the Fruit would not fail to recommend it to the Curious, did not its delicious Taste absorb all other Merit; rendering it the Delight of our Tables . . . The Superiority of this Fruit over all others, in Taste and Excellence, has made it the great Article of polite Gardening.[50]

The final sentence is of particular significance: 'the great Article of polite Gardening'. All things 'polite' was what Carroll aspired to. In addition, he had the active support of his wife, Margaret Tilghman Carroll, a keen gardener herself.[51]

In October 1770, Mary Ambler of Jamestown, Virginia, was taken on a tour of the Mount Clare gardens by the estate gardener. The sun was strangely hot for the time of year and her new shoes had pinched her the whole day through, but there was one sight that she did not fail to note in her diary: 'there is a Green House with a good many Orange & Lemon Trees just ready to bear besides which he is now buildg a Pinery where the Gardr expects to raise about an 100 Pine Apples a Year He expects to Ripen some next Summer'.[52] This is one of the very few direct references to the existence of a pinery in a colonial garden.

Was the pinery built along the lines described in *Eden*? Since it details a structure designed to hold 100 plants, it seems probable. If so, it consisted of a bark bed covered with a frame and glass of about 30 feet long and 7 feet wide, calculated to hold about a hundred plants, as well as a stove with a bark pit to which the fruit were removed when they were about ready to ripen. For the two to three years that it took to grow a pineapple, presumably Hale's instructions were also followed in the main (which in turn were mostly based on Miller's *Dictionary*). What is extraordinary is that Carroll's gardener had the knowledge to proceed thus. The reason he did? He was English.

Chesapeake gentlemen often hired English or Scottish gardeners, since they were generally accepted to be by far the most advanced in terms of knowledge and experience. In January 1768, Carroll wrote to his English agent to inform him that, 'I am in want of a Gardener that understands a Kitchen Garden . . . Grafting, Budding, Inoculating and the Management of an orchard and Fruit Trees . . . under Indenture . . . for four or five pounds a year.' The other prerequisite was that he be over thirty, 'as they are more Likely to be Riotous and Troublesome if young'. But the candidate who turned up on the doorstep of Mount Clare later the same year by the name of John Adam Smith only partially fulfilled these credentials.[53]

Smith's brilliance is undeniable from the evidence at hand – even with Hale's instructions to help him, the construction of a pinery was an enormously challenging task. However, Smith was also a convict. This was not unusual – by 1770, over 10,000 felons had landed in the colony under Britain's transportation policy.[54] With Smith apparently rather difficult to keep track of, an advertisement placed by a disgruntled Carroll in the *Maryland Gazette* in May 1773 ran thus:

TEN POUNDS REWARD. Ran away . . . a convict servant man, named John Adam Smith . . . by trade a Gardener; has with him, it is supposed, a treatise on raising the pine apple, which he pretends is of his own writing, talks much of his Trade and loves liquor.[55]

The gardener was all talk: by 1773, the only published treatises on the pineapple were those by John Giles and Adam Taylor. Perhaps the basis on which he got the job was a promise that he would produce pineapples for his master. A thorough knowledge of the subject had become almost a prerequisite amongst the upper echelon of English gardeners – though once subjected to the little-understood climate of the colonies, it is likely that most found previous experience of this fruit of less use than they had thought.

Whether any pineapples actually ripened at Mount Clare is not known, but that Charles Carroll was at the forefront of the race to do so is no surprise. Not only had his education given him a profound affinity with England, but he also needed to assert himself socially, economically and politically: this was a period of genuine uncertainty in Maryland, as well as for the other twelve colonies, with the political direction of the nation still very much up for grabs. Carroll was responsible for framing Maryland's Declaration of Independence, adopted on 3 July 1776, while the following November he was elected to Congress: even those central to the Independence movement often did not see themselves as anti-English, *per se*. In fact, many respected the nation immensely, in particular its political system – so much so though that, understandably, they wanted the right to self-determination for themselves.

A third gentleman who took a courageous step towards home-grown pineapples is Henry Laurens of South Carolina. Like Carroll, Laurens had been packed off to London at a relatively young age to get an education in the hope that he might return, in the words of his stepmother, 'polished and quite polite'.[56] He retained an interest in the city, returning on and off throughout his life, since he made his money through commerce: as well as being the leading American agent for British investors seeking to buy land in the south, the stalwarts of his business were rum, indigo, rice, deerskins and slaves, a business that soon netted him vast profits.

The pre-Revolutionary period was one of extraordinary prosperity in South Carolina, in particular Charleston, almost entirely due to trade with England. A visitor in 1773 was astonished by how 'in grandeur, splendour of buildings, decorations, equipages, numbers of commerce, shipping, and indeed in almost everything it far surpasses all I ever saw or ever expected to see in America'. However, what its inhabitants aspired to most desperately of all was less tangible – refinement. More than anywhere else in the colonies, it emanated an almost unsurpassed admiration, even reverence, for English high society, a state of affairs noted by almost every contemporary visitor.[57]

In 1764, Laurens took up residence in a house in the Ansonboro area of Charleston. The four acre garden was overseen by 'a complete English gardener' named John Watson, who was brought out to the Americas especially;[58] and by October 1767 Laurens was able to boast in a letter to James Grant, the Governor of East Florida, that 'I lately cut 4 Pine Apples in my Garden'.[59] Yet again, the master of the house unfailingly appropriated the hard-earned achievements of the gardener in his pay. A year or so later, Laurens tried to expand his collection with 'three or four growing Pine Apples in large tubs' brought back from Jamaica.[60] By this method, he had access not only to the crowns but also to the suckers – he was in this for the long haul. However, in 1779, following a stint as President of Congress, he was dispatched to Holland to negotiate a treaty. While at sea, he was captured by the British, only to be charged with high treason and thrown in the Tower of London. The night before he lost his freedom, the politician Sir William Meredith gave him a pineapple as a present to try to cheer him up. It was the last one he was to see for fourteen and a half months.[61] Thus released, he remains both the first and the last American ever to be imprisoned there.[62]

There is absolutely no doubt that colonial America in the brief period from about 1760 until the beginning of the American Revolution boasted many more pineries than the ones detailed here. Evidence for this is limited – since few plans of colonial gardens survive, all our knowledge has to be gleaned from diaries, letters and other documents. It has never before been investigated in detail and there is still much more to be done on the subject. For example, the lack of data makes it difficult to ascribe differences within the individual colonies: pineries seem to have been more common in the southern colonies than in less wealthy New England, but otherwise, it is mostly a matter of extrapolation.

And yet, such structures were not nearly as ubiquitous amongst the highest echelons of society as they were in England. The craze for pineapples patently did not reach the maniacal proportions that it had there. In particular, its relative absence from the (albeit scarce) American art and literature of the period suggests that it barely made a mark on the wider public consciousness. Why was this? While the plethora of high-quality imports might be thought a disincentive, this slightly misses the point. The home-grown pineapple was in a league of its own in the excess of wealth it denoted.

One contributing factor was that gardening was just not as popular as it was in England. As the German traveller Johann David Schoepf observed as late as 1783, 'The taste for gardening is, at Philadelphia as well as throughout America, still in its infancy . . . Gardens as at present managed are purely utilitarian – pleasure-gardens have not yet come in . . .' The reason for this? '. . . the American cares little for what does not grow of itself, and is satisfied with the great yields of his cherry, apple and peach trees, without giving a thought to possible and often necessary betterment'.[63] The implicit suggestion is that the national character was a lazy one. 'The American planters and farmers [are] the greatest slovens in Christendom' was the verdict of the author of one 1775 gardening manual.[64]

Those who had developed a taste for gardening, however, faced the major problem of a chronic lack of books. While scores of these deluged the bookshops of the mother country each year, the colonial gentleman felt fortunate to have even a single one in his library – Philip Miller's *Dictionary*, perhaps, or Richard Bradley's *New Improvements of Planting and Gardening*. Knowledge was scarce, disseminated only through personal correspondence or word of mouth, both usually involving arduous days riding along long, dusty tracks – at least for those who did not live near a waterway. Yet tried-and-tested knowledge was a necessity for all but the very bravest gardener, since the alternative was trial and error, a risky business when even a successful attempt took two to three years to make itself known.

Since no vernacular literature emerged to supplement Miller's *Dictionary* until after Independence, even if you did have a book, the limited written advice that was available was dismally inadequate. The instructions set out by English texts were sound in theory, but they were of little relevance to the specific needs and problems of American colonial gardens.[65] Trained gardeners were in chronically short supply: by the 1760s, London newspapers like the *Public Advertiser* featured regular advertisements specifically for gardeners to go to North America – 'A Quarter's Wages paid them before they embark'.[66] When they did deign to come, they rarely stayed long, in part frustrated by a lack of tools and equipment to sustain their exertions – all supplies had to be ordered from England. Glass was hard to come by, as were seeds both in terms of quality and quantity, for transatlantic shipping was notoriously unreliable. Acres of land untilled, unenclosed, scattered with alien native plants, with few tools, seeds or personnel to help him: looking out the window, the American colonial gardener was faced with a very different prospect to his English counterpart.

Most problematic of all was the weather, a phenomenon that it took the colonists quite some time to appreciate. The assumption was that Virginia's climate was similar to that of southern Spain – it was on the same latitude, after all. In fact, it did not have the benefit of the ocean to temper seasonal extremes: instead it had cold winters (often with snow), hot summers, humidity and dramatic temperature changes. There were also wide variations from year to year and from colony to colony. It was a climate that was little understood and for a plant as delicate as the pineapple outside its native territory, this was a disaster.[67]

In addition to such practical considerations, there were a multitude

I. 'Brazilian Landscape', by Frans Post, 1655

II. A plate from *Metamorphosis Insectorum Surinamensium* by Maria Sybilla Merian, 1705

III. John Rose presents Charles II with a pineapple, attr. Hendrick Danckerts, c.1670

Agnes Block and her family in
the garden of her country estate,
Vijverhof, by Jan Weenix, c.1690

... By Theodore Netscher, 1720.
The Latin inscription reads,
'To the perpetual memory of
Matthew Decker Baronet, and
Theodore Netscher, Gentleman.
This pineapple deemed worthy
of the Royal table, grew at
Richmond at the cost of the
former, and still seems to grow
by the art of the latter'.

VI. A Wedgwood teapot and
tea caddy, c.1765

VII. The Pineapple at Dunmore Park
(currently let for holidays by the
Landmark Trust)

VIII. 'The Cabinet Dinner or a Political Meeting'
by C. Williams, 1804

IX. 'Lady with a Parasol
and a Pineapple', c.1840

X. A selection of labels for canned pineapple, c.1930

THE MARKET GARDEN OF THE TROPICS — MALAYAN PINEAPPLES

XI. Poster produced by the Empire Marketing Board to promote
Malaysian canned pineapple, c.1930

XII. Pineapples at Heligan Gardens in Cornwall

XIII. A Chloe swimsuit, 2000

of ideological obstacles. Carroll's distant relative Charles Carroll of Carrollton wrote to a friend in 1772, 'An attempt with us at grandeur or at magnificence is sure to be followed with something mean or ridiculous. Even in England where the affluence of individuals will support a thousand follies, what evils arise from the vanity & profuse excesses of the rich!'[68] While many ignored this kind of clamour, it is evident from the way that people did not boast about it as they did in England that the doctrine of simplicity had to some extent taken hold. The home-grown pineapple was clearly tricky to justify. For it highlighted what could not be denied: to bother with a pinery, you really needed to have excessive amounts of time and money on your hands. In a way, it throws into relief what an absurd situation the English had got themselves into by elevating the pineapple to the status that they did.

Yet it was the War of Independence that really scuppered the pineapple's attempt to ingratiate itself into the gardens of the very rich. There had been rumblings for some time that such a statement of investment in the land as a pinery represented was perhaps not entirely sensible in view of the constant skirmishes – King George's War in 1744, the French and Indian War in 1755, Pontiac's Rebellion in 1763. However, it was not the fighting itself that was the problem, but rather one of the reasons for it – anti-Englishness.

Anti-English sentiment had been brewing for some time. Attempts to raise taxes from the colonists such as the Sugar Act of 1764 or the Stamp Act of 1765 had angered many. There was also a moral dimension: 'Alas! Great Britain,' lamented one onlooker in Virginia, 'their vices have been extended to America!'[69] Men like Samuel Adams were convinced that luxurious living was a plot by the mother country to corrupt the morals of the colonists: 'Nothing but FRUGALITY can now save the distress'd northern colonies from impending ruin.'[70] This was an era when not only did people seek to declare themselves independent of English rule, but also of English fashions.

As a result, the pineapple was very much implicated in the boycott movement that resulted in the Non-Importation Agreements. Its cultivation required a whole range of goods that had to be ordered from London – gardening tools, gardening manuals, the stove, the thermometer, even the plants that were supplied were said to be less prone to insect infestation than those shipped from the West Indies. Moreover, pineapple-growing required the importation of a whole range of English sensibilities – for fashion, for luxury, for extravagance way beyond what seemed reasonable in the circumstances. While for some like Abraham Redwood the home-grown pineapple had always been a reminder of life in the West Indies, for most, it was a reminder of a life in a far colder, rainier climate – England.

The Non-Importation Agreement affected not only imports from England, but soon those from English colonies like the West Indies too. The pineapple could not help but be implicated, on all sides. In August 1770, a Mr Applegate and a Mr Abrahams set off from New York City port to New Jersey to try to sell some recently imported pineapples. The trip was a disaster:

> The People of Brunswick, finding them to be Subscribers for Importation, treated them so roughly, that they judged it not safe to appear publicly, and being unable to sell their Fruit, a great Part of it spoiled upon their Hands; they were glad to get off privately, to avoid the Effects of the People's Resentment.[71]

The phrase 'Subscribers for Importation' haunted the pineapple in the period before, during and just after the War of Independence. While some clearly made a distinction between whether a specimen was home-grown or imported (as late as 1774, even Washington was apparently happy to indulge in goods eight weeks' journey away in the British islands in the West Indies), others were less generous. Regardless of provenance, the consumption of the fruit suggested not only a rampant materialism, but also a suspicious willingness to buy into foreign fashions. While private interests ignored these sentiments to some extent – in 1771, imports of luxury goods from Britain reached record levels – the theory at least of public virtue continued to hang in the air, very much to the detriment of the pineapple.

Then came the Revolution. This sounded a death-knell for the home-grown pineapple in the United States from which it would not recover for some years. While it was the transplanting of its intimate associations with the English aristocracy that had made the fruit so popular in the brief window between 1760 and 1775, this very attribute proved its downfall in the aftermath of the bitter war. Just as the craze was gaining momentum, it was abruptly halted. Luckily for the pineapple however, back in England, the Victorians were about to embrace it with a zeal not seen before or since.

8

'And as the race of pine-apples, so is the race of man'

William Makepeace Thackeray (1850)

The pineapples at Chatsworth, the residence of the sixth Duke of Devonshire, constituted one of the most impressive collections in Victorian Britain. The pineries were first constructed in 1738, just as the fashion for them was gaining momentum; but the ensuing years saw them much neglected.[1] All this changed, however, when in 1826 an up-and-coming 22-year-old named Joseph Paxton took up the position of Superintendent of the Gardens. He found the pineries in a sad state of disrepair – '4 pine houses, bad,' the Duke recorded ruefully in his notebook when Paxton first arrived.[2] But from 1828 the pineries were renovated and extended, and over the decades that followed Paxton made it one of his main projects to make them productive once more to the extent expected of an estate of Chatsworth's size and grandeur.[3] Right here in this smelly and humid palace made of glass was evidence of the nascent industrial revolution – not only in terms of the vastly increased scale of the enterprise, but also in the extraordinarily advanced technology.

Paxton's education in the art of pineapple cultivation was a matter he took seriously. In 1840, for instance, he wrote to the Duke to regale him at length about tips he picked up on a trip with his wife to see the pineapples at Versailles.[4] While much of the labour involved was delegated to his team of gardeners, it was still a very time-consuming element of his job – for like many others in the same profession, it was a matter of personal pride: 'The talents of Gardeners have on many occasions been measured by their competency in producing this princely fruit, and there are few gentlemen in the possession of sufficient means to keep up a garden establishment, who do not aim at the production of pine apple; either considering their cultivation necessary to complete their ménage, or as an essential delicacy without which no dessert can be complete.'[5] To Paxton's delight (even relief), it was not too long before the pineries began to flourish.

The results were spectacular. As an American journalist noted with awe in 1858, 'The domain of the Duke of Devonshire would cover one of our largest counties . . . There are thirty greenhouses, each from fifty to seventy-five feet long. We went into three or four containing nothing but pineapples, ripe . . . We saw pineapples weighing ten or fifteen pounds each.'[6] This may be an exaggeration for journalistic effect, but still – a hundred years earlier, you were deemed a success

22. The pineries at Chatsworth, illustrated in the *Gardener's Chronicle*, June 1887.

if you had a dozen pineapples that weighed two or three pounds each. No wonder then that the Chatsworth pineapples won medals at almost every horticultural show.

It may well have been this element of competition that drove Paxton on. It certainly did his friends and neighbours. Take George Stephenson, the brilliant inventor of the first steam locomotive engine, a revolutionary development in itself. In about 1845 Stephenson embarked on an ambitious project to build himself not only a 68 foot long pine house but also a separate 140 foot long pine pit at his home Tapton House in Chesterfield in Staffordshire. For a man with a life-long interest in progress, it was certainly a fitting way for him to spend his retirement. Yet this was not his only motivation. According to Stephenson's Victorian biographer Samuel Smiles,

> At one of the county agricultural meetings, [Stephenson] said that he intended yet to grow pineapples at Tapton as big as pumpkins. The only man to whom he would 'knock under' was his friend Paxton, the gardener to the Duke of Devonshire; and he was so old in the service, and so skillful, that he could scarcely hope to beat him. Yet his 'Queen' pines did take first prize at a competition with the Duke.[7]

This must have been a triumphant moment: nationally renowned, the Chatsworth pineapples were very much the ones to beat. But the real point to note is that here were two icons of the Victorian age engaged in a fierce and determined battle over . . . pineapples.

While in the United States, the fruit's associations with the English aristocracy had largely halted the onset of a fashion for growing pineapples, it was these very associations that allowed the mania to reach new heights back home. England, it was felt, had become its spiritual home. So what if it originated in Brazil? Who cared if it flourished most easily in the West Indies? To the late Georgians and early Victorians, England's soil had cared for it, nurtured it and cajoled it. Only in England did it receive write-ups like this one by Charles Lamb that appeared in the *London Magazine* in 1821:

Pineapple is great. She is almost too transcendent – a delight if not sinful, yet so like sinning that really a tender conscienced person would do well to pause – too ravishing for mortal taste, she woundeth and excoriateth the lips that approach her – like lovers' kisses she biteth – she is a pleasure bordering on pain, from the fierceness and insanity of her relish.[8]

Once again cast in the role of an Eve-like figure, but this time of extreme, almost masochistic sexual temptation, no wonder it appealed to the average repressed English gentleman. For crucially, the readership of such accounts was changing.

The whirlwind that surrounded the pineapple emanated from a core of distinctively English values. While pineries were in evidence in Scotland, Wales and Ireland, it was almost always at the instigation of a decidedly English aristocrat. This is reflected in the literature of the period that unfailingly refers to the 'English' pineapple, the 'English' garden and so on. The prevailing prejudices of the period dictated that this was where polite society was located. Everywhere else was seen to be peopled by Celtic barbarians, more likely to throw a pineapple at you than to display it at dinner. This was a manifestation of the school of thought that pervaded many of the activities of Victorian England: the English were a mightily superior race, created by God to capture and control the world's treasures – whether it was a palace in India, a river in Africa or a decidedly non-indigenous fruit back on the ancestral estate.

As the century progressed, the English aristocracy found it necessary to embark upon more and more excessive displays of wealth in order to distance themselves from an increasingly moneyed and powerful middle class. With a booming economy, no major wars to finance and a drop in income tax of two pence in the pound, not only was there more disposable income available to the middle class, there was inevitably also more social competition. While this was by no means a new phenomenon, in Victorian Britain it was even more pronounced than ever before. An enormous greenhouse was an increasingly popular acquisition, but an enormous pinery declared a level of wealth attainable by only a tiny minority. For an upper class whose cultural hegemony was so threatened by the Reform Act of 1832, it was also a statement of investment in the land.

And with more upper-class money around than ever before – whether old money (from the agricultural improvements made by the generation before), new money (from the industrial boom) or a happy combination of the two – it was an investment that was no problem to finance. As a result, pineries stocked with several hundred plants at a time became a not-uncommon feature of the British landscape, while the pineapples themselves were being grown to ten, twelve, even fifteen pounds. From the experiments made on the fruit by Thomas Andrew Knight, President of the Royal Society, on his Downton Castle estate in Herefordshire in the 1810s, to the pineapple pits 400 feet long at Eaton Hall, the Cheshire seat of the Marquis of Westminster, in the 1840s, to Lord Leconfield's gardener dispatching forty pineapples from Petworth in West Sussex in one go for preserving in the 1860s, all the usual suspects pursued the pastime with a by-now accustomed doggedness.[9]

The distinguishing feature of the cultivation of pineapples in this period was that etiquette had come to dictate that it was no longer sufficient merely to produce them in the summer months; they had to be available all year round. In order to maintain pineapples at different stages of growth at different temperatures, few could get away with building just one pinery that housed the entire collection: any respectable estate had to have not only its own pineapple pit but also a separate pineapple stove and succession house, in addition to all the other accoutrements like a store room that a delicate fruit like the pineapple requires. A successful fruiting depended on the successful manipulation of a multitude of factors: 'Even in that conservatory existence where the fair Camelia is sighed for by the noble young Pineapple, neither of them needing to care about the frost or rain outside, there is a nether apparatus of hot-water pipes liable to cool down on a strike of the gardeners or a scarcity of coal' was how George Eliot put it.[10] It was imperative that all risk factors were efficiently controlled. This soon became possible – but only because technology was to make it so.

In 1826 the influential garden writer J. C. Loudon commented that 'the most general mode of heating hot-houses is by fires and smoke flues'.[11] However, since 1684 when this system had first been introduced at the Chelsea Physic Garden, the fumes it generated had remained a problem to the respiratory systems of both plants and people. The first innovation in this sphere came with the use of steam, a technique first successfully attempted by a Mr Butler at Knowsley Hall in Merseyside in 1792, while a couple of years later another gardener, John Hay, proved it was even able to meet the challenge of the Scottish weather with a steam pineapple stove at Preston Hall in Edinburgh. Its major advantage was that it was much cheaper, both in terms of materials and labour, than maintaining a fire all the time.

However, while steam was briefly in vogue to heat hothouses in the 1810s, the boilers proved rather too prone to explode. In an age where every new idea was welcomed as a potential stroke of genius, the editor of the *Dumfries and Galloway Courier* put forward an alternative system he claimed was common in Russia that depended solely on the breath of cattle. It did not catch on.[12] Instead, the conundrum was solved with the introduction of hot water pipes through which heat circulated (the basis of today's central heating systems). These had been in evidence in some of the very grandest homes for some time, but it was only in the 1820s that the invention was put into use in the garden. Efficient, reliable and backed up by coal-fired boilers that were much easier to operate than before, the result was that the gardener had increased control over the elements of Nature under his jurisdiction. While they did not do away with the need for the near-constant supervision of the thermometer, or for a big-biceped garden boy to keep the boiler stoked, nonetheless, hot water pipes were an innovation from which the pinery benefited particularly.

But it was no longer enough just to own a pinery. It had to be huge. This reflected a broader trend in gardening that dictated that greenhouses of all kinds were longer, wider, taller. The first step forward was the invention of sheet glass in 1833. One firm, Chance Brothers of Birmingham, produced sheets which, at thirty-six inches, were over fourteen inches longer than had previously been possible. This was the beginning of various improvements in the way glass was manufactured that made it increasingly feasible to build ever-larger structures, helped by the new use of iron in sash-bars, which gave them a new strength and flexibility. This allowed more leeway to be creative with the design – a dome, a half-dome or a box? The choice was yours.

As the horticultural writer Henry Phillips had prophesied in 1820, 'This fruit was long confined to the tables of the rich and luxurious, on account of the expense of raising it in stoves, but . . . Should . . . the duty on garden glass [be] relinquished, we shall soon have African gardens of great extent on the banks of the Thames, and pine-apples cried through our streets for two a crown.'[13] He was not wrong.

The expense of glass had been the principal reason why the construction of pineries had been so expensive. Manufacturers paid a licence fee of £20 a year for each works, imported materials were taxed on entry and the glass itself was assessed at three pence per pound in the melting-pot or six pence per pound once removed. In 1845, however, the Glass Tax was abolished. The potential effects of this were immediately recognised: 'An elasticity will be given to the trade, and new enterprises will embark in it . . . Private individuals also will be able to have conservatories; and we hope to see the majority of town residences adorned with cases for containing plants.'[14] This is indeed what happened.

Structures dedicated to the cultivation of pineapples were soon spotted all over the British landscape. Since nowadays the only garden in England that boasts these facilities is the wonderful Heligan Gardens in Cornwall, it is hard to appreciate just how prevalent they were 150 years ago. Every summer saw the construction of scores more, as the number of people attempting to grow their own spiralled ever upwards. To visitors from abroad, it was like a feature from an alien landscape. In July 1846 a visitor to Knowsley Hall, the seat of the Earl of Derby, noted that, 'His gardener estimated that there were two thousand pineapples in various stages of growth in the hothouses.'[15] In all such accounts, one gets a definite sense of the gardener's enthusiasm to show off the facts and figures of his endeavours. And why not? The entire enterprise was geared around the intrinsically human desire to show off. This was its very *raison d'être*. As Mrs O'Dowd boasts so obnoxiously in William Thackeray's *Vanity Fair* (1847), 'We have an acre of hothouses, and pines as common as pays in the sayson.'[16] The pineapple was very much the snob's choice.

For the royal gardens to exclude themselves from this frenzy would have been inconceivable. Throughout the nineteenth century, Sandringham in Norfolk maintained three pineapple houses, each 100 feet long.[17] Under the capable direction of William Aiton, by 1822 pineapples were produced in both Kew Gardens and Kensington Palace Gardens all year round and 'equal to any within ten miles of London' in the august opinion of J. C. Loudon: 'the presence of such a rare fruit at an uncommon season, accords well with the pomp and splendour of a royal table'.[18] While Loudon admitted that those fruited in winter did not taste quite the way they should, he conceded that normally by the time the pineapple was brought to the dinner table, most guests were too drunk to notice – or, as he more delicately put it, 'a few drops of alcohol are already transferred to the ventricles of the brain'.[19]

News soon spread of these various developments. Many (relatively) cheap and accessible books were published to help the stressed gardener fulfil his master's extravagant demands. Of this, Loudon in his best-selling and comprehensive *Encyclopaedia of Gardening* (1822) was well aware: 'The fruit being reckoned the most delicious of all others, and gardeners being valued by the wealthy in proportion to their success in its cultivation, we shall here lay before the reader a copious view of the present modes of cultivation.' Sure enough, the sections on the cultivation of the pineapple are among the most detailed.[20] Further income was generated for Loudon with the appearance the very same year of his *Different Modes of Cultivating the Pine-apple*.[21] The science of horticulture had come to be taken more seriously than ever before and with it, the highest point of its expression, the cultivation of pineapples. Because of this, Loudon was by no means the only one to write on the subject. To cope with the

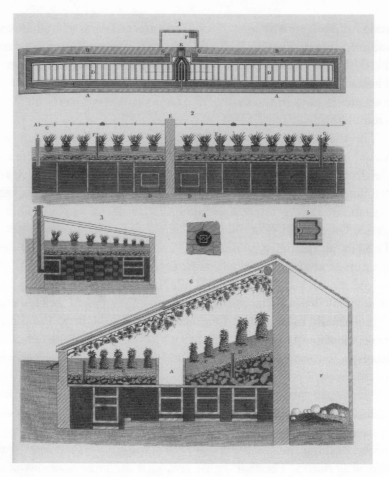

23. A system for growing pineapples advocated by J. C. Loudon. By
J. Pass, c.1829.

demand, as the century progressed, a continuing slew of books on the
subject of the cultivation of pineapples appeared.

William Griffin (1806), George W. Johnson and James Barnes
(1847), David Thomson (1866) – all cashed in by publishing their own
top tips on how to produce juicy pineapples the year round, and this
was in addition to the paragraphs on the subject that had become a
standard feature in all the more general gardening books of the

period.[22] Most writers were taking advantage of accolades they had acquired through practical experience. While in the employment of the Duke of Buccleuch at Drumlanrig near Dumfries, David Thomson successfully grew 200 pineapples a year, claiming in his book that 'Its superior cultivation is reckoned one of the greatest triumphs of the horticulturist.'[23]

The thirst for knowledge about pineapples gave some ideas that reeked of over-ambition. In 1818, Thomas Baldwin, the Marquis of Hertford's gardener at Ragley Hall in Warwickshire also had a go at penning his tips: *Short Practical Directions for the Culture of the Ananas, or Pine Apple Plant*, he called it.[24] He failed to sell many copies, however, by asking the extortionate price of a guinea a copy.[25] To be fair, he had reason to hope to be taken seriously in the field – in 1817, he produced a pineapple of 4 lbs in less than fifteen months.[26] It was because of such horticultural feats that many considered him the most talented British pineapple grower of his day.

It is phrases like this that force one to step back for a moment. 'The most talented British pineapple grower of his day'? That such an accolade even existed in Britain is bizarre from today's perspective. As a nation famed for its grey, cold, wet weather, there is no reason why a fruit like the pineapple could hope to find itself propagated here. And yet, for a few delicious moments in its history, this not only came to pass, but did so to a spectacular degree.

One of the most fashionable books was Mr R. Glendinning's 1839 treatise, *Practical Hints on the Culture of the Pineapple*. It contained two main innovations. The first was that the pineapple should be supplied with only a little heat and moisture at first in order to make it grow slowly while developing its constitution so that when older it would produce bigger fruit when more heat and moisture were allowed. The second was to use warm rather than cold water to water the plants.[27] Neither may seem particularly radical to the non-gardeners amongst us, but such was the level of detail and competitiveness involved that every little tweak and twiddle counted. Glendinning's method was adopted at Longleat in Wiltshire (among other gardens) with great success.

But many were suspicious of these various advances. An 1845 review of *Treatise on the Culture of the Pineapple* by George Mills, gardener to the Baroness de Rothschild at Gunnersbury Park in Middlesex, enthusiastically praised the fact that 'There is no mystery here – no preposterous mixtures of all manner of unmentionable substances called a compost – no crochetty schemes for rendering the buildings dear or unmanageable – no ignorant recommendations of operations to which reason in the first instance, and experience afterwards, are alike opposed. The foundation of the author's success is common sense.'[28] It is somehow a very Victorian instinct to praise common sense above all other virtues. But then, if common sense was really key, he would not be in the business of trying to grow pineapples in the first place.

The crucial point here is that these are accounts written by mostly middle-class writers for a mostly middle-class audience. For the pineapple, it proved a turning-point. In the same way that the printed word had served the pineapple so well in its early excursions into Europe, the democratisation of literature in the nineteenth century presented an opportunity to spread the gospel to an ever-expanding readership. Magazines, newspapers, books for a sixpence – the news was spreading.

However, this was not necessarily entirely to the advantage of the pineapple, for much of the mystique surrounding its cultivation dissipated. Looking back on this a few years later, one horticultural expert commented that, 'By degrees . . . the culture of this fruit became extended, and the more general diffusion of garden literature enabled most people to comprehend that, after all, no secret was involved in the matter, and that no extraordinary management was necessary to attain a moderate degree of success; but that the whole affair was one of pocket.'[29] The suggestion is that there is nothing inherently special about the pineapple as a commodity; it is its associations which give it its status. The passage also places significant emphasis on the economics of the situation. In contrast to, for example, Lady Mary Wortley Montagu's denial of the pineapple as an economic entity in 1716, the Victorians were intimately concerned with the material conditions in which it came to appear at the dinner table.

At the forefront of the trade in pineapple plants was Joseph Knight's shop. Opened in 1808, it covered two acres stretching between the King's Road and the Fulham Road in Chelsea. Other shops catered to those who wanted fully grown fruit. A prosperous entrepreneur, James Gunter lived in an enormous house in what was then the village of Earl's Court near London, surrounded by acres of nursery gardens, fruit orchards and hothouses, with the latter supplying the pineapples he sold in his newly acquired shop The Pineapple in Berkeley Square. According to *The Epicure's Almanac* of 1815, 'Mr Gunter has had for many years the high honour of supplying the Royal Family with articles from his shop. Some of the Royal Dukes condescend occasionally to give Mr Gunter a call for the purpose of tasting his pines.' Such celebrity endorsement must of course have been a boon for business. Perhaps it is for this reason that James Gunter was less than punctilious about making sure that they settled the debts they ran up: when the Duke of Sussex died in 1828, he owed Gunter nearly £700.[30] As more people simply had more money to spend, the commodity culture of Victorian Britain spread even to the bottom of the garden.

In 1841 there appeared of the first modern weekly gardening newspaper, the *Gardener's Chronicle*. Edited by Joseph Paxton (the pineapple owes him a good deal), it is a barometer of trends in gardening; and, throughout the 1840s and 1850s, the pineapple dominates its pages. Typically for the Victorians, the level of detail is astounding. There are endless debates about how to speed up the growth process, letters about the most impressive varieties, accounts of the enormous pineapples seen. A particularly heated controversy of 1847 centred around what kind of manure worked best. We learn that Joseph Hamilton, author of the acclaimed treatise *On the Hamiltonian System of Cultivating the Pine Apple* (1844), advocated undecayed tan; Isaac Oldacre, gardener to Joseph Banks's widow at Spring Grove, liked powdered bones; while Mr Brown, gardener at Merevale Hall in Warwickshire (owned by the Dugdale family, who also owned many coal mines in the area), was in favour of peat.[31] After trawling its pages, it all begins to seem utterly barmy. The pineapple may be only a fruit, but to gardeners at the time, it meant infinitely more.

Another issue that aroused passionate partisanship was pineapple stove design. In 1843 Mr J. Jones, architect to R. H. Clive, MP, at Hewell Grange in Worcestershire, submitted a plan of a new kind of pineapple stove that supplied the bottom heat with hot water in gutters but the atmospheric heat as usual with flues;[32] while in 1850 G. Fleming at Trentham Hall near Stoke countered this with a method that used hot water both in a tank and in flues.[33] From John Richardson, gardener to Henry Sharples of Oswald's Croft near Liverpool, to Peter Marsland of Woodbank near Stockport, to George Cherry, gardener to James Fenton of Bamford Hall in Lancashire, the geographical distribution of the players in the whole debate is astonishing.[34] Such was the onslaught of information that more and more people were successful in their quest to propagate pineapples.

The pages of the *Gardener's Chronicle* make it clear that by the 1840s it was not just the Marquis of This and the Duke of That who were involved in the struggle to cultivate pineapples, but increasingly the richest elements of the middle classes too; and not just in London and the surrounding area, but all over Britain. The importance of this is illustrated in an episode in *Ruth* by Elizabeth Gaskell (1853).

The first day at dessert, some remark (some opportune remark, as Mr Bradshaw in his innocence had thought) was made regarding the price of pine-apples, which was rather exorbitant that year, and Mr Donne asked Mrs Bradshaw, with quiet surprise, if they had no pinery, as if to be without a pinery were indeed a depth of pitiable destitution. In fact, Mr Donne had been born and cradled in all that wealth could purchase, and so had his ancestors before him for so many generations, that refinement and luxury seemed the natural condition of man, and they that dwelt without were in the position of monsters.[35]

A crisis of confidence, merely because he was unable to supply pineapples grown in his own garden? Apparently so.

Winter or not, English pineapples were famous for being the best in the world. While in Tahiti in 1835 on his momentous voyage round the world on board H.M.S. *Beagle*, Charles Darwin noted in his diary that, 'Pine-apples are here so abundant that the people eat them in the same wasteful manner as we might turnips. They are of an excellent flavour – perhaps even better than those cultivated in England; and this I believe is the highest compliment which can be paid to any fruit.'[36] This was by no means merely an expression of homesick pride. Even the French recognised the superiority of English pineapples, a state of affairs brilliantly depicted by Charles Dickens in his essay *A Flight* (1858). Sitting in the stifling heat of a carriage of a boat train about to depart for Paris from London Bridge, the narrator gasps,

> Whew! The hothouse air is faint with pine-apples. Every French citizen or citizeness is carrying pine-apples home. The compact little Enchantress in the corner of my carriage . . . has a pine-apple in her lap. Compact Enchantress's friend, confidante, mother, mystery, Heaven knows what, has two pine-apples in her lap, and a bundle of them under the seat. Tobacco-smoky Frenchman in Algerine wrapper . . . carries pine-apples in a covered basket. Tall, grave, melancholy Frenchman . . . has the green end of a pine-apple sticking out of his neat valise.[37]

In 1847 a debate raged in the horticultural press over specimens grown in the gardens of Louis-Philippe's château in Meudon,* a suburb of Paris, by the head gardener, Monsieur Pelvilain. Reports were emerging that his were larger than those grown in England.

---

*The area around Meudon had been the centre of pineapple cultivation in France for some time. In 1838–9, the writer Honoré de Balzac worked out that by cultivating pineapples at his nearby villa Les Jardies, he could make a profit of 400,000 francs a year 'and not a word to write'. He went to look for a shop to rent in Montmartre, for which he already had the shop sign designed: painted black, with gold embellishment, 'Ananas Des Jardies' is what it would read. According to his close friend Théophile Gautier, 'To Balzac, the lacy plumes of those hundred thousand pineapples were already visible above their plump golden cones, arrayed in rows beneath huge vaults of glass he saw them in his

English gardeners were horrified, but it was their own fault: Pelvilain learned English for the specific purpose of being able to read all the English treatises on the subject. To the immense relief of most gentlemen concerned, however, the *Gardener's Chronicle* was soon able to establish that, although the Meudon pineapples may have been larger, they were by no means tastier. The verdict was that 'there is in reality no ground for anger or annoyance on the part of English gardeners. They are not beaten yet . . . The English may console themselves that they are still unrivalled for quality.' The sense of victory emanates off the page. This was an era of fervent patriotism and the pineapple was just one more direction to channel it towards.[38]

A real crowd-pleaser, an English pineapple remained the primary attraction at the most prestigious horticultural shows, a newly popular phenomenon that provided an additional public context for the fruit to display itself. The American traveller Harriet White Paige recorded in her diary in 1839 how, 'By previous invitation, and arrangement, we drove to Chiswick, to visit the Horticultural exhibition . . . The *flavour* of the pineapples growing within, was very powerful and agreeable, but an approach to the tables, for *seeing* the pines, we found, in consequence of the crowds, entirely impracticable.'[39] Such shows undoubtedly encouraged the competitive instincts of those involved, much to the advantage of the pineapple, whose cultivation reached ever-increasing heights of perfection. In the 1830s in the language of flowers, the pineapple came to signify, 'You're perfect'.[40] In this way, the Victorians found a way to codify a cultural association that had in fact been tacit for centuries.

In 1839 R. Glendinning asserted that, 'The Pine apple has for a number of years justly become the most conspicuous article at the

mind's eye, glowed in the warmth of the greenhouses and with nostrils passionately distended breathed their exotic scent; and even when he was back home, leaning on the window-sill and watching the snow fall silently on that bare slope, he scarcely lost the illusion.' He hoped it would be the answer to his money worries, but Gautier quickly managed to persuade him out of the project. See Claude-Marie Senninger (ed.), *Honoré de Balzac par Théophile Gautier* (1980) 87. The translation is from André Maurois, *Prometheus: the Life of Balzac*, tr. Norman Denny (1965) 359.

Dessert, and at all assemblies of the noble and the rich a most indispensable luxury.'[41] One of the most prominent stages on which the pineapple appeared was at public banquets such as one in the Guildhall in York on 2 November 1850, where it was much in demand to perform to rapturous audiences – herein lay yet another chance for it to seduce a much wider range of people than ever before both in terms of numbers and class. Partly the pineapple is the most suited of fruits to fill this position, with its distinctive fountain of spikes that allows it to tower over its neighbouring oranges or melons. But the English pineapple had also come to represent a certain way of life of which the other members of the fruit world could only dream. As a reminder of the enormous quantities of glass, heat and labour the host could afford, it was an uncompromising visual representation of wealth. As a result, it was not only at public but also at private occasions that the pineapple was a potent statement of intent.

A cursory glance over diaries of the period confirms this. Take the artist Joseph Farington's, written between 1793 and 1821. It reveals

24. A banquet in the Guildhall in York, 1850.

that even in the first two decades of the century, whether he was at dinner with Sir Martin Ffolkes at Hillington Hall near Massingham, with Lord Lonsdale at Lowther Castle in Westmorland, or with the political writer John Penn at Stoke Park in Buckinghamshire, English pineapples were ubiquitous – alongside venison, champagne and ice-cream, they were an absolute essential.[42] Farington also recalls how, on the stroll back from dinner with Lord Lonsdale, he discussed with his friend Edridge how 'He knew his Lordship when he was only Sir William Lowther, and that there had not been the least alteration in His manner since he became possessed of the vast Lowther property, & attained his present high rank.'[43] I bet his stock of pineapples increased, though.

It remained the case that a pineapple was more likely to be put on display than to be eaten, as a work of art rather than a consumable of nature. 'Six Pines upon the table – 2 cut', noted Farington after dinner with John Julius Angerstein, the founder of Lloyd's bank, at Woodlands House in Blackheath near London.[44] It is this which explains the newly emerging obsession in this period with size, rather than taste. The trend had a certain legitimacy bestowed upon it in 1821, when a 10 lbs 11 oz pineapple grown on Lord Cawdor's estate was considered so impressive that it was a centrepiece of the banquet for George IV's coronation.[45] But as the century progressed, such achievements began to reach previously unheard-of proportions.

A controversy raged in the pages of the *Gardener's Chronicle* throughout 1843 over a report that Mr W. Dawson, gardener to Lord Rolle at Bicton in Devon, had cut pineapples weighing up to 6 lbs 2 oz.[46] Many wrote in to question this, but Dawson stood by his story. This was also what caused the stir over the Meudon pineapples. People simply refused to believe that the cultivation of pineapples had really progressed so dramatically (though this was nothing compared to those produced later in the century of up to 15 lbs). This was recognised in a parable of progress that appeared prominently in the *Gardener's Chronicle* in November 1843 warning against those individuals who 'have been standing still, while the crowd has been rolling on'. It ran,

Take, for instance, the pine grower. He was thought something of thirty years ago who could make his Queens average 2 lbs, and a 2½ lb. Fruit was a prodigy . . . Then when they see in the newspapers that heavier Pines are procured in this place and that, some of them shake their heads and doubt, others flatly contradict the statements, while some cry out at the injury they occasion them.

The newspaper sought to warn its readership: 'These are the persons who lag behind, and are so soon lost to view by the crowds who advance with the stream of discovery.'[47] For really, the fuss over size masked the battle over another issue: industrial progress.

Progress was the maxim by which Victorian Britain functioned. While there were far more protagonists of progress than critics, many were pessimistic about the problems they predicted it was going to bring in the future. Commentators like Thomas Carlyle and John Ruskin fretted about 'the wilderness of our manufacturing world' of which the certain result was going to be that 'the fatal cycle will continue to revolve with more intense force and rapidity – speculation, prosperity, over-production, glut, distress' (H. H. Milman, 1848).[48] This was a moment of moral crisis; and the state of the cultivation of pineapples was just one, albeit illuminating, example of the very dramatic changes brought about by the industrial revolution that made many so anxious.

But despite this, few felt they could afford to be the ones to lag behind the unflinching march of progress, whether in the machinery they chose for their factories, the materials they chose for their clothes, or the heating techniques they chose for their pineries. In 1844 the *Gardener's Chronicle* was moved to comment that 'Perhaps there never was a time when more interest was felt in the cultivation of the Pine-apple, than at present; or when the spirit of competition ran higher among cultivators generally, than it is likely to during the coming season.'[49] And so it was that just one obstacle remained between the pineapple and the masses – the crippling, extortionate, disproportionate expense of the whole enterprise. Glass, coal, labour – it all added up, and quickly.

Yet while middle-class gardeners would have loved to have given it a go – this is evident from J. C. Loudon's decision to write about it, for he was a middle-class enthusiast aimed at a middle-class audience – the economics of the situation prevented them. There was just no way to make it substantially cheaper to produce, despite tweaks in the process here and there.

For the majority of the population, then, the English pineapple remained an imaginative adventure, with at least one appearance in (for example) almost every single work by Charles Dickens and

25. Wallpaper by Augustus Pugin, 1848, used in the Houses of Parliament.

William Thackeray, the foremost social chroniclers of the period. Its ability to inveigle itself into the art and culture of the age is a clear indication of its cultural importance in comparison to other commodities. It had earned itself an enduring role within the English consciousness. One memorable example is a number of wallpapers designed by Augustus Pugin in the 1840s. Interestingly, it was a replica of one of these that caused such a storm in 1998 when it was revealed that Lord Chancellor Derry Irvine had paid a total of £59,000 to have it in his redecorated chambers in the House of Lords. Was he too trying to make a statement about his status? Or was it his prickliness that he hoped to highlight?[50]

However, forces were circling that were beginning to shift the way the pineapple was perceived. Among the first to notice this was William Thackeray. The May 1850 instalment of *Pendennis* sees the eponymous hero muse upon the extraordinary progress made over the past few decades in the way women in London went about their day-to-day business. The analogy he uses for this?

> Ye gods! How rapidly we live and grow! in nine months, Mr Paxton grows you a pine-apple as large as a portmanteau; whereas a little one, no bigger than a Dutch cheese, took three years to attain his majority in old times. And as the race of pine-apples, so is the race of man.[51]

To Thackeray's primarily middle-class readership, the analogy was an alluring one. The nineteenth century indeed saw the progress of pineapple cultivation become a powerful metaphor for the nation's industrial growth. More than any other guest of the English garden, it made certain that it benefited from the hundreds of technological advances ushered in in this period. It was amongst the most blatant displays around of the advanced state of British innovation.

Yet Thackeray's cultural perspective allowed him to have a more critical stance on the pineapple than most. Born in Calcutta, he was not easily seduced by expressions of the exotic: 'Pines – I've seen 'em feed pigs on pines,' splutters a Colonel just back from service in India while at dinner with Pendennis.[52] The suggestion is that the pineapple has no inherent quality that makes it exalted beyond all others; it is merely the associations that have grown up like weeds around it that have made gentlemen and gentlewomen worship at its altar. Thackeray wrote in a letter around the time *Pendennis* was published, 'The present writers are all employed as by instinct in unscrewing the old framework of society, and getting it ready for the Smash'; and he participates in this himself. Just as Thackeray elevates the pineapple as a metaphor for progress, he also ridicules its role in society as an expression of luxury.[53]

It is Thackeray's comparison with a 'portmanteau' that exposes the sense of subversion contained in this passage. In contrast to De Rochefort's assessment two centuries earlier that 'Nature may be said to have been extremely prodigal of what was most rare and precious in her Treasury to this Plant', the pineapple, so long portrayed as the 'container' of so much cultural capital, was now essentially empty – a vacuous and ephemeral obsession of the privileged, almost all it had to recommend it now were the labels which it carried with it on its travels. Indeed, with the portentous statement, 'And as the race of pine-apples so is the race of man', Thackeray surely parodies the era in which he lives which sees fit to elevate what is after all only a fruit to a position of such profound resonance.

Attacks like Thackeray's by no means left the home-grown pineapple unscathed. By the 1860s and 1870s, in an age of relative sobriety, pineapple-growing began to seem a somewhat ridiculous proposition, redolent of bygone extravagance. While this by no means prevented the very rich from continuing to indulge themselves, it did make such excesses begin to seem like an anachronism. In 1875 at Cyfarthfa Castle in south Wales, the seat of the iron magnate Robert Thompson Crawshay, a stock of no less than 3,000 pineapple plants were maintained throughout the year in the estate's four pine stoves and nine succession houses. One hundred ripe pineapples were regularly cut for the Crawshay family Christmas alone – always lavish affairs.[54] Being just a few minutes' walk from the centre of Merthyr Tyfvil, overlooking one of the largest ironworks in the area, ensured a steady supply of easily available coal to feed the furnaces that heated the pineries. Nonetheless, it remained an amazingly remote location to which to transport all the various other materials required. The costs involved in the upkeep of this many pineapples make the mind boggle. Crawshay's desire to recreate the tropics on a hill that overlooked the smoke and dirt of a nineteenth-century ironworks apparently remained powerful enough to overcome such practical considerations. But while fifty years ago, such excess reigned supreme, to many it now seemed like the last throe of a dying art.

'Although a noble Pine is an ornament to any table, it becomes rather commonplace when it is seen too often, and I have heard of one going the round of a series of west-end dinner parties for some weeks. It might have been used in the same way longer, and been equally useful, if it had been made of wax or cast-iron,' wrote J. Robson in the *Journal of Horticulture* in 1872.[55] Clearly a Victorian home-grown pineapple transcended its actual taste, smell or nutritional value. However, it was the resulting clamour for it that was, sadly, to lead to its demise. For from the mid-nineteenth century, it was forced to contend with a daunting new challenger: imports.

9

'Desire makes all things flourish; possession withers them'

Marcel Proust (1896)

'A penny a slice! A penny a slice! A taste of paradise for just a penny a slice!' Thus became a commonly heard cry on the grimy streets of Victorian London. By 1850, 200,000 pineapples were being unloaded on to London's docksides every year. Suddenly, the pineapple came within reach of those outside the secluded world of the British upper classes. With the advent first of steamships and later ships with refrigerators, high-quality, low-cost imports from Britain's colonies became so widely available, not only in London but in all the big cities, that pineries began to seem like a folly without justification. By eliminating problems of supply, imported pineapples gained the ascendancy with astonishing speed. A drastic drop in prices meant that they became available to (almost) everyone – a startling development that was to transform the pineapple's existence forever.

It was in the summer of 1820 that the first large-scale cargo of pineapples arrived in Britain. Four hundred luscious pineapples from the Bermudas were bought by the fruiterer Mr Mart for his shop on Oxford Street in London. However, since at this date the journey still took at least six weeks, not even two-thirds arrived in a saleable condition.[1] It was only steamships that finally solved this problem.

The first successful crossing of the Atlantic by steamship took place in 1819 when the *Savannah* sailed from Georgia to Liverpool. The

172

1830s saw a boom in the industry, with the launch of the first such ship to make the journey regularly, the *Great Western*, which took just over fifteen days. Soon steamships plied all the world's major trade routes, presenting an unprecedented opportunity for the pineapple. It had constantly had to face up to the problem that once plucked from the plant, it no longer ripened but merely decayed. Of all the produce of the West Indies, it was one of the most delicate. Speed was of the essence and this is what the steamship delivered.

The first to spot the potential profit to be made from the mass import of pineapples was a London firm called Keeling and Hunt, based in Monument Yard in the City of London. In 1842 1,000 pineapples from the Bahamas were imported into the busy port of Liverpool by Claypole and Son: some were sold at the point of entry, but most were transported by railway to Keeling and Hunt's warehouse in London.[2] Thereafter, stacks of crates of pineapples became a regular feature of Britain's ports, no doubt further encouraged by the repeal of the Corn Laws in 1846 which encouraged free trade – each shipment averaged from about 2,000 to up to 50,000 as the century progressed. In the summer of 1850 *The Times* calculated that a total of 200,000 pineapples had been imported in the space of just three months.[3] The result was that, eight short years since the inauguration of the trade, the pineapple was available to buy in unprecedented quantities.

Throughout the century, newspapers carried reports of the arrival of the first pineapples of the season. These came from every corner of Britain's ever-expanding empire: 1852 saw the first consignment from Africa in the form of a parcel of pineapples sent to Keeling and Hunt from Sierra Leone, for instance, having been introduced to the region by the Portuguese in the sixteenth century.[4] The huge majority, however, had been nurtured under the blessed West Indian sun – some from St Bartholomew's, some from Antigua, but most from the Bahamas, in particular the islands of New Providence and Eleutheria. The British had managed to uncover yet another way to plunder the New World of its treasures.

Depending on its exact provenance, a steamer from the West Indies faced a voyage of between three and four weeks. On board, the pineapples were stowed in galleries at the fore and aft, 'so extravagantly fragrant that it has to be ventilated to abate the odour'.[5] Ventilation was key – the ship's hatches were left open for the duration. Some consignments arrived at Southampton or Liverpool, to be transported onwards by railway: the boom of the industry meant that, by 1845, 2,441 miles of railway tracks criss-crossed the countryside. There was often no need, however, to take advantage of this innovation, since most arrived in London.

When a steamer carrying pineapples arrived at one of the Thames wharfs, the delicacy of the cargo meant that it was imperative that it was unloaded as fast as possible. Sometimes special measures were taken to ensure this. In August 1847, a cargo of 1,048 dozen pineapples from Nassau arrived in London aboard the *Shamrock*. According to *The Times*, 'In order to afford every facility in the landing of the cargo from the hold of the vessel, especial permission was granted by the proper authorities for the discharge to continue beyond the legal and regular hours of business, in order that the fruit might not become deteriorated by unnecessary delay in the delivery to the importers' private stores.' The crew were forced to work through the night, but hopefully they understood that the cargo was worth a little extra effort. At least it smelled better than fish.[6]

But sometimes it did not all go according to plan. In September 1849, a ship bound from Nassau under the command of Captain George David, the *Ace of Trumps*, was forced to make an unscheduled docking at Plymouth harbour. Appalling weather meant that the journey had taken much longer than expected: not only had the crew run out of food and water, but most of the pineapples (on which their wages depended) had decayed. The other casualty was a consignment of an alternative delicacy, sea turtles, most of which had to be thrown overboard, while all the others remained 'in a dying state'. The tables of the obscenely rich must have been rather sparse that month.[7]

Once the cargo had been successfully unloaded ashore and reported at the Customs House, destinations varied. There was considerable demand in prosperous cities like Manchester or Bath, while there are

GREAT SALE OF WEST INDIA PINE-APPLES.

26. A sale of West Indian pineapples in London, 1847.

reports of some being re-exported the same day to France. Most, though, were destined to be sold in London, sometimes by the importers themselves: in 1847, the *Illustrated London News* recorded that, 'A cargo of this hitherto valuable and delicious fruit, consisting of the immense quantity of 35,000 Pines, has, within these few days, been received,' to be auctioned off at the Keeling and Hunt warehouse for between ten and forty shillings per lot of twenty.[8] Another reliable outlet was the Jewish brokers in the streets around Duke's Place next to the Bevis Marks synagogue, the centre of the Jewish community in London at the time. Today it sits uneasily on the margins of the City, hiding its glory behind a photocopy shop and a cheap flights outlet. It is hard to imagine the flurry of activity that was precipitated by the arrival of a ship from one or other of Britain's colonies.

The largest public sales were arranged by brokers in Covent Garden market. Beneath the red glow of the early morning sun, the nearby streets were jammed with 'carts of all sorts, sizes and descriptions, from the heavy lumbering wagon, with its four stout horses, to the jingling costermonger's cart, with its consumptive donkey'.[9] The pavements were nowhere to be seen, buried beneath mounds of fruit and vegetables waiting to be whisked off to the greengrocers. Men and women elbowed their way through the crowds 'with their arms bowed out by the cauliflowers under them, or the red tips of carrots pointing from their crammed aprons, or else their faces red with the weight of the loaded head-basket'.[10] Many were the hazards to watch out for – the walnut husks scattered carelessly all over the cobblestones slipped up more than a few market traders in a hurry. While the air smelled amazing, an eery quietness hung heavy: tradition deemed that business was done in a subdued murmur, rather than with the cacophony of shouting that less prestigious markets had to endure.

Public sales of pineapples usually took place on Saturday mornings in the north-eastern corner of the market. Charles Dickens described how, at about ten o'clock, the auctioneers clambered on to boxes to begin.[11] It was a sight closely associated with Covent Garden: 'The supplies of fruit and vegetables sent to this market, in variety, excellence, and quantity, surpass those of all other countries. There is more certainty of purchasing a pineapple here, every day of the year, than in Jamaica and Calcutta.'[12] Nowhere else were they displayed in such extravagant quantities. In Dickens's *David Copperfield* (1850), David recounts how, when he first started work at Murdstone and Grinby's, 'We had half-an-hour, I think, for tea. When I had money enough, I used to get half-a-pint of ready made coffee and a slice of bread and butter. When I had none, I used to look at a venison-shop in Fleetstreet; or I have strolled, at such a time, as far as Covent Garden Market, and stared at the pine-apples.'[13] For a boy like David, it offered a glimpse into a world of unimaginable opulence.

The finest specimens sold at Covent Garden were bought whole-sale by hotels, restaurants or shops like Owen and Bentley, a luxury fruiterer at the north end of Bond Street. Here each one retailed for up to ten shillings. Many, however, found themselves piled high upon the barrows of the costermongers, the fruit and vegetable hawkers –

by 1851, a tenth of all pineapples sold were sold in this way. Never before had it flaunted itself in such an unashamedly public context. It is the costermonger that the pineapple has to thank for the fact that it became available not only to the middle classes, but in time to the working classes too: 'but for the trade having become part of the costermonger's avocation, hundreds and thousands in London would never have tasted a pine-apple'. Much of our information about the way the pineapple found its way into these homes comes from Henry Mayhew's wonderful contemporary work of philanthropic journalism, *London Labour and the London Poor* (1851).[14] Mayhew vividly evokes the costermonger's day, spent pushing his barrow of precariously balanced pineapples through the uneven cobbled streets,

" PINE-APPLES, A PENNY A SLICE "

27. A London trader selling 'Pine-apples, a penny a slice' from a barrow, c.1850.

trying to avoid the tramps, drunks and piles of rubbish. Just to keep his stock all aboard was challenge enough.

Pineapples were one of the most profitable staples of the costermonger's trade: 'They made more money "working" these than any other article . . . One costermonger assured me that he had taken 22s. a day during the rage for pines, when they first came up.' Selling 20,000 pineapples on the streets at an average of 6d. each, when wholesale they went for about 4d., generated a total net income of £500 a year, a not inconsiderable sum. The speed with which imported pineapples established a grip on the streets of London is extraordinary – this really was a radical explosion of exotica.

In the beginning, most of them were sold to 'gentlefolk'. According to Mayhew, 'The public were not aware then that the pines they sold were "salt-water touched", and the people bought them as fast as they could be sold.' In other words, they tended to be bought under the misconception that what was on offer was a home-grown specimen but at a bargain price – here was a stab at social status for only a couple of shillings a go. However, by the time Mayhew came to write his book, most of those buying a pineapple from the costermonger were typical middle-class types – the suburban wife of an artisan, a modest-sized shopkeeper or a clerk. In these circles it was an instant hit, often brought home to the family for a treat, perhaps for a birthday or Christmas. In Mayhew's view the housewife was the most demanding type of customer the costermonger had to deal with – not necessarily due to a sense of household thrift, but rather in a bid to ensure she had a penny left over at the end of her shopping trip to spend on a glass of gin to fortify her before she trudged back to her husband. Colloquially known as the gin penny, it sounds like a fabulous institution.

The costermonger's job was not always an easy one, however. In a letter to *The Times* of 23 August 1856, for example, Keeling and Hunt took up a 'case of great injustice':

> On the 9th of this month a man named George Gee, while plying his trade in Tottenham-court-road, was rudely assailed by an inspector of the Board of Health named Newman, who condemned his barrow of

pineapples and smashed them, entailing a loss to the amount of 4l or 5l, which we need not say was tantamount to ruin to the poor man.[15]

Smashing up the offending fruit seems a little excessive, even if it was fantastic street theatre for all the shoppers passing by. Keeling and Hunt's protest at the unfairness of it all was of course not entirely altruistic – the costermongers sold their firm's produce on the streets. The first Food and Drugs Act of 1860, a direct response to these kinds of problems, was an attempt to regulate the food industry at a time when poor quality produce was widespread and of great public concern.

To cater for the recently sparked middle-class interest in the fruit, it popped up more and more in contemporary recipe books. Since the publication of Richard Bradley's recipe in *The Country Housewife* (1732), other recipes had followed sporadically – one for preserved pineapple in Elizabeth Raffald's *Experienced English Housekeeper* (1769) and one for pineapple ice in Richard Dolby's *Cook's Dictionary* (1833), amongst others – but they remained relatively uncommon: so precious was this commodity, it seemed like a waste to present it bereft of the powerful signifier of its crown.[16] Imports changed all this, however. The publication of Mrs Beeton's *Book of Household Management* in 1861 provided the middle-class housewife with access to recipes that include the pineapple as a central ingredient: the first edition featured pineapple fritters, pineapple chips and preserved pineapple. For pineapple fritters, proceed thus:

Ingredients – A small pineapple, a small wineglassful of brandy or liqueur, 2 oz. of sifted sugar; batter . . .
Mode – . . . Pare the pine with as little waste as possible, cut it into rather thin slices, and soak these slices in the above proportion of brandy or liqueur and pounded sugar for 4 hours; then make a batter . . .; and, when this is ready, dip in the pieces of pine, and fry them in boiling lard from 5 to 8 minutes; turn them from the lard before the fire, dish them on a white d'oyley, strew them over sifted sugar, and serve quickly.[17]

It was now officially in the mainstream. Mrs Beeton did add the sensible caveat that it should only be attempted when West Indian pineapples are available, since substituting English pineapples renders the dish decidedly uneconomical.

For those unable to afford even a shilling or two for a taste of the exotic, all was not lost. The cannier costermongers also developed a roaring trade in pineapple slices at a penny each. According to Mayhew, 'The poorer people – sweeps, dustmen, cabmen, occasionally had pennyworths, "just for the fun of the thing".'[18] Had the third Duke of Portland been able to travel forward in time to see it sold in this way, imagine his surprise. No longer was it necessary to get into debt just for a taste of this much-talked-of fruit. They were now available just a hop, skip and a jump away from the urban doorstep. The result was the emergence of an entirely new customer base.

Pineapples sold by the slice tended to be those of an inferior quality, as explained in a letter to *The Times* in 1856: 'The quantity of pineapples brought in a vessel necessarily causes many to be discoloured and the sale of them to be forced, which will account for so many finding their way into the streets, the sale of which at a reduced price has afforded many a costermonger the means of providing for his family and the poorer classes of enjoying a luxury hitherto unobtainable.'[19] While such democratisation had many happy consequences, it was also by this route that the pineapple lost much of its social cachet. When sold in slices, it no longer had its crown and armour to sustain its reputation as the king of fruits. With its position as a 'perfect' fruit thus undermined, it inevitably lost much of the kudos it gained from its arresting appearance. This was just the beginning of an encroaching disrespect for its finery.

For the lower and middle classes, imported pineapple was a way of comprehending the emerging British empire for those participating in it imaginatively, as consumers, rather than physically, through travel or government. The nineteenth century was one of almost continual imperial warfare by British troops, with all the associated financial demands. The pineapple was a tangible affirmation of the benefits of this – bringing the wonders of the empire to the doorsteps of the

KING OF FRUITS 181

many. It may not have had the economic clout of sugar or tobacco, but just one whiff of its smell or glimpse of its crown brought a world of sunshine into the fusty, dusty dining rooms of Victorian Britain. As a declaration of Britain's superior global power within the intimate realm of the dining room, it worked brilliantly.

The main source of imported pineapples in this period was the Bahamas. Previous studies have concluded that the pineapple was first introduced there by Palatinate refugees in the 1720s. However, this is undoubtedly misleading. There is no doubt that it found its way to these lovely islands many centuries earlier. It is possible that this happened under the aegis of the Arawak Indians when some of them migrated there from the Greater Amazonia around 800 AD. From them sprang the Lucayans ('small-island people'). Their staple crop was maize, but this was supplemented by a wide range of other cultivated foodstuffs – amongst them sweet potatoes, chilli peppers, peanuts and, it seems highly likely, pineapples. While the area suffers from a lack of fertile soil, there are pockets of the famous 'red loam' known locally as pineapple soil. It is likely that the Lucayans, experts in making the most of their resources, found this out for themselves long before they became the first native American tribe to greet Christopher Columbus when he landed on the Bahamian island of San Salvador in 1492. Alternatively, Las Casas claimed that it was thanks to the Spanish conquistadores that the pineapple was introduced from the islands to the south. But whether it was the Arawaks, the Spanish or some more complex process of contacts and trade with the many other islands in the Caribbean that we know boasted the pineapple by the time Columbus arrived, there is no doubt that they were growing in the Bahamas before the 1720s. [20]

A trip to the Public Records Office threw up a document that proves this. In a missive of 19 July 1701 written to the Council of Trade and Plantations back in London, the island's Governor, Elias Haskett, notes pineapples 'in abundance' on the Bahamian island of New Providence; this is before he goes on to voice his concerns that his attempts to subdue the pirates in the area 'may cause them to serve me as the Spaniards did one of the Governors of this place, which was to ro[a]st him alive'.[21] The only possible conclusion is that the Palatinate refugees in the 1720s were not the first to introduce the pineapple to the island, but the first to engage in its cultivation. For the Bahamas, this too is an important milestone.

The first two decades of the eighteenth century saw life in the Bahamas dominated by a moral and social economy imposed by pirates like Blackbeard (Edward Teach), with up to 1,000 pirates at a time using the Bahamas as a base. But after Captain Woodes Rogers arrived in July 1718, he made it his mission to restore and expand the legitimate economy. By the time of the census of 1734, the total population was 1,378, yet the scope of the island's trade remained minuscule, with most of the twenty small vessels that plied the island engaged in the transport of provisions, including pineapples, to South Carolina.[22] 'Their pineapple is thought to be the best in America,' commented a report by the Council of Trade and Plantations.[23] It was a verdict that was to attach itself to the Bahamian pineapple for some time.

Throughout the century, the Bahamas continued to trade pineapples with the North American east coast: 1772 saw the export of about 6,000 dozen in total. Even so, because the island's primary product was cotton, pineapples, though cultivated, were not given serious attention. Wrecking, turtling and fishing made up the other major occupations, with the minimum of farming and only a few plantations. However, the aftermath of the American Revolution saw an influx of American loyalists (along with their slaves), many of whom were farmers. The island's total population trebled. In 1787 John Murray, the fourth Lord Dunmore, was installed as Governor – not only had he apparently recovered from his traumatic experiences in Virginia, he also felt able to drag himself away from his beloved Pineapple at Dunmore Park for a few years. The recompense, perhaps, was that he was now surrounded by fields and fields of the real thing. While he stood up for the rights of slaves (as he had in the American colonies), he was very unpopular, due to nepotism, crooked land speculation and a strange obsession with building expensive new forts for no reason. Few were surprised when he was recalled in 1796: the eccentric Dunmore had failed in his brief – yet again.

Yet Dunmore did help to oversee a period of major expansion. The area of cultivated land in the Bahamas increased from 3,434 acres to 16,322 acres between 1783 and 1788 and much of this was cotton. But while the climate was great for this crop, the soil was totally inadequate – productive in the beginning, it was so thin and sparse that it was very quickly exhausted and by 1800 the cotton plantation economy had collapsed. Salt from the country's twenty-five major salt ponds filled the economic gap up to a point, but this still left the inhabitants without a plantation staple and the planters were forced to diversify. It was a troublesome process. As the island's Governor commented in 1832, 'The real truth is that these islands with the exception of salt do not offer any real encouragement for the employment of capital. Pine-apples to a very large extent have lately been cultivated; but they only answer in particular situations, and in a particular soil.'[24] Indeed, pineapples are very choosy about the soil in which they will deign to grow. But the island's abundance of red loam, which provides just the nutrients it demands, meant that many decided it was worth the risk – for there was clearly money to be made, particularly to meet the demand from American high society.

Following the abolition of slavery in 1834, some ex-slaves chose to buy land specifically for the purpose of growing pineapples. Most, however, were forced to work on it under the share-cropping system. This meant that while farmers were able to lease land from the landlord, they had to give him a share of the profit in return, a share that varied between a third and a half, depending on soil conditions. The result was that most remained virtually hired hands, with limited independence or choices and little improvement in their economic and social lot. It was a miserable existence – the hands that harvested the Bahamian pineapple were not happy ones.

Farmers also had to deal with those who marketed the pineapples to ships' captains. After a stint as the island's Magistrate in the 1860s and 1870s, Louis Diston Powles penned a withering attack on the tactics of the local merchants that he had witnessed. 'The Nassau merchant', he fumed, 'appears on the scene with his pack of rubbish on his back, and establishes a temporary store. Like "the flowers that bloom in the spring", he appears with the pine-apple season and disappears with it; save that instead of a flower he is a upas-tree, blasting and withering wherever he sets his accursed foot.' For while the merchant received payment in cash, he bartered with the pineapple farmers not with cash but with quantities of rice, salt, pork or cotton that were invariably worth much less than claimed.

Since the farmers had no choice but to comply, the results were devastating. In the course of one investigation into this common malpractice, Powles told how 'When I arrived at the settlement in question, the haggard looks of the poor folk told their piteous story far more eloquently than the flood of words in which they poured it out to me. This conduct was absolutely inexcusable, for plenty of vessels call every year for pine-apples, and there is never the slightest necessity to ship a cargo without cash down.' This was certainly not the Eden that many consumers of the pineapple back in Britain imagined it to be.[25]

Following the successful export of pineapples to Britain in 1842 and again in 1843, in 1844 over 10,000 additional acres of land were set aside in New Providence for the cultivation of the same. A year later, the smaller island of Eleuthera followed suit.[26] While exports to America had sustained the island up to a point, the opening of a whole new market in Britain made it clear that this was a major commercial opportunity, to be taken advantage of by all who dared. For Bahamian farmers it was literally a life-saver, now that experiments had proved that cotton was no longer a feasible economic option.

Since in the early days of the trade many pineapples arrived 'ill-grown', in 1846 1,000 'offsets' of some of the most popular varieties at this time were sent over from Britain to be planted in the Bahamas, accompanied by 'several parties well versed in the cultivation of this fruit [who] have proceeded thither to turn that knowledge to a profit'.[27] The pineapple had been so appropriated by the English that they clearly had few qualms about establishing themselves as experts in its cultivation, even on an island that had produced the fruit for centuries longer. As a ploy, it proved very successful. In 1864, 61,500 dozen pineapples to a value of £8,516 were exported from the Bahamas to Britain, almost all from New Providence and Eleuthera.[28]

Knowledge was not all that the British had to offer. In 1856, Thomas C. Harvey, assistant surveyor-general to the Bahamas, wrote a report for the Governor that included a wide variety of recommendations, many of which were intended specifically to benefit the pineapple industry. On the subject of the Glenelg Settlement on Eleuthera, where about 25,000 pineapples were raised every year, Harvey noted a paucity of roads:

> Another road is much wanted for the benefit of those towards the eastern side of the Island, who are extensively engaged in cultivating pineapples, and have no road; in consequence of which, the only way that a number of proprietors have the power of transporting the produce of their fields to the seashore is, by the laborers carrying them in baskets on their heads – a laborious and expensive mode, and at the same time one so tedious that the delay it occasions in loading a vessel, often obliges much fruit to be cast aside. Such drawbacks as these naturally dispirit the cultivator and retard the extension of pine cultivation, which, considering that this fruit obtains its utmost perfection in the Bahamas, is to be deplored.[29]

It was a situation swiftly remedied by British civil servants. In this way, the Bahamian pineapple industry was one more sphere in which the British empire chose to wield its influence and power.

The newly opened market for pineapple in England presented Bahamian pineapple farmers with other advantages too. Firstly, it allowed them to demand a fairer price for their product. According to *The Times* in 1846, 'The advantage accruing from the importation of this article is, that the whole of the proceeds are remitted from this country in manufactured goods, principally for clothing the natives, who hitherto had the Americans only for customers, who obtained the produce in question for a mere trifle, but since the import to England the price has been enhanced nearly double.'[30] It also gave them easy access to the various manufactured products for which Britain was

28. White plantation owners survey the pineapple fields in the Bahamas in 1879.

famous. As an 1856 report summarised: 'The increasing demand for this article from the mother country is materially improving the prospects of the planters in the Bahamas.'[31] It is a fascinating glimpse into Britain's commercial relationship with its colonies in this period.

In August 1843, after a second successful season of imports from the Caribbean proved to even the most committed sceptics that the trade was no fluke, the *Gardener's Chronicle* warned that, 'It is understood that large numbers are to be expected.' However, it went on to attempt to reassure its readers with a rather disparaging report of the cargo that had arrived to such a fanfare from most other quarters: 'They are small, and mostly ill-grown, many not weighing more than half a pound, and none that we have seen exceeding two pounds . . . English Pine-growers need not, however, be alarmed at present, for unless future importations improve in quality, those accustomed to English Pine Apples would not place them on their tables.'[32] The English pineapple not only had the advantage that it grew all year round, in contrast to imports in this period which were only available in June, July and August. More importantly, a consensus remained that imported pineapples were simply not as delicious as the home-grown variety.

On 21 July 1873 *The Times* printed a lengthy and damning article, deadly serious in tone, on the supposed moral dubiousness of the imported pineapple.[33] Beneath the headline 'Social Hypocrisies', it railed against a practice that was apparently becoming worryingly common among fruiterers. Customers buying a West Indian pineapple were being offered a British crown to go with it in order to make it appear home-grown – in other words, to deceive dinner guests into thinking that the whole pineapple had been grown in their host's hothouses:

> This may be considered a small matter by ladies who think it no dishonesty to wear chignons so artfully constructed that the keenest observers will oft times fail to discover the deception practised on them and imagine that the luxuriant tresses which excite their imagination are really their own, but it is a doubtful policy to introduce the fashions of the London world into the hitherto innocent vegetable world.

Levelled at the pineapple in this passage are all manner of accusations that again reveal a considerable degree of continuity with those thrown at it a century, two centuries, even three centuries before.

One of these is that of artifice – worse still, the kind of artifice practised by Victorian womanhood who are said to conspire in a 'deception' to enhance their attractions. 'Innocent' no more, the fall from godliness is thus characterised in sexual terms: a British, virginal (female) has been illicitly stolen by a threatening West Indian foreigner to 'excite' the onlookers' 'imagination'.

Yet the writer has not finished his attack. National identity was also at stake, apparently: 'A West India pineapple has no more right to wear a British crown than an apple or a peach has to employ rouge for the purpose of concealing its pallor or heightening its bloom.' The social threat which the intrusion of such artifice presents is characterised as the presence of the racial 'other' within British society, the Satan within Paradise. This strain of thought may in part be related to a contemporary rise in patriotism – it was around this time that the apple enjoyed a resurgence in popularity in an expression of this. But whatever the subtext, what is certain is the way the pineapple has the enduring ability to elicit this kind of passion. It is hard to imagine The Times devoting a similar number of seething columns to the grape, for instance.

While the last quarter of the century saw imports of pineapples from the West Indies decline somewhat, this was only because they were usurped by those from Africa, Florida and, in particular, the Azores. It was an industry relatively new to the Azores – pineapples had grown there for two centuries, but it was not until 1864, with the failure of the orange groves due to disease, that pineapple cultivation was embarked upon on a grand scale. Though attempts were made on the islands of Pico and Terceira, producers on St Michael were the first to make a success of it. To reach the tables of the British took only a few days by steamer and because of this, from the 1870s, the Azores became the most common origin of pineapples imported to England.[34] In February 1873, for instance, The Times announced the arrival of 150 dozen pineapples from St Michael aboard the steamer Ocean, which were then sold at public auction for between ten and thirty shillings per crate.[35]

In 1881 there came a dramatic new development. The year saw the first successful import of goods by refrigerated ship – after 98 days at sea on board the Dunedin, 5,000 sheep carcasses from New Zealand, frozen with the use of a system invented by the Bell-Coleman Mechanical Refrigeration Company, were unloaded in London 'in fine condition', according to a letter written to The Times a couple of days later. Thereafter the use of such ships became common, with the result that it became possible to import pineapples of immeasurably improved quality. Fresh-tasting, sweet-smelling, sun-drenched – what chance did the home-grown pineapple have when challenged to compete with this oh-so-desirable interloper direct from the tropics?

The English home-grown pineapple was simply no longer able to compete: having conceded the one advantage on to which it had clung, its freshness, the fight was all but over.

It seems that the *Gardener's Chronicle* had been right to alert its readers to the threat of imports. For over 100 years, the successful cultivation of a pineapple had been the pinnacle of a gardener's career. To present it at dinner was to eschew any confusion about the fact that not only was the host rich as rich can be, but his gardener was worth his weight in gold too. Now, all of a sudden, startling advances in the pineapple trade augured disaster. It seemed that the days of the pinery stocked with 2,000–3,000 fruit were numbered. For while it might have managed to withstand attacks like Thackeray's, it now faced a far more powerful force: industrialisation, with all its ensuing effects. The more pineapples that flooded the insalubrious streets of Britain's cities, the less socially advantageous their display became – with the result that the investment in home-grown varieties could no longer be justified in the way it used to be. This affected every British horticultural enthusiast, for whether they grew pineapples or not, it was clear to all that this development heralded the end of an era: as the *Journal of Horticulture* put it in 1872, 'large quantities of fruit from tropical countries arrive here at a time when home-grown fruit of other kinds is also plentiful: hence both the market and the appetite are glutted, and the once-aristocratic pineapple figures on the coster-monger's barrow, and is retailed at the lowest figure imaginable'.[36] 'Once-aristocratic'? Yikes. The pineapple had, quite literally, been cheapened.

As Proust was to write: 'Desire makes all things flourish; possession withers them.'[37] The cheaper, more plentiful and more widely available the pineapple became, the more its cultural clout declined. I blame Mrs Beeton's pineapple fritters. A world away from a time when Charles II himself deigned to cut up the fruit at the royal dinner table in full view of the French ambassador, the mere existence of this recipe of hers in the middle-class domain was evidence of how spectacularly prevalent the pineapple had become. The trade-off for this, however, was that it was forced to eschew most of its more aristocratic supporters. Having dominated English gardens for over 100 years, the glory days of the home-grown specimen were well and truly over.

But the pineapple was not going to give up without one final fight. As long as it still had its crown, its sword-like leaves and its armour-like shell, it was, after all, well-equipped for one. The difficulty was how to find a way for its crown to rise above the deluge of other exotic novelties that attempted to grab the attention of the average turn-of-the-century consumer while, at the same time, clinging on to those very attributes that had made it so culturally significant in the first place. One option was for this ever-restless fruit to shift the geographical location of its primary cultural battleground in the West. The obvious choice? America.

10

'Lead me to that delicious clime
Where the anana swells and grows'

James Gates Percival(1865)

The eager young journalist from the *American Gardener's Magazine* had visited John Perkins Cushing's garden in Watertown, Massachusetts, a number of times before. The greenhouses were legendary the state over for their truly spectacular array of exotic plants. But this trip – it was May 1835 – was different. This time, his editor had heard a rumour that pineapples had been successfully fruited. As he waited in the rain outside Boston's Hancock Tavern for the stagecoach to take him out of town, his heart raced with excitement. While he had seen pineapples being unloaded at Boston docks before, he had never (nor had his readers) seen them growing, smelling, sprouting right off the plant, just an hour and a half's dusty ride away from this throbbing, bustling city of dirt and debauchery. Come to think of it, he did not even know how they grew – On a tree like a banana? In the ground like a tuber? This was something that the chattering classes of the east coast had never had the chance to read about over breakfast.

However, though news of Cushing's pineapple may have boosted the magazine's circulation that month, the journalist did not hold out much hope for the pastime becoming anything like a national craze. While he had heard tell that, in England, improved technology had resulted in gardens that boasted 100, 1,000, even 5,000 pineapples at a time, closer to home, other obstacles were apparent. The struggle to popularise the home-grown pineapple coincided with the struggle for the heart and soul of America. In an era of constant change, it had to take on new associations in order to find a place in this assertively independent nation that refashioned every symbol to meet its needs. Yet this proved difficult – the competition from imports was intense. Nineteenth-century America was becoming subject to the powerful forces of the industrial revolution; there was not a single commodity that escaped it.

After George Washington's election in February 1789 as the first President of the United States, prospects for the home-grown pineapple had looked hopeful. Relations with England were a little less fraught: the fruit had established itself among the ultimate in luxury goods and also maintained the air of having been snatched straight from Nature's 'Treasury', as Christopher De Rochefort had characterised it many years before. It was a prize to be fought for above all others, according to Philip Morin Freneau, the most prominent American poet of the Revolution:

> The prince of fruits, whom some *jayama* call,
> Anana some, the happy flavoured pine;
> In which unites the tastes and the juices all
> Of apple, quince, peach, grape and nectarine,
>
> Grows to perfection here, and spreads his crest,
> His diadem towards the parent sun;
> His diadem, in fiery blossoms drest,
> Stands armed with swords, from potent Nature won.[1]

Its 'diadem' on display, leaving not a soul in doubt of its superior status, it is depicted (as anthropomorphically as ever) as a warrior, 'swords' at the ready to defend itself not only from Nature's constant attempts to retain one of her most impressive creations, but also from all the other predators who sought to challenge the way it is 'drest'. This by now oft-repeated incarnation allowed it at least a valiant attempt at establishing a permanent presence in the households of the rich and famous in the way that it had done so astonishingly successfully in England.

With the burden of debt at last lifted, in the decades following the Revolution American society had seemed blessed by 'unparalleled prosperity . . . there is not a nation under the sun enjoying more present prosperity, nor with more prospect', according to Thomas Jefferson.[2] Merchants were free from restrictions placed on them by the British and revenue flowed freely into their pockets – earned from trade not only overseas, but also with an ever-expanding hinterland. Local lawyers cashed in too, ready to address the squabbles that inevitably ensued.

Thus a whole new class of suddenly wealthy professionals had sprung up to replace all those who in the course of the upheavals of the last decade had lost their keys to the colonies' coffers. These *nouveaux riches* ardently embraced the representation of the pineapple in their homes, with the 1780s and 1790s seeing a dramatic peak in its popularity in silverware, with sugar bowls, teapots, coffeepots and the like designed and manufactured by some of the most celebrated silversmiths of Philadelphia and Baltimore.[3] Furniture became more elaborate, jewellery more encrusted, food more indulgent, pets more fluffy. Similarly, local newspapers burst with advertisements for the construction of greenhouses, not only in the major cities but also to prospective clients further out of the slipstream of fashion.

By their very nature, greenhouses tend to fade from the view of the historian, a phenomenon comprehended even at the time: 'The greenhouse lover is like an actor, remembered by his contemporaries, and by them only.'[4] As a result, most examples of this ephemeron exist only in paintings or diaries. Glimpses of dedicated pineries are rarer still – they sneak up here and there, tantalisingly so – but one is always left with the impression that there were many more that have since been obscured by the passage of time. Post-Revolution, the undisputed centres of horticulture were the urban areas of Massachusetts, Pennsylvania and, to an extent, Maryland, and these are where pineries were most often found.

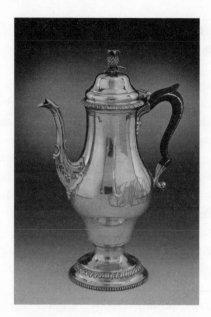

29. A silver coffeepot with a pineapple finial, by John Letelier. Philadelphia, 1775–95.

In 1794, the English textile merchant Henry Wansey had the pleasure of visiting two Massachusetts pineries, one owned by lawyer Ashton Harvey in Salem and one by merchant Joseph Barrell in Charlestown (now Somerville) – Barrell's was almost 200 feet long and heated by two stoves imported from England.[5] Three years later, pineapples were noted (along with lemon trees and coffee trees) on Robert Morris's lavish estate The Hills on the eastern banks of the Schuylkill river near Philadelphia – as the largest private property owner of the period, as well as the primary financier of the Revolution and a signatory of the Declaration of Independence, he certainly had the finances to indulge what became one of his pet hobbies.[6] Come 1800, another pinery pops into view – the one built by Theodore Lyman in his garden at The Vale. Having made a stack of cash trading with the Far East, Lyman had purchased thirty acres of land in Waltham, Massachusetts, upon which to build his dream home. The result was English in inspiration, inside and out, with the garden no exception – he even hired an English gardener named William Bell.

Yet compared to Britain, the home-grown pineapple remained a singular sight. While up to a point this served to enhance its symbolic power, at the same time, for the pineapple itself, it meant that opportunities to reproduce itself simply did not present themselves. The principal problem remained inadequate access to instructional literature on the subject. Help was at hand, however, in the form of an Irish immigrant with a talent for exotic horticulture by the name of Bernard M'Mahon.

M'Mahon emigrated to America in 1796 to pursue the interest in plants that had dominated his life since he was a child. By 1804, he had set himself up just outside Philadelphia with a well-respected nursery, as well as a busy shop on the east side of Second Street that was overseen by Mrs M'Mahon, a cheery but formidable saleswoman with an all but impenetrable Irish accent. The pinnacle of his career came in 1806 with the publication of his *American Gardener's Calendar*. This was a turning-point in the history of horticulture in America. Utilising knowledge gleaned from a combination of training in Ireland, meticulous study of works by experts like Philip Miller and William Speechly (he was particularly a fan of a method of eradicating insects detailed in Speechly's 1779 treatise) and a plethora of personal experience of the idiosyncrasies of the American climate accumulated in his own muddy but flourishing patch of earth, he became the first to tailor his advice to the plants he dealt with.

M'Mahon was also the first American writer to give clear directions on the cultivation of the pineapple. These are not dissimilar to earlier writings (by Miller in particular): he advises a hothouse of dimensions of between 20 and 100 feet long, 12–16 feet wide and 10–14 feet high on the back wall, 5–6 feet high on the front wall, with a roof made entirely of glass and flues on all sides, accompanied by plenty of personal attention to the fruit from start to finish. As the century progressed, modifications were made to this technique; but few diverged far from the one he originally prescribed. Trustworthy, accurate and characterised above all by common sense, the *Calendar* went into eleven editions.[7]

In one notable passage, M'Mahon drew attention to the 'great expence' of growing pineapples – for good reason. His decision to feature the fruit was part of a grand plan to encourage an 'air of grandeur and magnificence' in American gardens, which up until then had almost all been solely practical in intent. However, it was not until the 1830s when A. J. Downing, one of the most noted designers and writers of the antebellum period, waded into the debate that attitudes genuinely began to shift.

In Downing's view, gardening was still so little-practised because 'we Americans are so particularly *practical*, and so possessed of the demon of trade, that nothing is valuable which cannot be sold'.[8] He sought to combat this by bestowing upon gardening a reinvigorated moral dimension – a pastime of undeniable purity, where the goal was the recreation of Eden. Herein lay a cure for the moral woes of the nation, distanced from the greed that was seen to be subsuming America's upper class. All of a sudden, an hour spent down the bottom of the garden monitoring the thermometer had a higher purpose then just the neighbours' approbation. A fruit like the pineapple fitted perfectly into the central paradox of this vision – with Edenic connotations and little value on the open market due to the competition of imports, as a nutrient it was also just functional enough to be acceptable within the aggressively republican and mercantile northern states.

It was not long before this theme seeped into a number of the magazines that began life in this period, aimed primarily at a middle-class readership. While just 100 magazines existed in America in 1825, by 1850 this figure had risen to six times this, with a fair proportion dedicated to the natural world.[9] One of the most influential was the *American Gardener's Magazine*, founded in Boston in 1835 by Charles Hovey. The first genuinely American horticultural magazine, it provided a real spur to the advancement of related matters: it not only disseminated knowledge and reported on recent achievements, but it also provided a forum for gardeners to write in with specific questions, as well as to stoke the fires of competition that so often accompanied such discussion.

In its first year of existence, the *American Gardener's Magazine* had the good fortune to stumble upon an exclusive: a tale of rivalry, rakes and coal in the wealthiest enclaves of the Boston suburbs, it implicated a number of the city's most prominent citizens. The cause? Pineapples, for goodness' sake.

Boston in the third decade of the century was experiencing an economic boom. In the period after the Revolution, many of the wisest local business heads in town had turned their attentions to trade with China, with the result that 1830 saw over 1,000 ships dock in the course of the year, generating a revenue of about $11 million. The opening of three railways (to Lowell, Worcester and Providence) further increased the flow not only of goods but also of ideas and fashions. All this was supplemented by a growing investment in factories. Massachusetts was the most thoroughly industrialised state in the country, beaten in the world only by Britain, a state of affairs much encouraged by entities like the Boston Associates, a conglomerate of businessmen who built the world's first integrated textile factory.

Also some time around 1830, a consolidated élite of merchants, lawyers, railroad men and the like established a hegemony in Boston once and for all. Most rewarded themselves with a country estate, and while these did not come close to the astonishing scale of the Castle Howards of the day, they were unashamedly modelled on the style of life so treasured by the British upper class. These men had few qualms in presenting to the world a distinctly aristocratic disdain for the range of values that had so often been trumpeted since colonisation: parsimony, simplicity and so on.[10] Nowhere was this more true than in the realm of horticulture. While the Hudson valley had initially led the way here, the area around Boston was soon at the forefront: in 1837, the *Horticultural Register* noted the 'rapid strides of improvement which Horticulture has made, within a few years, in the vicinity of Boston' – manifested in part by a widespread mania for pears in this period.[11]

However, in July 1835, the *American Gardener's Magazine* featured a momentous announcement: 'Two pine apples were cut at Belmont Place, by Mr. Haggerston, a few days since, perfectly matured.'[12] Belmont Place was an estate in Watertown, Massachusetts (now the Boston suburb of Belmont, named after the house) owned by John Perkins Cushing. At the age of just sixteen, Perkins had been charged with overseeing the Canton office of his uncle's trading company in China, Perkins & Company. When he returned to Massachusetts in 1827, he was an exceedingly wealthy man. His next mission was to ensure that the 200 acre estate he had bought reflected this fact in its furnishings, books, hothouses, the lot.

Cushing's was the first pinery in the United States to produce pineapples of a reliable quality and quantity. In the fetid atmosphere that surrounded the plants, this was a world the like of which the journalist we met at the beginning of this chapter had never before experienced. It represented the investment of more cash than he could even conceive of – he might as well have been on a jaunt down a diamond mine. Sweating a little under his overcoat, he crouched down to smell a fruit, then paused to wonder: where had Haggerston, Cushing's head gardener, disappeared to? To check the thermometer? He wanted to have the chance to shake his hand before he had to go and file his report.

Over the coming months, the magazine continued to print a highly excitable commentary on the progress of Haggerston's pineapples. A visitor in August 1837 found one stove that contained over eighty pineapples about to fruit, many weighing up to six or eight pounds: 'It is gratifying to see such a fine number of plants, and we may date the present time as the commencement of the taste for growing this "king of fruits", as it has been justly and truly denominated . . . we hope that every gentleman who is fond of fine fruit will possess a pinery.'[13] A few weeks later, Haggerston also 'agreeably entertained' a journalist from a rival magazine, the *Horticultural Register*, who was equally impressed by the 'perfection' of what he saw: 'It is much to be hoped that every success will attend the pine-apple, under the above cultivation; as it is certainly one of the noblest acquisitions to the Hot

House, and forms one of the most prominent features on the table as a dessert.'[14] Happy to collude with received wisdom, the local media thus stirred up a frenzy around the home-grown pineapple that was not to go unnoticed by the more competitive of Cushing's peers.

Thus Cushing was not allowed to bask in the reflected glory of Haggerston's achievements for long. Just a month after the public was told of his triumph, the *American Gardener's Magazine* noted 'some fine healthy looking' pineapple plants at John Lowell's garden at Broomley Vale in Roxbury, Massachusetts.[15] John Lowell was a highly successful lawyer and agitator, as well as President of the Massachusetts Agricultural Society from 1823 to 1828. Another visit in December 1836 threw up further amazement at the leaps and bounds made in the science of 'This most excellent of all fruits': 'We were astonished when Mr Lowell's gardener informed us that several fruit had been cut during the past year.'[16] Not for the first time, there is the sense that the gardener is especially keen to show off this aspect of his daily labour. However, his is a knowledge still in its infancy: the magazine notes that the relatively small size of the fruit on display is due to a paucity of bottom heat, an error by now universally appreciated by English gardeners to be severely detrimental to the crop.

Word was spreading amongst the salons of Massachusetts high society. It was also in 1835 that Marshall Pinckney Wilder declared his intention to leap into this spirited race. Wilder was a major influence in the horticultural activities of the state – the first to import azaleas, he was also a founder of the American Pomological Society and President of the Massachusetts Agricultural Society from 1841 to 1848. His plan was to grow 'this greatest of all luxuries' on his Dorchester estate, Hawthorn Grove, by turning his greenhouse into a forcing-house, 'to include a peachery, a grapery, and, perhaps, a pinery'.[17] Presumably the qualification depended on whether finances permitted.

With horticultural activity now an accepted arbiter of status, many were continually on the lookout for ways to trump the neighbours – even when the neighbours were three days' ride away. In 1836,

Thomas Handasyd Perkins did this by building a separate and dedicated pinery that consisted of a pit, a succession house and a fruiting house (in contrast to the ones at Belmont Place and Broomley Vale where a pre-existing greenhouse had merely been converted). With the help of his head gardener, William H. Cowan, Perkins heated it with a system he developed himself.[18] Perkins had made his money from the same place that his nephew, John Perkins Cushing, had: China. He purchased Brookline, then in a small village outside Boston, in 1800, then proceeded to wile away his days doing his utmost to transform it into the exotic paradise he craved. In the maintenance of the gardens alone, he invested $10,000 a year. His taste for the extravagant was no secret (Madeira wine was a favourite), but with his stern expression, complemented by ruddy cheeks and bushy grey eyebrows, contemporary portraits of Perkins suggest he was a man for whom the no-nonsense of the outdoors also had a special appeal.[19]

At the 1837 Massachusetts Horticultural Society annual exhibition, fruits from the gardens of Cushing, Perkins and Lowell jostled for space on the centre table.[20] For what was the point unless you showed off about it? Rivalry hung heavy in the air. Like many others before them – the Duke of Portland and the Earl of Carlisle to name just two – these were ambitious, energetic and also somewhat profligate men keen to make a place for themselves in the world. The pineapple helped them express this in public.

By 1838 the *American Gardener's Magazine* (by this time renamed the *Magazine of Horticulture* in order to appear more sophisticated) was in buoyant mood: 'We hail these as the first steps towards the general cultivation of this "king of fruits" by the wealthy gentlemen and patrons of gardening in this country.'[21] In addition to innovations in the realm of horticulture, the 1830s saw many seminal technological inventions (Samuel Colt patented his design for the revolver in 1835), social changes (1837 saw the establishment of the first college for women, Mount Holyoke) and moral shifts (the American Antislavery Society was founded in 1833). Times were a-changing.

An additional theme emerges when you study the type of careers that many of these pinery owners had carved out for themselves. One factor that they have in common is that they had all spent a considerable chunk of time in some of the world's most exotic locations – China, for instance. Was the decision to build a pinery in some way a homage to this? A world where fantasy met reality, a controlled environment in which to meditate upon the source of their fortune? Boston's impossibly harsh winters may also have encouraged this search for a reminder of warmer climes. What is in evidence here is the changing relationship between the United States and Britain. This was a nation trying to establish its own identity on its own terms, rather than on terms inherited from elsewhere. The home-grown pineapple was thus relocated within the cultural landscape – no longer a symbol of the motherland, it was now back where it belonged as a symbol of otherness.

Yet despite the flurry of activity in Boston in the 1830s, pineries remained a novelty, even in richer and more fashionable cities like Philadelphia and New York. Again, all we have are hints here and there – since this period saw the explosion of greenhouses, constructed by anyone who was anyone, there is no doubt that pineries experienced a similar surge in popularity. In 1851, 'highly flavoured' pineapples were grown by Caleb Cope, President of the Pennsylvania Horticultural Society, on his estate Spring Brook near Philadelphia.[22] By 1856, there were supposedly only two successful pineapple cultivators in all of Pennsylvania – John Anspach and John Tucker: 'They produce as good pines, at least, as are ever seen in Covent Garden market, or on the tables of the nobles of England.'[23] It was not unusual for a note of competition with English pineapple growers to creep into such accounts, in part to encourage others. In 1858, pineapples were displayed at a horticultural show in Connecticut for the first time – James Stebbins, a gardener employed by the inventor and industrialist Samuel Colt of Armsmear, Hartford, was the one to take the glory.[24]

In all of this, most gardeners tended to defer to the techniques of their English counterparts. In 1838 William Haggerston was sent to

England 'to ascertain every thing new in relation to farming and gardening', to the approval of the *American Gardener's Magazine*: 'We are yet but in the very infancy of agriculture, and, unless we are willing to profit by the experience of others, we shall make but slight advancement to that state of perfection to which it has been carried in Great Britain.'[25]

'Within the last twenty years there has been a great advance made in the successful cultivation of the Pine-apple' was the verdict of *The Horticulturist*, a popular magazine founded by A. J. Downing, in 1860, using in evidence the fact that there were now four pineries in the vicinity of New York and more purported to be on the way.[26] In the magazine's opinion, this was to be attributed in part to improved knowledge of the subject, but also to recent advances in greenhouse technology. The first greenhouse in America known to use iron in its rafters instead of wood, for example, had been built by William Resorr of Cincinnati in 1849 to house his grapes.[27] The result, as in Britain, was the construction of ever-more beautiful and delicate structures – no longer just like glass boxes in form, curvilinear became the in-thing: 'It was like entering fairy land.'[28]

Then came the Civil War. Although war had historically signified trouble for the home-grown pineapple, this one was different. While the south was utterly devastated by the bitter and prolonged fighting, the impact on the north and the west was relatively slight. Thus even in September 1862, Sarah Butler, the wife of the northern Civil War general Benjamin Franklin Butler, made sure that she kept him up to date with the fact that 'The pineapple plants arrived today, looking very well.'[29] A central tenet of Victorian society, leisure time remained a top priority, only minimally affected by the carnage elsewhere.

Just before the war, one journalist predicted that 'Ere long we shall see the pine-apple grown here for the public markets to a much greater extent and perfection than is now done in Europe. What a glorious sight will be the Fruit Palace of America, with its noble centre, glowing with its golden pine-apples, and the sweet honey-dew dripping from its luscious cheek.'[30] But he was wrong. Although it is remarkable in itself that anyone at all attempted to grow pineapples in the north, the passion still failed to catch the nation's imagination in the way that it did in Britain. Why? What was it about American high society in this period that chose to reject the home-grown pineapple once again, even now that it was no longer hindered by its connotations of Englishness?

In part, it was still true that horticulture was an exclusive, rather than popular, pastime, and that there was a lack of literature. Few of the horticultural texts of the nineteenth century contain a reference to the pineapple – the pinnacle for most was grapes or peaches.[31] As Geo N. Stack, gardener to John Bridgeford in Albany in New York State, asked in 1865, 'Very few places seem to have the Pine-apple. Why is it so? . . . I think the answer is simply this: expense and ignorance.'[32] Those texts that sought to dispel this 'ignorance' were soon out of date due to relentless technological advance, while turning to English works on the subject, as noted in the earlier years, was no solution.[33] Similarly, the sun's rays played a different game in the differing latitudes. There were other practical obstacles: since glass was imported from Belgium or France until long after the Civil War, much of it arrived uneven, warped and blistered – a recipe for disaster, with many plants burnt by concentrated rays of sun before they had even had a chance.[34]

Many recognised that the onward march of the industrial revolution, with its side-effects of increased production, innovation and mass consumerism, also benefited the onward march of 'civilisation'. As a result, one magazine tried to encourage the cultivation of pineapples thus: 'We want to see what *can* be done in all the arts, and especially in the useful ones: and besides, when wealth accumulates to a certain amount, (the great difficulty is to know *what* that is), the sooner it overflows in almost any direction, irrigating poorer and dryer objects around it, the better for the public.'[35] A flood of letters protested at the article, deemed to be pointless: why not devote the page to turnips or potatoes or 'sich like' instead?[36] 'The culture of the pineapple is very expensive and troublesome' was how one magazine dismissed it.[37] In its different guises, the spectre of the anti-luxury movement is one that appears in every age, whatever form it takes – social, political or religious – and now it was resurrected by contemporary American philosophers like Henry Thoreau and Francis Wayland. The pineapple was a victim of an enduring contradiction in American popular thought: admirably idealistic, but at the same time unashamedly materialistic. It fulfilled both these instincts because while some might justify it in terms of the pursuit of Culture, for others, it was merely a gross indulgence.

Such protests resonated most loudly in the south, despite the fact that 'Men, women and pine-apples, I am inclined to think, flourish with a more kindly growth in the fervid latitudes.'[38] This is not to say that there were not some in the south who saw the appeal of the fruit: for example, 'J.S.' of Daufuskie Island in South Carolina wrote to a magazine to boast of the success he and his neighbours had with it in 1850.[39] But in the main, pineapples were not to be found in the number one might have expected. This was partly due to practicalities – there were only two plant nurseries of note in the entire region – but also to a number of problems peculiar to the south.

Horticulture in general was less popular in the south than in the north: landscape gardening in New Orleans was said to be fifty years behind everywhere else.[40] One journalist explained the south thus: 'Even with the wealthiest planters, those who count their slaves by hundreds and their acres by thousands, and have the incomes of the nobles of England, a garden seems a superfluity.'[41] Indeed, many visitors noted how even the grandest plantation houses, so opulent on the inside, were seemingly happy to leave the immediate exterior to degenerate into a playground for the family's horses. This was in part because cotton and tobacco generated so much revenue that they consumed almost all the energies directed towards the land, in contrast to the north which was always on the lookout for more and different crops. In addition, the shortage of railroads, canals and turnpikes presented logistical difficulties. The final straw, however, came with the Civil War which smashed the south to pieces – economically, socially and politically – with the result that with surplus cash in short supply, there were more important things to think about than tanner's bark.[42]

As in Britain, on estates like Cyfarthfa Castle, in the period after the Civil War the cultivation of pineapples began to have a somewhat anachronistic air even in the northern states. Take S. L. M. Barlow, a wealthy New York lawyer. Barlow took possession of a mansion in Glen Cove in New York State when one of his clients, the English engineer Thomas Kennard, was forced to sell it to him to extricate himself from financial crisis. Glen Cove already boasted a number of hothouses, but for a man like Barlow who 'spends his money like an American, and lives like an English lord', this was apparently not enough. He chose to dedicate one of the largest ones to the cultivation of pineapples. It was a successful scheme, bearing some 'delicious' fruit – but so it should be, given its team of three dedicated gardeners who were employed to shovel the more than 100 tons of coal a year that it required.[43] Here was one manifestation of a pattern of ostentation of which the *nouveaux riches*, ever-more Eurocentric in their attempts to be sophisticated, were becoming increasingly fond. With no income tax or death duties to pay, the post-bellum period saw the wealthier elements of American society free to indulge themselves in a spending spree of some magnitude.

Yet this grandeur by now felt out of date. The chief reasons lay stacked up in crates on the docksides of the east coast ports. While Britain was not presented with this option until the 1840s, here imported pineapples were a contender right from the beginning. They were distinctly second-rate in terms of the way they tasted, but they were indisputably cheaper, more plentiful and more widely available to purchase (at least, when they were in season). In a way, the struggle between the two mirrored the struggle between the old America and the new – while the home-grown pineapple represented increasingly archaic values like privilege, hierarchy and royalty, the imported pineapple was a more democratic manifestation of progress and trade.

Imported pineapples had been available since the mid-eighteenth century. Not even the War of Independence had managed to halt the influx: in July 1776, in the same breath that the *Pennsylvania Gazette* reported that Lord Dunmore was suggesting an exchange of prisoners, it also featured news of a ship from Providence captured in Hampton Creek in Virginia that was carrying 'a large quantity' of West Indian pineapples.[44] With peace came the explosion of imports. Ships from the West Indies arrived with 'festoons of fragrant pineapples' hung all over the deck in order to make the most of the available storage space.[45] These must have been quite a sight to behold in the grim, grimy American cities of this period as they expanded, industrialised and dramatically increased in population: in 1790, out of a population of nearly 4 million, only 202,000 lived in towns of over 2,500 people, but by 1825 this figure had risen to 1,000,000 out of a total population of 11,252,000.[46]

Before long, the introduction of steamships eliminated dependence on the winds, as well as a whole host of other difficulties that affected this delicate cargo. By the late 1820s, they were a common sight trundling up and down the east coast and into the Mississippi river. The journey time was so decreased that, with the risk of decay much diminished, it became possible to import pineapples from Caribbean islands further away than the Bahamas – Cuba, for example. At the same time, trains made it easier to transport them from the seaports into the country's interior. The first railroad, the Baltimore and Ohio, began carrying goods for revenue in 1830. Thus millions, not only in the north but also a fair way inland, had a taste of the tropics for the first time.

Travellers reported pineapples in abundance in the markets of all the major cities of the Atlantic coast. Those sold in Charleston impressed a journalist for *Frederick Douglass' Paper* in 1853: they 'reminded one of Oriental stories of luxuriance . . . If Adam and Eve were as sorely tempted by the apple, there is more apology for them than we had supposed.'[47] This was not the first time that they had elicited such a reaction, of course. Prices remained pretty steady throughout the century until the 1870s at about 20 cents in season (about $4 today) or 50 cents out of season (about $10 today) when purchased in one of the metropolises, but sometimes up to as much as

$3 when purchased in the more outlying areas. Some were sold by hawkers – Caroline M. Kirkland was struck by a 'stout Irishman, lazily pushing the pine-apple cart' in New York City in 1852[48] – while specimens of a higher quality were sold in shops.

Imports did not have an entirely easy journey into the larders of the American people, however. Fruit in general was viewed by many with suspicion: in the presidential campaign of 1840, Martin Van Buren was pilloried for his decadent taste for the stuff.[49] And not all fruits are created equal, apparently: as Henry Thoreau noted in his diary, 'Do not think that the fruits of New England are mean and insignificant, while those of some foreign land are noble and memorable. Our own, whatever they may be, are far more important to us than any others can be. They educate us, and fit us to live in New England. Better for us is the wild strawberry than the pineapple.'[50] In this way, the pineapple was cast as the choice of the unpatriotic, the undemocratic – in other words, everything that America sought to stand against.

A more practical argument against the consumption of fruit also surfaced. In 1832, its sale was banned by various city councils due to the cholera epidemic. It was a stance upheld by even the most respectable physicians: Dr Martin Payne argued that 'those who would escape the disease in the United States should restrict themselves to lean meat, potatoes, milk, tea and coffee'.[51] Prices were adversely affected for some years. 'Pine-apples and newspapers are rather cheap here! The first (and *fine* ones) at a penny a piece (owing a good deal to the prevalence of cholera, which makes people afraid of eating them)', exclaimed Lady Emmeline Stuart-Wortley in 1849 of the pineapples for sale in Gloucester, Massachusetts.[52] Thinking had shifted little since seventeenth-century physicians like Jacob Bontius had thrown identical accusations at the pineapple because of what they had learned from South American natives.

In the long term, such fears made little difference. If anything, the Civil War boosted demand for imported pineapples – at the tables of rich Confederates, in particular. For the economies of those countries able to supply them, like the Bahamas, this was a golden age. In 1864, a total of 229,226 dozen pineapples were exported from the Bahamas to the United States alone, to a total value of £21,299 (about £1.1 million today).[53] It was just the kind of present that Rhett Butler might have brought home for Scarlett O'Hara.

The enemy attempted to prevent this: in September 1863, a schooner called the *Etta* was seized with a cargo of pineapples from Nassau.[54] But newspapers all over the south triumphantly recorded the arrival of those that avoided such a fate. In December 1861, the *Theodora* managed to sneak past a Union blockade ship at Fort Johnson and Fort Caswell in North Carolina to deliver a cargo of pineapples, bananas, oranges, salt and coffee to the Confederate troops embedded there. It was quite a sight. The blockade ship gave chase, but the *Theodora*, 'one of the fastest steamers on the Continent', managed to make its way to safety under the guns of Fort Caswell and Fort Johnson – 'It was a very exciting race. We could see it distinctly from both Forts, and hear the booming of the enemy's guns, answered by the shrill and defiant whistle of the *Theodora*, "Catch me if you can".' Success! 'I wish I could send you some of the fruit,' lamented Thomas Rowland when he recounted the incident to his mother.[55]

Most of this went to the rich. The memoirs of the glamorous Confederate spy Belle Boyd regale the tale of how, in 1865, she dined with General P. T. Beauregard and some of his officers in Charleston, South Carolina, on a feast of fresh lemons, oranges and pineapples. In all honesty, though, she was more interested in 'a very handsome parrot, which I contrived to take home with me'. It indeed made its way as far as Richmond.[56]

As soon as the war was over, newspapers again began to feature advertisements placed by local grocers for pineapples.[57] The period saw a dramatic increase in the demand for all kinds of tropical commodities, in part due to a rise in the national incomes of the leading industrialised states of the continent. The improved transport technology of the post-bellum period, on land as well as at sea, made it possible to indulge this clamour: as early as 1868, refrigerated railroad cars were being used to transport peaches from the Midwest to the east coast, after which the practice became more and more common in the attempt to preserve fresh foods.[58] As in Britain, pineapples were now sold in such quantities that the American middle class was able to get in on the act: in 1874, 4,937,125 pineapples were sent to New York from the Bahamas (of which 30 per cent perished on the way).[59]

Unlike the home-grown pineapple, the imported pineapple tended actually to be consumed. At banquets, they were mostly eaten fresh. But with the fruit increasingly available to those a little lower down the social scale, other uses were soon sought. The most common recipe to feature in early American cookery books was, not surprisingly, preserved pineapple. One method suggested by the celebrated cookery writer Eliza Leslie in 1828 went thus:

> Pare your pine-apples, and cut them in thin round slices. Weigh the slices, and to each pound allow a pound of loaf-sugar. Dissolve the sugar in a very small quantity of water, stir it, and set it over the fire in a preserving-kettle. Boil it ten minutes, skimming it well. Then put in it the pine-apple slices, and boil them till they are clear and soft, but not until they break. About half an hour (or perhaps less time) will suffice. Let them cool in a large dish or pan, before you put them in their jars, which you must do carefully, lest they break. Pour the syrup over them. Tie them up with brandy paper.[60]

A later book by Leslie, *The House Book* (1837) featured more of a variety, with not only preserved pineapple but also pineapple ice-cream, pineapple sorbet and pineapple marmalade, in addition to detailed instructions about how to prepare fresh pineapple.[61] Leslie was one of the first to write about food specifically for the American middle classes – 'Who live well, but moderately'.[62] Her recipes for the pineapple were echoed by recipe books throughout the century, as well as by such mainstays of the American housewife's bedside table as *Godey's Lady's Book* and *Good Housekeeping*.[63]

Up until now, it has been possible to track our relationship with the pineapple through the way artists and writers responded to it over the centuries. In the United States, however, the nation's attempts to assert itself within the cultural sphere were relatively late in coming. Only around 1850 did stirrings of a great national literature become evident, and a vernacular fine art was equally slow. The result is that, to later generations, the pineapple's cultural significance to the American people in this era is hard to pin down. It still denoted luxury, but more and more this came to merge with expressions of welcome. The provenance of the imported pineapple also linked it with the earthly paradise that was seen to be the West Indies: 'Lead me to that delicious clime / Where the anana swells and grows' was how James Gates Percival put it in his poem 'Come From Thy Home in the Far Blue Sky' (1865).[64] Representations of it remained popular throughout the century. One I particularly like is at West 20th Street in New York City. Built in 1839–40 by a dry-goods merchant named Don Alonzo Cushman, it is a gorgeous Greek Revival townhouse with a pineapple on each newel. I went to have a look the day after a heavy snowfall – it was like a flash of the tropics amidst the sludge of the city. However, as imports flooded the market, the pineapple began to lose some of its more powerful

30. A gatepost at West 20th Street in New York City, c.1840.

associations, especially with royalty. While these still clung on, it was no longer able to depend on them to bolster its appeal the way that it had for the past 350 years.

Cheap and plentiful as these imports were, they presented quite a conundrum in terms of taste: 'People accustomed to the miserable stuff sold in the markets for Pine Apples, have no idea of the delicious character of cultivated fruit, as grown by gardeners.'[65] Period cookbooks prescribed the addition of tablespoon after tablespoon of sugar. When Mary Lawrence, the wife of the captain of an American whaling ship, had the chance to try some in the Cook Islands that had only just been harvested, it became clear why: 'I never had the pleasure of eating as much pineapple as I wished before. Oh, how luscious they are! It would be a mockery to put sugar on them as we do at home.'[66] What on earth was the solution?

One answer was simply to grow them closer to home. By 1858, pineapples were under cultivation in the counties of Santa Clara and Solano in California. However, this was soon overshadowed by the enormous success of the pineapple industry in Florida. Large-scale commercial production began there in the 1880s, and soon everyone was keen to join in. In January 1881, a Floridian reader wrote to *Gardener's Monthly* to ask about where to get pineapple plants. Since the magazine knew of no firm that had them for sale, it replied that 'If they have, it would be an advantage, we think, to make the fact known.'[67] In 1893, the state produced more pineapples per acre than anywhere in the world: it was estimated that about 4,500,000 were shipped to New York alone (a figure that did not even include those transported by railroad).[68] There they tended to fetch from between 8 and 16 cents each, the lowest price they had ever been.[69]

But the problem of transport remained, despite fast-improving methods of transport and storage. The challenge was on. Home-grown pineapples were ridiculously expensive to produce, but pineapples that had had to travel some distance – even those from Florida or California – were variously flavourless, unreliable and, to those outside the transport hubs, still sold at prices beyond what most households could afford on an everyday basis. The distances in this enormous new country were still simply too great for a pineapple to endure with ease. What to do? The answer was to be found in canning.

The principle of canning, by definition, removes a foodstuff further than ever before from the realities of how it came into being. Detached from the effort and earth of its growth, the product of nature becomes the product of industry.[70] Canning was first successfully attempted by a French inventor named Nicholas Appert in the hope of winning a reward of 12,000 francs offered by Napoleon Bonaparte to whoever could invent a way to provide his starving troops with fruit and vegetables all year round. Appert's technique was to seal the fresh produce in airtight glass jars, then heat them. In 1811, a year after details of Appert's method were published, the London firm Donkin and Hall modified this with cans made of iron sheet dipped in molten tin. This was the first canned food to find its way into shops.

Attempts were made to can pineapples in the Bahamas as early as 1857, but it was not until 1876 that a firm named Smith & Wicks managed to make a success of it. The 1880s saw the advent of similar

31. Pineapples being canned in the Bahamas in the 1880s.

small, hand-operated factories in Malaysia and Singapore, followed by Thailand, China and the Philippines. However, the first place really to make a success of canned pineapple on a grand scale was Baltimore. Baltimore had been at the forefront of the production of canned food for some time and by 1865, firms that specialised in oyster canning had begun to give pineapples a go too. It was not an immediate success: a local newspaper commented that the produce 'resembled pine cones and had about the same flavor and texture'. Production was limited by the lack of specialist equipment for preparing the fruit – peeling, coring and slicing. But all this changed in the 1890s.

The Zastrow Machine, patented in 1892, removed the fruit's core then sliced it up; it couldn't peel, though, which was a drawback. A year later came the Lewis Peeler that did exactly this, at a rate of four per minute. While a few of the specimens subjected to this indignity came from Cuba, the majority were imported from the Bahamas. This added an element of risk to the enterprise – the long journey (the return trip took about a month) meant that it was not uncommon for schooners to unload an entire cargo of fruit so rotten that it had to be dumped straight into the harbour for only the fish to feast upon. All the same, 1886 saw 190,503 dozen fresh pineapples imported into Baltimore, a figure that had almost doubled just five years later (New York City was the other main destination). A stalwart of the city's import trade, they generated an enormous amount of revenue: 'the fruit, like the peach, is gradually being looked upon more as a necessary than, as heretofore, a luxury', commented the British consul. In 1900 the production of canned pineapple peaked at 250,000 cases.[71]

But the legacy that the Baltimore pineapple canning industry left was a significant one. As the international centre of technological innovation in the realm of food processing (albeit for just a fleeting few years), the Baltimore industry paved the way, conceptually and technologically, for the monster enterprise in Hawaii. This was to transform Man's relationship with the pineapple once and for all. For while in the beginning even pineapple in cans retained the multiple associations that had come to surround the fruit over the past few centuries, once stuffed into tin receptacles, produced in thousands and flogged to the masses, it was sadly forced to concede some of them – much as the pineapple companies scrambled to suggest otherwise. For it was in their hands that the fruit's image in the twentieth century essentially came to reside.

I I

'Here the total artifice reveals itself
As the total reality . . .'

Wallace Stevens (1947)

Of all the Edens ever conceived by the human imagination, pre-human Hawaii probably comes closest to a real-life version. This fecund tropical paradise, a riot of dense forests and diverse wildlife, knew little of predators: it was blighted by no snakes or mosquitoes and largely free of any plants with thorns or poisons. Colonisation changed all this, however. Today, a typically Hawaiian scene, such as the verdant lower mountain slopes of the five main islands of the Big Island, Oahu, Maui, Lanai or Kauai so frequently featured on postcards, looks completely different to the one that greeted European adventurers when they first dropped anchor. Out of 1,935 flowering plant species identified in Hawaii today, 902 are not indigenous but rather artificially introduced.[1] This includes the pineapple. That it even found its way from South America to this archipelago 2,000 miles away from the nearest continental land mass was a matter of chance, yet out of this apparently random encounter came the pineapple's defining relationship of the twentieth century, one that was to define percep-tions of the pineapple for years to come – primarily because of the highly effective intervention of the advertising men of Madison Avenue. Nonetheless, it remains a mystery how or when the pineapple came to be in Hawaii in the first place.

215

Linguistics hold one clue. The name by which it is known in Hawaii's native language, *halakahiki*, translates as a pandanus plant (*hala*) from Tahiti (*kahiki*). However, while contact was made between the two islands from around 400 AD, these epic voyages ended in around the fourteenth century, by which time the pineapple was not even known outside South America, let alone in Tahiti. This suggests that the alternative translation of *kahiki* as foreign in the general sense is more helpful. But from what foreign land? And introduced by whom?

One contender is the ever-intrepid Spanish. With their aptitude and energy for trade and exploration, they dispersed the pineapple to many other parts of the world: they appreciated its attributes, in particular its ability to avert scurvy, and it was often to be found in ships' holds amongst the wine barrels and the homesick rats. A Spanish shipwreck in 1527? A visit by explorer Juan Gaetano in 1555? On both these occasions it is feasible that wild pineapples collected on the South American continent somehow floated ashore.[2]

Another possible source is Captain Cook. While neither he nor his botanist Nelson mention in their diaries that they planted pineapples when they landed in Waimea Bay on Kauai in January 1778, they had previously done so on a number of other Polynesian islands, namely Tahiti, Tonga and the Society Islands, which 'were in a fair way of succeeding without any assistance before we left the place'.[3] Intended to strengthen the islands' strategic and commercial usefulness, this sort of plant introduction was an integral aspect of British imperialism in this period.[4] However, the pineapples in question were highly evolved varieties provided at the start of the voyage by Sir Joseph Banks from the stock in the hothouses at Kew Gardens – whether a Queen Pine, a Sugarloaf Pine or perhaps a Smooth Green Pine, they were certainly not of the wild variety. This suggests that while Cook may well have brought certain new varieties of pineapples to the island, he was not the first to introduce the species.

So the mystery remains. The earliest reference to the pineapple in Hawaii appears in the diary of the adventurer Don Francisco de Paula Marin – completely seduced by his first visit to the island, he had deserted a Spanish naval ship to settle there. On 21 January 1813 he noted: 'This day I planted pineapples and an orange tree.'[5] It may not be the most florid of statements ever made about the fruit, but it will do, for it was just the first of many. Missionaries, whalers and other foreign visitors soon flocked to the various islands of the archipelago, many of whom were presented with a gift of a pineapple by the Hawaiian royal family. This influx of white settlers ensured that change was afoot: the mid-nineteenth-century population explosion, both in Hawaii and on the mainland, was the first step in the pineapple's dramatic transformation into a truly global commodity.

The Gold Rush started it all. In the summer of 1847 California boasted a population of just 460; but with the news of the discovery of gold at Sutter's Mill in the Sacramento Valley on 24 January 1848, this rocketed to 80,000 in the course of just a year and a half. As hordes descended on the west in search of a fortune, the demand for fresh pineapple also soared. In time-honoured fashion, this came mostly from those keen to use the context of the dinner table to parade their success – newspaper proprietors, steamboat operators, wagon-makers and even those with wives (women were so scarce in the early days of the settlement of California that some paid as much as $5 to attend a wedding just to get a glimpse of one). Between July 1850 and July 1851, 21,310 pineapples were shipped from Hawaii to California, while many more (usually the ones of a lesser quality – wild varieties like the Wild Kailua still grew in abundance all over the island, in addition to the cultivated kind) were sold to passing whaling ships.[6] With its volcanic soils and tropical climate, Hawaii was ideally suited to the crop.

However, transportation remained tricky. A considerable proportion of the cargo arrived on the mainland bruised, beheaded or rotten. And since this was a seasonal enterprise, the windows of opportunity were all too brief. What entrepreneurs needed was a more efficient means of bringing this luxury into the west coast's smartest dining rooms all year round. The answer was to preserve them, just like American housewives had been doing for years. The first recorded attempt to do this commercially was in 1882: Messrs Akerman and Muller of North

Kona peeled each fruit by hand then sliced, sugared and cooked it on a kitchen stove. It was a slow and laborious process and they soon found they were unable to produce anywhere near sufficient quantities to make it profitable.

Once again, it was a slightly eccentric Englishman who came to the pineapple's aid: John Kidwell was his name, and he was the first to see the potential of the Hawaiian pineapple canning industry. Just as the English had introduced America's east coast to the wonders of the fruit, so they persuaded the west coast that it was worth the effort it posed not just to grow but also to eat. (Perhaps as a nation the English are more impressed than most by the fruit: with the look, taste and smell of a world where the sun always shines, it contrasts dramatically with grey skies and drizzle.)

John Kidwell was born on 7 January 1849 in the village of Marwood in Devon. At twenty-three he emigrated to San Francisco to set up as a nurseryman, but ten years later he uprooted himself once again to Hawaii, widely perceived at the time to be a land of infinite opportunity. It was clear that there was money to be made, not least from fresh pineapple: in the 1880s it continued to be sold at extortionate prices to the most exclusive elements of San Franciscan high society. 'The pineapple is one of the most neglected resources of the country,' commented a Honolulu newspaper in 1882.[7]

Kidwell obviously agreed. In 1885, having bought five acres of land on Oahu, he made his first tentative plantings from slips he had obtained from Kona. However, as he later recalled, there was a hitch: 'The old pines were like Topsy; they just grew. Being a wild product, they naturally were of an inferior quality, replete with acid and fibre and apt to bruise and rot at the slightest touch.'[8] Much of the history of the pineapple in Hawaii has been motivated by this instinct to 'civilise' what is perceived to be overly 'wild', savage or out of control. Kidwell's profoundly colonial attitude is typical of a man born at the height of Victorian imperialism.

Kidwell also experimented with pineapple slips from Florida and Jamaica, but neither satisfied him in terms of taste or appearance. In 1886 he ordered four specimens of all thirty-one known varieties of pineapple, many from Kew Gardens in London, still known to harbour the finest the planet had to offer. In tests the Smooth Cayenne produced the best results and became the centrepiece of the commercial venture. But the market for fresh pineapple remained limited. Canned pineapple, on the other hand, definitely had potential, a fact already demonstrated in Baltimore.

Kidwell was a shrewd operator. In 1892 he established the first pineapple cannery in Hawaii: five years later, the annual export of fresh pineapples from Oahu, Maui and Kona amounted to almost $14,000 worth. It was widely accepted that Hawaiian pineapples simply tasted better than others – the flavour was much superior, as they had been allowed to ripen fully before being picked. But still it was not commercially viable. All the cans had to be made by hand, but more cripplingly, there was a tariff of 35 per cent on all processed food products shipped from Hawaii to the US mainland. This was a major obstacle, not only to Kidwell but to all those who gave canned pineapple a go in the early days – men like Byron O. Clark and A.W. Eames.[9]

'Sometimes I do as many as six impossible things before breakfast': the Queen of Hearts' pronouncement in *Alice Through the Looking Glass* is one with which these early Hawaiian pineapple growers would surely have sympathised. That an attempt was made to develop an entirely uncharted business, thousands of miles away from the markets of the world where the facilities did not exist and neither did the expertise, is to be marvelled at. It was a huge gamble. In the dogged pursuit of an enterprise apparently so unsuited to its environs, these early pineapple pioneers recall their forebears in England: like William Speechly, Robert Teesdale and the like, in the face of circumstances that made it anything but easy, they were determined to make it work. But the pineapple has always had the ability to inspire genuine devotion in its mentors, the like of which other fruits have rarely been able to match. As one magazine rhapsodised in 1911: 'The history of the Hawaiian pineapple reads like a romance in which a number of heroes struggled with the unknown forces of inanimate nature and the better-known vagaries of insect and human nature, and finally won the victory.'[10] It had become the stuff of legend.

In 1898, however, to many it seemed as if they were backing a loser. Kidwell gave it all up to go into the sugar industry instead, a decision he would soon come to regret. It was in this year that Hawaii became a territory of the United States: not only did this mean that the crippling tariff was lifted, it also opened up a whole new American market. For the first time the pineapple was a significant economic proposition. No longer did it have to fight for the chance to reproduce itself over and over again; in no time, others clamoured to do this for it. For 1899 saw the arrival of one of the pineapple's most famous champions – James Drummond Dole.

Dole has been the subject of so much hagiography over the years that it is tempting to be cynical about the path he chose. However, the evidence does suggest that he had the kind of vision, energy and brains that only the very luckiest are born with. The son of a Massachusetts Unitarian clergyman, he arrived in Hawaii fresh out of Harvard aged twenty-four, one of many white settlers lured there at the end of the century: a pamphlet issued in 1893 trumpeted not only the island's unique resources but also the potential to live 'a languorous life of ease and plenty'. It is not difficult to see the appeal.

Dole had planned to give coffee production a go, but after further investigation, he decided that the pineapple was where the real money was to be made. Even he had no idea how true this was. In 1900 he purchased sixty-one acres of land in Wahiawa, twenty-three miles north-west of Honolulu on the island of Oahu, where he bedded down 75,000 pineapple plants. At first, the business was intended to focus exclusively on the production and export of fresh pineapples, a venture of which many were understandably sceptical – at the time, it was a product enjoyed only at the tables of the privileged few. 'If pineapple paid, the vacant lots near town would be covered with them . . . export on any great or profitable scale is out of the question,' sneered an editorial in the *Honolulu Advertiser*.[11] But Dole was only too aware of the difficulties he faced. As he later recalled, 'Pineapples mature with a rush at certain seasons of the year, steamers were uncertain and infrequent, and it would be almost impossible to get large quantities of fresh fruit to the mainland in marketable

32. James Dole surveys his pineapple fields, c.1920.

condition.' He realised instead that the instincts of the defeated Kidwell had in fact been correct. With just enough funds to buy a boiler, an engine and a pineapple sizer and slicer, Dole had all the machinery with which a fortune was to be made. In 1902 his first cannery opened, under the rather uninspired banner the Hawaiian Pineapple Company (it was only some years later that it was renamed the Dole Corporation, after its founder).[12]

In 1903, the Hawaiian Pineapple Company packed 1,893 cases of canned pineapple. A year later, this reached 8,810; a year after that, it hit 25,000; two years after that, 125,000. With the mass-production of the fruit at last a reality, James Dole was in business. From this moment on, the story of the pineapple became the story of twentieth-century corporate America. Other Hawaiian pineapple companies emerged – among them the California Packing Corporation (later renamed Del Monte), Libby McNeil & Libby and Maui Land & Pineapple – until by 1940, Hawaii was the world's biggest supplier of canned pineapple with a 70 per cent share of the market. With places like Baltimore and the Bahamas simply unable to keep pace, Hawaii's economy boomed: released from its dependence on the sugar crop, it also benefited from an endless stream of tourists from the US mainland, keen to see the pineapple's new spiritual home. For the first time, the 'king of fruits' was no longer a primarily symbolic article of trade, but instead an international player with real economic weight. Forced to sully itself thus with the prosaic realities of grubby money matters, however, it was inevitable that its cultural resonances would eventually suffer.

The fields, canneries and offices of the pineapple companies generated an enormous number of new jobs for Hawaii's inhabitants, in particular for its female population: 23 per cent of the women in employment in 1928 worked in the islands' twelve pineapple canneries.[13] A typical example is Kame Iwatani. Born in Japan, in 1922 she sailed for Hawaii to enter into an arranged marriage with a pineapple field worker named Kumediji Iwatani: 'I didn't know too much about pineapple. Since Mr Iwatani's father was in Hawaii long ago, I was told that he lived in a pineapple-cultivating area, and that

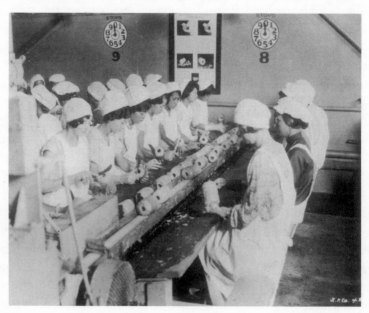

33. Women in the Dole canneries in Hawaii, c.1940.

pineapple was a delicious thing.'[14] In 1920 42 per cent of the island's population was Japanese, by far the largest ethnic group amongst the Hawaiians, Chinese, Portuguese, Filipinos, Koreans, Puerto Ricans and Americans who made up the rest, a breakdown mirrored by the labour force of the pineapple industry.[15] It seems fitting that the Hawaiian pineapple, an immigrant to the island itself, was produced almost entirely by a labour force made up of the same.

The workers were housed in dedicated pineapple towns built by the Hawaiian pineapple companies. Up by about 4 a.m., they were collected by buses ready for a 6 a.m. start. Those who worked in the fields, rather than the canneries, were considered the lucky ones: as one Japanese worker, Motoe Nihei, put it, 'Pineapple, while you working, you can see all the outside. Skies. And you get a nice air. But sugar cane, when you're in the tall ones – you under there – how can you see the outside?'[16] Lunch lasted just half an hour, during which some liked to chop the crown off any discarded pineapples they came across, then use their knives to mash up the flesh inside. Left for a few

34. Labourers in the Dole pineapple fields in Hawaii, c.1925.

days, the mash fermented to create a sort of pineapple wine, not dissimilar to the one the Tupí-Guaranís had discovered many years earlier. Most were allowed home by mid-afternoon, at which point the first task was to change into normal clothes: 'Even after I started wearing uniforms, when I go home, the kids know I'm coming. They smell pineapple.'[17] The rest of the day was spent doing housework, training cocks to fight or, from the 1950s, watching television. By 8 p.m., everyone was in bed.[18]

Man's relationship with the pineapple was altered merely by the material circumstances in which most of the crop was now produced in the West. Fields of fertile red soil stretched for miles, with row upon row of pineapple plants basking in the kinds of constant tropical temperatures of which Chatsworth's junior garden boy had only dreamed. Out under the open skies all year round, there was no glass barrier to fend off those lower down the social scale keen for a taste. Once harvested, conditions inside the canning factories were hot, smelly and deafening, while all who worked in them commented upon the sheer vastness of the enterprise. It was a world away from the great country house kitchens of the eighteenth and nineteenth century that had previously been charged with the preparation of the pineapple for consumption. Accordingly, the context in which each specimen now forged its first connection with Man was mechanised, impersonal and in no way conducive to perpetuating the anthropomorphisation of the fruit.

Similarly, the context in which it was consumed – the dinner table – was transformed by this mass production. At the height of the early mania for the fruit in the 1770s, the whole point was to ensure that the experience of eating a pineapple was overtly and intimately connected with the extravagant circumstances of its production in the estate's hothouse. One hundred and fifty years later, the opposite was true. With a can, the ugly, distinctly unromantic circumstances of its production were all but hidden from those who consumed it.

Within each can was a story of unequal social relations predicated on the kind of economic exploitation from which huge profits are possible. The hours were long and the wages were low, and it was back-breaking work for the workers to produce the pineapple in sufficient quantities. This was no paradise. And because most workers stood at the trimming and packing tables barefoot, deep in the copious juice that dripped off them on to the floor, bromelein's ability to digest flesh resulted in feet that were often covered in open sores by the end of the week. If this was the pineapple's revenge for the indignity of canning, its targets were unfortunate.

Yet the grim realities of the fruit's newly mechanised existence were completely swamped for most Western consumers by the onslaught of propaganda let loose by the Hawaiian pineapple companies. In the first fifty years of the twentieth century they overwhelmingly prevailed in shaping the pineapple's image on both sides of the Atlantic, regardless of the actual origins of what came to be served at dinner. The aim, as with all advertising, was to appropriate, modify and use pre-existing meanings that swirled around society in order to increase consumption. And of course, the pineapple had a larger cache of these than most upon which to draw – compared with, say, Welch's Grape Juice or Coca-Cola, other big spenders on advertising over the same period. Of all the pineapple companies, the Hawaiian Pineapple Company led the way, its strategies generally representative of those adopted by the others. For this reason, in addition to the fact that its company archives are by far the best preserved, the advertising choices it made are the ones described here.

In the first two decades of the twentieth century, spending on advertising increased sixfold. The Hawaiian pineapple companies contributed considerably to this. The first advertisements for Hawaiian canned pineapple appeared in magazines just before Christmas 1908 in response to a dramatic drop in the market caused by the financial panic that engulfed the nation in 1907. Luxury items were the first to be hit, and sure enough – 400,000 cases of canned pineapple were produced, but orders were received for a meagre 12,000. Weeks went by with the wharves strewn with homeless produce. It became clear that what was called for was a marketing strategy of revolutionary proportions. Indeed, the one that was adopted was the first of its kind in the world. The Hawaiian Pineapple

Company formed an alliance with the other pineapple canning companies on the island to undertake a joint programme of innovative and aggressive advertising to promote the product by origin rather than by specific brand. 'Don't Ask for Pineapple Alone' exhorted the advertisements, 'Insist on Hawaiian Pineapple'. Placed in all the major women's magazines, the ensuing eighteen months saw consumption of Hawaiian pineapple quadruple.

In the heady early days of the industry, one problem urgently needed to be addressed. How did you eat a pineapple, whether fresh or canned? As with bicycles or cameras in the same period, most American consumers needed to be taught how to approach this strange new entity – even Dole's grandmother thought they were just 'hard apples'. The result was advertisements like this one of 1909: 'It cuts with a spoon – like a peach.' In an echo of the way that early explorers frequently compared the pineapple to the pinecone, the artichoke or the aloe in order to place it in context, the advertisements supplied a point of reference with which the early twentieth-century consumer was already familiar.

It was not long before the Hawaiian pineapple companies also began to produce recipe books to help people figure out what to do with this unusual addition to the kitchen cupboard. Since the increasing geographical dislocation of a now industrialised society meant that fewer and fewer new brides were able to turn to the wisdom of a nearby mother or sister for culinary advice, alternative sources were much in demand. In 1923, 223,631 requests for recipe books were received by Dole alone. Typically of this period, many helpfully propounded the idea that cooking pineapple will help you keep a husband. One promotional recipe that appeared in women's magazines in 1931–2 ran: 'If you want to give the head of the house a treat that will make him smack his lips in real he-man enjoyment, just bake a pineapple pie!' In this way, the copy deviously correlates the purchase of canned pineapple with a sense of pride at being the perfect wife.

With a growing number of women now at work, as early as 1909 convenience was becoming a major issue. Initial snobbery against cans gradually dissipated, with the result that canned food became respectable even when served at dinner parties. The result was an element of 'keeping up with the Joneses'. An advertisement that appeared in newspapers in 1934 depicts one housewife exclaiming to another, 'I don't know what to have for dinner,' to which her friend replies, 'Pineapple, my dear, pineapple! We have it every day. It's refreshing and gives you a lot of summer energy.' Drawing on the very human fear of feeling left out, canned pineapple is here presented as a means of entry into genteel society.

The central character in all communications by the Hawaiian pineapple companies with their consumers, however, was that of Hawaii itself. As James Dole explained, the intention was to 'by means of advertising . . . make "Hawaiian Pineapple" mean to the country for pineapple what "Havana" means for tobacco'. There is no doubt he succeeded, so much so that this association remains in evidence right up to the present day, even now that only about 2 per cent of the total amount of pineapple consumed in the world is produced there. It was not just any old Hawaii that was featured in almost every advertisement, but a mythical vision of Hawaii where the sun always shone, native girls were always half-naked and life was a series of glamorous fun and larks – archetypally, unflinchingly, indisputably exotic. The intimation was that here was a taste of Paradise, available to all for just a few cents a can. Aided by the publicity material of the Hawaii Tourist Board – 'the world's enchanted playground' was how it described the islands – it presented them as a fantastical escape from everyday life rather than, as they were in reality for many, the location for the drudge of everyday life itself.

One weapon in this assault was a can's label. 'Treasure Island' and 'Paradise Island' were typical names given to different Dole varieties of canned pineapple, accompanied by the depiction of some kind of beatific scene (colour plate x). It is really just a visual representation of what chroniclers like Richard Ligon had attempted to express in the pages of their books centuries earlier. Print advertisements then filled in the rest. Take this one from *Good Housekeeping* in 1929: 'Just look at this tempting fruit, the treasure of the tropics – gorgeous in colour,

35. An advertisement for Dole canned pineapple, 1952.

tender in texture, perfect without and within!' Or here is another from a 1952 edition of *Life*: 'From glamorous Hawaii to your table comes Dole's Royal Family of delicious pineapple products – all field-ripened all richly mellow with tropic sunshine.' In order to maintain the illusion, the canning stage is conveniently excised from the picture, as are those workers who facilitate it, with the emphasis instead on the supposedly all-natural qualities of the fruit. This reinforcement of its Edenic credentials was a technique applied more than any other in the course of its career in Hawaii.

The Brazilian cabaret singer Carmen Miranda's famous pre-dilection for elaborate head-dresses topped by the fruit also helped. For the first time in quite a while, Western art and literature associated the pineapple less with the privileged existence encap-sulated by the hothouses of the European aristocracy than with the wonders contained in Paradise, just as it had in the sixteenth and seventeenth centuries. It had come full circle. The paradox was that this occurred only with the injection into the island of the very elements that meant that Hawaii edged further and further away from this idyll. Money, power, industry: progress it was, but at a price. The arrival of European settlers led not only to an 80 per cent decline in the native Hawaiian population, mainly from new diseases, but also the destruction of much of the indigenous language and culture, as well as of the natural resources and landscape.

One other asset upon which the Hawaiian pineapple companies shamelessly capitalised was the pineapple's royal heritage. Dole's company slogan for a while was 'By Nature Crowned the King of Fruits'. 'King of Hawaii', 'Tropic Queen', 'President', 'Ambassador': all were brands available from Dole alone. 'Pineapple, the "King of Fruits" was once the "Fruit of Kings" – a novelty, rare and expensive,' proclaimed one advertisement of 1939. The pineapple is a perfect example of the thesis, most famously propagated by Roland Barthes, that advertising works by drawing upon myths already entrenched in society, only to rework them to its own ends. Luckily for those ensconced in one of the glistening skyscrapers on Madison Avenue, the pineapple had these in abundance.

Yet it was a technique that needed to be handled very delicately: while the pineapple's historical associations were indeed useful, it was also imperative to emphasise to the American public the extent to which it had now been democratised for the first time. 'Thus, in this American community in the middle of the Pacific ocean, modern business, tropical climate and people from everywhere, combine to make pineapple, the fruit with nature's most refreshing flavour – the fruit that once only kings could afford – available to everyone, everywhere,' was the way a promotional pamphlet published by the Pineapple Growers' Association in the 1930s concluded its pitch. Thus integrated into 'this American community', the pineapple is trumpeted as being home-grown, yet still exotic – herein was the best of both worlds.

The pineapple was soon exposed to a new kind of royalty happy to bestow favour upon it: Hollywood movie stars. The pineapple companies made certain to enlist them without delay so that the fruit might bask in the reflected glamour of the early movie business. A feature in the *Honolulu Star-Bulletin* in 1933 captions one photograph, 'And here's "Buster" Crabbe, Olympic swimming winner and now doing "wild man" pictures at Hollywood, feeding canned pineapple to another figure of the films, Verna Hillie.' It is difficult to imagine any of today's movie stars being so willing to promote a canned product (other than caviar, perhaps).

An article in the *San Francisco Chronicle* the same year has this: '"Pineapple is delish!" said Pauline Frederick, star of stage and screen. "Of course," she added, "everyone knows that it's good for the throat. But, more important, it helps keep one slender."' The fruit's weight-loss properties became a more and more common theme through the 1930s – it is true that when eaten at the end of a meal, the bromelein contained in fresh pineapple (when canned it is destroyed by the heating process) does promote weight-loss since it aids with the breakdown and absorption of proteins in the stomach. It is not a very healthy programme, however, in addition to the fact that you would have to eat an awful lot of it for it to be effective.

A similarly contentious matter for the pineapple companies was the pineapple's associations with status: to what degree should this be exploited? The conundrum was how to capitalise on the fact that the pineapple was widely seen as a luxury food, while still reassuring the masses that this was a product within reach of the average housewife's shopping budget.

In the case of fresh pineapple, there was really no getting away from the fact that it was a luxury item, defiantly but definitely out of the reach of most. 'Hawaiian pines in fresh state should dominate over all competition this side of the Missouri at least, and be the favourite as a luxury on the tables of the wealthy clear to the Atlantic,' was the claim of one newspaper in 1904; but while some success was had getting fresh specimens on to the shelves of greengrocers in New York City, Washington DC and the bigger cities of New England, in fact, Hawaiian fresh pineapples never made a significant impact. There just was not a sufficient populace on the west coast to create a demand, while the east coast still presented difficulties in terms of the expense of transportation. High prices encouraged the public to view it as a special treat, rather than a regular purchase like apples or pears.

In the context of the dramatic social and economic upheavals experienced in the course of the twentieth century, the pineapple remained a symbolic focus in the worldwide struggle against social inequality. In this respect, little had changed since the narrator of George Walker's *Vagabond* asked in 1799 what right a man had to pay a guinea for a pineapple when another was starving. Thus while in prison in 1915, the Russian poet Mayakovsky wrote a scathing indictment of the world's capitalist élite: 'Munch on your pineapples, chew on your grouse / Your days are numbered, bourgeois louse!' He was later flattered to discover that this was the slogan chanted by Bolshevik sailors as they marched on the Winter Palace to topple the Provisional Government in 1917.[19] Again the pineapple is portrayed as the epitome of the privileged existence of the upper classes – an association that it was finding it difficult to shake off.

However, fresh pineapple of the kind so despised by those who fought for the rights of the working man (and, increasingly, woman) was not where the money was. The real treasure was to be found by struggling with a can-opener. A US government survey of 1901 revealed that for the poorest families, one can of pineapple represented 13 per cent of their weekly expenditure on food, whereas for the richest families, the figure was more like 3 per cent. It remained a luxury, but as incomes rose, it became a somewhat more accessible one: 'It is true that pineapple is fairly expensive, but it is easily within the means of the average family occasionally . . . Keep a few cans in the pantry for special occasions or the unexpected guest,' was one food writer's advice in 1925. By then, the American public were consuming an annual average of seven cans per family, compared to one can for every two families in 1910.[20]

Up to a point, there were advantages in the perception that canned pineapple, just like fresh pineapple, was a more luxurious, glamorous product than most. 'Hawaiian canned pineapple puts any meal in a party mood!' ran one advertisement of 1939 – not only did this appeal to the housewife worried that the meals she served were dull but in addition, just like 200 years before, the implication is that a party is not really a party unless a pineapple is present. But it was a precarious route to navigate, and it became all the more so with the onset of the Depression.

Though the Hawaiian pineapple industry was not greatly affected by the Depression at the start, when it struck, in 1931, it was utterly disastrous. Housewives simply stopped buying pineapples. Between 1931 and 1932, production fell from 12.8 to 5.1 million cases, while Dole alone made a net loss of $8.5 million. This was 'partly the fault of the advertising methods', explained one Hawaiian newspaper in June 1932:

> They were represented as almost too good to be true! The psychology of the family which felt the need of retrenchment was to cut out the things that were unnecessary and extravagant. 'Cut out the fancy stuff. We can get along without pineapples until times get better'. No wonder the market collapsed. The public had the wrong idea and no effort was made to correct it.

What had been an asset had become a millstone. While for many years the industry had gleefully associated its product with luxury, it became clear that in order to protect itself from future financial crises, it also needed to emphasise that here was a slice of luxury available to all. In the short term it was able to recover its market share through aggressive advertising that focused on the upper end of the market where consumers still had money to spend on luxuries, as well as through the development of a new product in the form of pineapple juice that, with the repeal of Prohibition in 1934, became an instant success. But it was clear to all concerned that the Depression had been a crucial turning-point for the industry. Only with democratisation would a truly reliable and constant profit be achieved.[21]

The power of advertising meant that the pineapple in Britain in this period was subject to exactly the same manipulations as it was in America, a manifestation of the country's increasing Americanisation.[22] It also, however, saw additional forces contribute to the fruit's attempts to find itself a suitable role in the confusing and contradictory world of the twentieth century.

By 1900, the home-grown pineapple was already a rare sight: with the end of World War One, it became all but extinct, with more and more pineries left to the ravages of ivy. Lack of money, manpower and resources resulted in the severe reduction in scope of many of Britain's most legendary and luxuriant gardens. For their owners, it was nothing short of heart-breaking: when the Duchess of Devonshire was asked in 1938 how many gardeners she employed at Chatsworth, she replied, 'We used to have seventy but now we manage with fifty. We have to be economical.'[23] 'Economical'? It was a word that was simply not in the vocabulary of Joseph Paxton when he was in charge there.

While the wealthier elements of British society were still able to support their habit with the purchase of pineapples imported from the Azores, for most, they remained a rare treat. In *Greenery Street* by Denis Mackail (1925), a wonderful novel about the first happy year of one couple's married life, the one piece of news that persuades Felicity Foster to accept a dinner invitation from her neighbour is that

36. The pinery at Cannon Hall today.

pudding is purported to be a pineapple.[24] Almost unheard of during World War Two, in September 1946 2,000 pineapples from the Azores were unloaded at the London docks, the first that most children of the war had ever seen, followed by a further 20,000 a month later, with the result that recorded imports in the second half of the year totalled £153,106. In the context of continued rationing, this created uproar: as the Earl of Portsmouth told the House of Commons in February 1947, 'Our shipping exchange should be used for importing feeding stuffs and not pineapples and mimosa.' A couple of months later, the Communist Party organised a march through London in protest: 'Apples for the many, not pineapples for the few', read one of the banners. Real-life fresh pineapples remained an exceptional sight until well into the 1950s.[25]

Canned pineapple, however, became more and more widely available every year. Britain was the second biggest consumer of Hawaiian canned pineapple after the US, but its primary supplier was Malaysia. The industry in Malaysia was founded in 1882 by a Frenchman named Mr Landau based in Singapore, with such success that by 1929 it supplied 82 per cent of all the canned

37. A stall at Covent Garden market in 1912 selling pineapples imported from the Azores.

pineapple sold in Britain (colour plate XI). While it was widely acknowledged that it did not match the quality of the Hawaiian product, it had the edge in terms of price, and for many British shoppers this was the primary consideration, often regardless of income. By 1939, Britain consumed about 2.5 million cases of Malaysian canned pineapple a year (in addition to about half a million cases from Hawaii and elsewhere).[26] In view of the frequent contemporary references to the sheer monotony of food in this period, no wonder so many sought to fill their basket with a product that was a little out of the ordinary. Some even came to prefer this to the fresh alternative: 'no junglegrown pineapple ever smacked like the whoppers you shook out of Ananias' cans . . .'[27] In most respects, then, canned pineapple took a similar route to the one already traced in the U.S., but with one major difference: in the States it was bought mostly by the upper echelons of society, but a more entrenched sense of snobbery towards the principle of canning

38. Cartoon by Joseph Lee in the *London Evening News*, 5 April 1947. The caption that accompanied it read: 'I wish the Ministry of Food would buy something sensible like coconuts rather than all these flipping pineapples!'

meant that in Britain, it remained for some time a distinctly working-class purchase.

In World War One the Allied governments placed enormous orders of canned pineapple in order to help feed the troops. Although shipping costs were higher, sales increased by 33 per cent. As James

Dole commented in early 1918, 'Hawaiian pineapples are today being shipped to almost every civilised section of the globe.' Many soldiers were introduced to it for the first time this way – a glimmer of sunshine during dark days in the trenches. Once demobilised, they were able to spread the word back home with the result that, when the war ended, demand was maintained on both sides of the Atlantic. World War Two proved similar in this respect. Two-thirds of all the Hawaiian pineapple produced in this period was shipped to the armed forces, all the cans sprayed with olive green paint to make them less noticeable to enemy planes when discarded in forward areas.[28]

On the Home Front, however, it was a different story. In 1942 in Long Island, Dorothy Atkinson Robinson dreamed of the feast that she hoped to concoct for her son: 'If I ever catch up with another can of pineapple I'll have that dinner the first time Art gets leave.'[29] On both sides of the Atlantic tinned pineapple was a treat to be saved for a rainy day, in part because most of the pineapple factories around the world were brought to a standstill by the fighting, with Malaysia particularly badly affected.

Post-war, new sources of canned pineapple were developed, including the Ivory Coast, South Africa and Australia: in 1947 the future Queen Elizabeth received 500 cases of canned pineapple as a wedding present from the Government of Australia.[30] It was not long before canned pineapple was one of the most democratic of foodstuffs. By 1950, the average annual consumption in the US was 3 lbs per person (the second most popular after canned peaches), compared to just over half a pound per person of the fresh product (the eleventh most popular after almost everything), despite the fact that the period saw sources of fresh pineapple for North America such as Cuba and Mexico hugely expand their operations.[31]

Figures in 1950s Britain told a similar story in a nation that was in the midst of a dramatic shift from post-war austerity to baby boom affluence. Ham or gammon and pineapple became a ubiquitous feature of the average housewife's repertoire of dishes (the rationale for the pairing is that the bromelein in the pineapple tenderises the meat). The result was that the fruit stooped to new levels of degradation. This is encapsulated by one particular recipe that frequently appeared in advertisements towards the end of the decade: canned pineapple and baked beans.

> Preheat oven to 400 degrees. Then for each pound of canned baked beans, stir in 2 tbsp brown sugar, 1 tbsp syrup drained from Dole Pineapple slices, 1 tbsp catsup and 1 tbsp prepared mustard. Bake for 30 minutes, then top with drained Dole Pineapple slices and bake for 30 minutes more. Elegant enough to serve company – easy enough to fix just for the family!

Can you imagine anything more disgusting? Compared to the glamour that had emanated from the pineapple 200 years before, the situation in which it now found itself was little short of pathetic. Yet somehow it managed to retain some traces of its former self: as Betty Crocker proclaimed in a widely syndicated article in 1953, 'Pineapple gives a glamour-look to meat, salads, desserts and bakings.'

It is the reasons for this that the American modernist poet Wallace Stevens investigates in 'Someone Puts a Pineapple Together' (1947).

> It is something on a table that he sees,
> The root of a form, as of this fruit, a fund,
> The angel at the center of this rind,
>
> This husk of Cuba, tufted emerald,
> Himself, may be, the irreducible X
> At the bottom of imagined artifice.
>
> . . . There had been an age
> When a pineapple on the table was enough,
>
> Without the forfeit scholar coming in,
> Without his enlargings and pale arrondissements,
> Without the furious roars in his capital.
> . . .

[A pineapple is one of] The small luxuriations that portend

Universal delusions of universal grandeurs,
The slight incipiencies, of which the form,
At last, is the pineapple on the table or else

An object the sum of its complications, seen
And unseen. This is everybody's world.
Here the total artifice reveals itself

As the total reality.

In this brilliant meditation on the multiple meanings that inhabit every element of our world, what Stevens recognised was that the complicated mêlée of associations that the pineapple had acquired since its emergence into the Western world had made it one of the most refined examples of this phenomenon – 'An object the sum of its complications, seen / And unseen'. This image, highly influenced by the work of Picasso during his Cubist period, paints not only a literal picture – as a *sorosis*, this apparently single entity of a fruit is indeed made up of 'the sum of its complications' – but a conceptual one too.

In order to try to ascertain 'the irreducible X / At the bottom of imagined artifice', Stevens wades into the debate about the fruit's not-so-noble 'complications'. 'There had been an age / When a pineapple on the table was enough'. Two hundred years later, however, things are different: 'Here the total artifice reveals itself / As the total reality.' The artifice of the pineapple as manifested in advertising had become the reality of its entire existence. The poet then breaks down different elements of the pineapple into twelve memorable snapshots:

1. The hut stands by itself beneath the palms.
2. Out of their bottle the green genii come.
3. A vine had climbed the other side of the wall.
4. The sea is spouting upward out of rocks.
5. The symbol of feasts and of oblivion . . .
6. White sky, pink sun, trees on a distant peak.

> 7. These lozenges are nailed up lattices.
> 8. The owl sits humped. It has a hundred eyes.
> 9. The coconut and cockerel in one.
> 10. This is how yesterday's volcano looks.
> 11. There is an island Palahude by name –
> 12. An incivil shape like a gigantic haw.

Which of these most resonates for you?

> These casual exfoliations are
> Of the tropic of resemblance.

In other words, the human imagination has a geography which can be mapped by visual images, cultural associations, long-held memories and so on. But then how is it possible to uncover 'The angel at the center of this rind'? The answer is that there is no such thing. Instead, there are many angels, all open to exploitation by Man's determination to find in the pineapple the meanings he wants to find. The pineapple is 'something on a table' which stands for 'everybody's world'.[32]

Within the maelstrom that enveloped the first half of the twentieth century, it becomes more and more difficult to get a moment alone with the pineapple. Despite this, it is clear that it underwent quite a barrage. In an era when image was all, canning dealt a severe blow to its cultural significance. However much the Hawaiian pineapple industry tried to claim otherwise – 1952 saw this monolith spend $1.75 million on advertisements alone – there is no doubt that canning removed the pineapple yet further from its mythical status. As thousands upon thousands of cans rolled off the assembly lines, each stage of the processing removed it further from the pedestal on which it had teetered for so many centuries. Personally I blame a young mechanical draftsman named Henry Gabriel Ginaca. It was Ginaca who back in 1913, while in the pay of James Dole, perfected the first machine that trimmed, sized and cored up to 120 pineapples a minute, the principal culprit of the hideous disfigurement suffered by the pineapple in this period. Decapitated, flayed and hacked to pieces: having been so unceremoniously stripped of so many of its most desirable attributes in order to be able to fit into cans, the pineapple was also stripped of an element of its identity. It was not only that it was now mass-produced. It was not even that it no longer presented a challenge to eat. Where was its crown, its appearance so reminiscent of royalty? Where was its shell, its smell so evocative of the tropics? It no longer had enough weapons to put up a fight and it was this that, in the end, changed Man's relationship with it.

'Now then, Sue, let's see . . . would you like a little cheesy-pineapple one?'

Mike Leigh, Abigail's Party *(1977)*

Not long ago a story appeared in the *New Statesman* that attributed the origins of cheese-and-pineapple-on-a-stick to a game invented by the Three Musketeers in the seventeenth century:

> Among the contests whereby they would show off their skills was one in which each man was required to catch a pineapple, launched across the great hall of the Palais du Luxembourg by a small military catapult, on the end of his sword, with grandiose flourish, perfect technique and minimum damage to the fruit. The next challenge was to catch a flying Camembert on the same sword. [1]

Oh, would that this were true! Actually, it was dreamed up in response to a challenge set by the magazine to bestow a bit of class on dishes often shunned by snobbery – a category into which cheese-and-pineapple-on-a-stick certainly fits. Some blame for this may be attributed to the play *Abigail's Party* by Mike Leigh, first performed in 1977. Its success ensured that cheese-and-pineapple-on-a-stick became an indelible feature of the decade's cultural landscape. The dish is one of an arsenal of weapons wheeled out by the play's central protagonist, Beverley, in her desperate bid to appear the sophisticated hostess: 'Now then, Sue, let's see . . . would you like a little cheesy-pineapple one?' 'Dainty' is how she describes them to the neighbours, just round for a drink.[2] As a satire on the aspirant social *mores* of English middle-class suburbanites, the play works brilliantly, but at the same time, perceptions of pineapple chunks were dealt a devastating blow – the preserve of the pretentious, rather than the prosperous.

Pineapple out of a tin has been damned to naffness ever since, not helped by the way it tends to be paired with the most seemingly eccentric of partners. Ham or gammon and pineapple is a case in point – though this is currently enjoying a minor revival. According to Nigella Lawson,

> For all that we try and put the blame on the Hawaiians, there does seem to me to be something ineffably, if embarrassingly, English about the combination of ham and pineapple . . . You may smirk, but this is not intended as an ironic exercise in gastro-rehabilitation here . . . For all my robust internationalism – motto: if it tastes good, eat it – I do think that in the few warm weeks given to us, one wants food that reminds one of past summers, long ago ones, real or wistfully imagined.[3]

She also features a recipe for caramelised pineapple with hot chocolate sauce which I can highly recommend.

Pineapple does indeed remain associated with the Hawaiians. The truth is that, today, most pineapple is about as Hawaiian as I am. When I visited the islands in October 2003, I was surprised by how little evidence of the industry remains. Souvenir mugs, t-shirts, baseball caps: these are almost the only places that pineapples can be spotted by the casual tourist. Most locals looked vague when I asked where I might find the fruit being grown: in 2003 the crop commandeered 16,000 acres of land in total, but these are spread out across the islands and one doesn't just stumble across them. Drive inland far enough though and they are there. Sometimes they proclaim themselves from a distance by the vibrant red soil so well-suited to the crop, but when I was there most fields were draped in neat rows of unaesthetic black plastic sheeting. Intended to confine the pesticides, conserve moisture and help warm the soil, the black covering also rids the fields of any pretence that this is anything other than a commercial enterprise dependent not on Nature but on Man to eke all the quality and quantity possible out of Hawaii's increasingly tired soils.

The toppling of Hawaii's dominance is one of the most dramatic developments in the post-war period within the pineapple industry. Faced with an epidemic of mealybugs that threatened to decimate the islands' entire crop, in 1926 Del Monte established its first pineapple plantation overseas, in the Philippines. Dole eventually followed suit in the hope of benefiting from South East Asia's low labour costs, opening a plantation in the Philippines in 1963, followed by another in Thailand in 1974. Within a year, Thailand had surpassed Hawaii to become the largest producer of pineapple in the world, while Hawaii was all but abandoned by the very same companies who had once courted it: by 2000, it supplied just 2 per cent of the world's pineapple. These days, to describe a pizza topped with ham and pineapple as Hawaiian is a misnomer – Thai or Filipino is what it should really say on those delivery leaflets that drop through the letterbox so regularly. Promiscuous as ever, the pineapple had found yet another continent willing to embrace it as its own.[4]

Canning remains the principal source of income for the pineapple industry, but sales are static. The fresh fruit, however, has recently reasserted its iconic status with a growth in sales so unprecedented and so extraordinary that it is currently the envy of every comparable commercial sector. The fruit's future has not seemed so bright for some time. So where did it all go right?

The gradual resurgence of fresh pineapples began in the late 1950s when Caribbean growers lost their near-monopoly on the trade due to the improvement and expansion of refrigerated sea transport. Hawaii attempted to snatch a share of the sector, as did Taiwan and Costa Rica, with the latter receiving a significant boost in 1978 when Del Monte first established plantations there. Here was the globalisation

39. Harvested pineapples being loaded on to a lorry in Hawaii.

of the fresh pineapple trade happening in a way that even the most ambitious Portuguese, Spanish or Dutch explorers of the sixteenth and seventeenth centuries could not have foreseen.

Another key participant in the post-war trade has been West Africa, in particular the Ivory Coast. Pineapples began to be grown there on a significant scale in 1950, and after Independence a decade later the crop shifted into the forefront of the country's economy: a complex network of influence that linked the new president, Félix Houphouët-Boigny, with his cronies in the agricultural south meant that pineapples quickly became a priority. An extended period of stability under Houphouët-Boigny, encouraged by considerable foreign investment, allowed the Ivory Coast to become one of the more successful stories of modern sub-Saharan Africa, not least because of the focus on agricultural export products capable of producing significant revenues in vibrant markets – like pineapples, but also cocoa, coffee and timber – rather than on industrial development alone. With its modern, thriving port, the capital, Abidjan, soon buzzed with its grand boulevards, chic skyscrapers and bustling cafés.

By 1970, the Ivory Coast supplied approximately 95 per cent of all Europe's fresh pineapple imports.

By the early 1990s, the market for fresh pineapple had become very sluggish as it struggled to overcome the threat posed by other exotic pretenders like guavas and papayas. Most people were still not sure how to tell when a pineapple was ripe, compounded by the fact that even when it was, they had little idea what to do with it. Compared with the convenience of, say, a banana, by far the most popular fruit in the West, the pineapple is extremely cumbersome to prepare.[5]

Yet fresh pineapple refused to linger in this commercial rut. The market for fruit in general has increased in response to the trend towards healthier food, while exotic fruit has the added advantage of brightening up yet another evening of brown rice with a touch of the unusual. More specifically, pineapple has benefited from the increasing availability of pre-prepared snacks.

Changes in production practices have also had a significant effect. Crops are more reliable because of the use of increasingly sophisticated pesticides, as well as chemicals that ripen the fruit on demand. The efficacy of these was first discovered in the Azores in 1874 when a pineapple-grower decided to burn off all the dead leaves in his greenhouse in order to avoid insect infestation. To his astonishment, over the ensuing days all the nearby pineapples ripened at the same time, at the same speed, into a uniformly gorgeous golden colour. The leaves had released a natural gas called ethylene, exposure to which triggers the formation of the fruit.[6] Today, pineapples are sprayed with ethylene on a schedule designed to produce ripe fruit approximately six to seven months in the future. Where the weather is warm enough, the fruit can be forced into ripening all year round, a phenomenon that is unique to the pineapple (though there has been the occasional successful attempt on some varieties of mango). This regular harvesting means that, in the twenty-first century, the pineapple is always in season.

However, while these factors have undoubtedly contributed to the dramatic increase in sales since the late 1990s, one single invention has done more than anything else to revolutionise the world of pineapples:

a hybrid variety of the fruit known as the Gold. The story of how the Gold came into being is one of after-dark raids, anonymous benefactors and heated lawsuits. Of all the competitive struggles in which the pineapple has been embroiled over the centuries, this was among the most highly charged – at stake was a market worth over a billion dollars a year.

A variety of pineapple known as Smooth Cayenne had dominated the industry since the 1880s, when Kidwell made it the centrepiece of his commercial venture. But the increasing importance of hybrid varieties more resistant to pests has been one of the major shifts in the industry since World War Two – Australia, Taiwan and Malaysia are just three of the countries that have developed their own with a modicum of success. In the 1950s scientists at the Pineapple Research Institute, an organisation jointly funded by the Hawaiian pineapple companies, became engaged in experiments to improve upon the Champaka, a variety of Smooth Cayenne. Number 73–114, a hybrid developed in the 1970s that was a cross between two previous hybrids bred in 1958 and 1959, proved an instant hit.

The advantages of the 73–114 compared to the Smooth Cayenne were many. It tasted much sweeter, as well as less acidic and less fibrous; it also ripened to a bright golden yellow colour, in contrast to the dull green that the Smooth Cayenne remained even when at its ripest, often much to the confusion of the consumer. At long last, an assertion like Girolamo Benzoni's in 1555 that 'when ripe they are yellow' had become fact.[7] In addition, the 73–114 was more nutritious, with four times as much Vitamin C as the Smooth Cayenne; it was more resistant to parasites; its leaves were less prickly to the touch; and it could survive in cold storage for up to two weeks before it began to rot. Finally, it was very consistent in terms of quality, an essential for what was still a relatively expensive product. In sum, it was simply a better class of pineapple than anything that had gone before.

In 1987, the Pineapple Research Institute was disbanded and specimens of the precious 73–114 were handed over to its two remaining members, Del Monte and Maui Land & Pineapple. Del Monte used them to expand its plantings in Costa Rica with a new 15,000 acre site, protected by guards hired to watch over the plants twenty-four hours a day to prevent its rivals getting access to this secret weapon. Within a couple of years, small quantities of the new fruit were being sold in selected areas of the United States, with great success. It became clear that, to consumers, quality was everything, despite the higher prices. In 1992 Del Monte sought to patent the 73–114, by this time also known as the MD-2. However, this proved tricky. First, the fact that it had already been offered for sale was contrary to patent rules. Secondly, rights to it were still co-owned by Maui Land & Pineapple, who refused a joint patent.

In 1989 the fresh fruit division of Del Monte split from the canning operations: it is now controlled by the family of the Jordanian businessman Mohammed Abu-Ghazeleh, the company's chief executive. In 1994, it applied for a patent for another hybrid pineapple, the 73–50, also known as the CO-2 or Hawaiian Gold. The CO-2 had been developed at the same time as the MD-2 – as genetic siblings, the two were almost identical. In this way, Del Monte effectively patented the MD-2. According to an internal memo written by a former vice-president of Del Monte, Mike Pereira, the intention was to 'confuse our competition' into thinking that the MD-2 was a 'proprietary variety'. Once the patent application was successful, Del Monte lost no time in writing letters to other companies growing versions of the MD-2 telling them to stop, the implication being that the MD-2 was covered by the patent, rather than just the CO-2 as was actually the case.

The MD-2 was launched worldwide in 1996 under the somewhat more catchy title of the Del Monte Gold. Unlike five or six hundred years ago, these days it is rare for a new product to appear in the fruit or vegetable world, and the effect was spectacular. Within months the Del Monte Gold became the world's best-selling variety of fresh pineapple with an 80 per cent share of the market, even though it is almost invariably more expensive than the Smooth Cayenne. At the same time it gave an astonishing boost to pineapple sales in general: in both Britain and the United States, consumption of fresh pineapple has more than *doubled* since its introduction – on average, two to three pineapples are now consumed per person per year.[8]

The Gold quickly proved too popular for Del Monte to be able to keep it to itself. With Del Monte basking in a decade-long head-start, its competitors urgently needed to catch up – especially as a pineapple takes at least a year to mature before it is possible to tell whether it is a success. As C. J. Ingles, an executive at one of Del Monte's smaller competitors, commented, 'You need two ingredients to grow pineapples. Patience and money. And it helps to be a little crazy.'

Subterfuge became the only option. With the Gold unavailable in Costa Rica's shops, local dealers took to selling its seeds on the black market. A string of Del Monte plantation managers resigned to set up their own operations, while rival companies found ways to lure Del Monte's field labourers away in order to pick their brains. In yet another twist, rumours emerged that competitors were flying to the U.S. for the day to buy boxes of Golds from a supermarket, only to discard all but the crowns at the airport on the way home: these were then smuggled back to Costa Rica. One way or another, Dole soon had the seeds it craved. It built a new pineapple plantation in Honduras which in 1999 started to sell its own version of the Gold called Dole Premium Select.

Within a year Del Monte responded with a lawsuit, accusing Dole of having 'misappropriated the most commercially valuable pineapple in the world'. It alleged that a plantation in northern Costa Rica called Cabo Marzo had stolen Gold seeds then sold them on to Dole. However, Dole fired back that it had obtained the seeds entirely legitimately: Gold pineapple was served at a dinner hosted by Del Monte that was attended by Dole employees, who afterwards went and retrieved the crowns from the rubbish.

Dole eventually admitted that it obtained some Gold seeds from Cabo Marzo, but in turn claimed not to know where Cabo Marzo got them. This is where the story gets really bizarre. Growers testified that Cabo Marzo obtained them from a 'stranger' who appeared at the farm with seven seeds that he wanted to sell on. It is these seven seeds

– like fairy-tale beans – that are believed to be the source for thousands of acres of Gold pineapples currently being planted by Dole. Nobody has admitted to knowing who this 'stranger' was and the mystery has yet to be resolved.

In 2002, a court in Miami ruled that Del Monte had 'intentionally committed a fraudulent act' by sending letters to growers that implied that the Gold 'was covered by the CO-2 patent, which Del Monte knew to be false.' Del Monte and Dole settled. The terms of the settlement were not disclosed, but Dole has since expanded its sales of Premium Select. Del Monte's difficulties continued, however, when it faced yet another lawsuit, this time from Maui Land & Pineapple after Del Monte also sent them a threatening letter demanding they stop selling a pineapple called Hawaiian Gold. However, as Maui Land pointed out, Hawaiian Gold was the same variety patented as the CO-2 that had been co-owned by Maui Land & Pineapple since the start. Again, Del Monte settled. In early 2003, Del Monte withdrew its patent, admitting that it was now invalid.[9]

The Gold has had a major effect, not least in terms of the opportunities it has provided for Costa Rica, the centre of Del Monte's fresh pineapple operations. Production of pineapples there tripled, and it quickly replaced the Ivory Coast as the largest exporter of fresh pineapples in the world.[10] This brought many benefits to the country's economy, not least the provision of thousands of jobs. However, Costa Rica's famously fertile land was also subjected to many of the environmental problems often associated with the large-scale cultivation of crops by a multinational: appalling pollution due to the vast quantities of pesticides pumped into the plantations; increased sedimentation in the rivers, caused by the erosion of the soil when the plants are ripped out of it, ready to be replanted every two or three years; and plagues of flies, drawn to the thousands of rotting pineapple plants.[11]

Costa Rica has been one of the first countries to rebel against such environmentally unfriendly agricultural practices. The government has introduced a series of policies to protect the land, in particular its rivers, while in 2002, a firm called Asoproagroin, an association of 150 small pineapple producers, began to export the world's first Fairtrade pineapples into Britain. Vilma Maritza Cambornero Badilla is the manager of the Asoproagroin packing plant, not far from its farms in Guanacaste, an area of northern Costa Rica with high unemployment and few opportunities, especially for women. Fairtrade, however, allows Vilma to support both her daughters: 'Working with Asoproagroin has helped me to improve my own and my family's situation,' she says. The pineapples in question are a little more expensive than Del Monte's, but just as delicious. Costa Rica remains the epicentre of the ethical battle over the fruit.[12]

Yet Costa Rica's position as the United States' principal supplier of fresh pineapple is a vulnerable one. With about 80 per cent of the market, it continues to dominate, but Central American countries like Mexico, Ecuador and Honduras that have a climate ideally suited to the Gold have also seen considerable investment. Exports from these areas have increased dramatically – in Ecuador, for instance, by 350 per cent between 1998 and 2003.[13]

At the dockside in Southampton, skirmishes over the market for fresh pineapples in Britain are played out almost daily, depending on the vagaries of the weather. Amid the clang of metal and the squawk of seagulls, crate upon crate is unloaded from huge container ships to a queue of waiting lorries, ready to be driven across the country to the distribution centres that supply the major supermarket chains. The country of origin proclaimed in bright colours on the side of each crate varies, however. The Ivory Coast has struggled to maintain its sales of Smooth Cayennes in the face of Costa Rica's storming success with the Gold, while the Ivory Coast civil war over the past six years has also at times made trade unpredictable.

The result is a brilliant opportunity for other West African countries equally close to the major European markets. With Del Monte's patent for the Gold no longer valid, thousands upon thousands of acres of Gold pineapples are being planted all across the region – not only by multinational companies like La Compagnie Fruitière but also by small independent farmers. Governments are beginning to realise that they too need ready access to Gold plants if they are to have any chance of keeping up. This is happening in spite of the fact that West Africa's climate is not nearly as well suited to the Gold as Central America's. One country to watch is Ghana. Wages there currently stand at about $30 a month, compared with $10 a day in Costa Rica, and while it lacks the necessary infrastructure (the port of Tema has yet to be modernised), the country is just beginning to emerge from years of misrule. In 2003 C.F.U.K., the British division of La Compagnie Fruitière, announced a huge investment plan to capitalise on this. Ghana is also pioneering organic pineapples, though this remains a small sector of the market. [14]

The main rival to La Compagnie Fruitière in the United Kingdom is J. P. Fruit. They supply, among others, Tesco, the country's leading seller of pineapples. Overall, the market for fresh pineapples increased by almost a third between March 2004 and March 2005, when it was valued at £30 million a year. According to Tesco, the principal obstacle to expanding the market yet further is consumers' lack of knowledge. The fruit continues to mystify us.[15]

Small-scale independent retailers still trek down to New Spitalfields Market, in the middle of nowheresville off the motorway in east London. Since the much-lamented closure of the fresh produce section of Covent Garden Market, soon followed by Old Spitalfields Market, this is now *the* place to buy pineapples at wholesale prices. I pitched up at 5 a.m. on a bright but blustery weekday morning to be faced with a scene of clinical efficiency. Security waved me through with a bemused smile, the only pedestrian among the long line of lorries that come and go through the early hours. The massive grey warehouses are strangely quiet, aside from the whirr of the fork-lift trucks – this is a place of business, not theatre. As I wandered round, the mildly grumpy traders I spoke to – Phil from M. R. London, Mike from Del Monte – seemed suspicious of my passion for 'the kinky gear', the term they use for all the exotic produce.

On the basic level of genetics, every plant has one priority: to find a way to make copies of itself, again and again and again. By this criterion the pineapple has been phenomenally successful. Today, eighty countries around the world harvest over fifteen million tons of pineapple each year (a figure that has trebled over the past thirty years), of which over two-thirds is consumed in the country of origin. Thailand remains the largest overall producer, followed by the Philippines, Brazil, China, India and Costa Rica.[16]

The average imported pineapple that you buy today simply is more appealing to Man's palate, as well as more nutritious, than it was a decade ago. Modern science has superseded Nature's best efforts, and herein lies a paradox. To consumers, science is increasingly cast as the enemy when it comes to food – with every new newspaper headline about preservatives, additives and genetic modification confirming this. But in reality, science has improved upon the modern pineapple. The kind we see most often on sale in the supermarkets is a fruit weirdly constructed by Man – well, by the man from Del Monte.

As Agnes Block put it in 1685: '*Fert Arsque Laborque Quod Natura Negat* ('art and labour bring about what nature cannot'). Since humans first attempted to cultivate it outside the Amazon rainforest, the story of the pineapple has, in different ways, been all about 'art'. Take the case of Heligan Gardens in Cornwall, which boasts the only working, manure-heated Georgian-era pineapple pit still in existence (colour plate XII). The estate was the home of the Tremayne family from the sixteenth century until World War One when the house and the gardens fell into a state of chronic disrepair, until they were rediscovered by Tim Smit and John Nelson in 1991. The pineapple pits excited them particularly, and work began almost at once to restore them to their former glory.

Smit and his team decided to base the pits on an 1822 design by Thomas Andrew Knight. They were stocked with suitably eighteenth- and nineteenth-century varieties of Smooth Cayennes and Jamaica Queens sourced from the gene bank of the Government Agricultural Research Station in South Africa, then fertilized with tanner's bark from a local leather tanner's. In October 1996 the first ripe specimen for over 100 years was cut: it was deemed 'a fizzy combination of tart, juicy and sweet' by those who had the privilege of a taste. Smit continues,

The second one went to Buckingham Palace, although it nearly didn't gain admittance. The police at the back gate thought the whole idea so unlikely that they insisted I unpack it before they would summon a lady-in-waiting. The fruit, the first of the ripe Cayennes, was packed in a cardboard box, nestling in a cradle of straw. The sight of the policeman lifting it out and tapping and sniffing it, before finally agreeing that it was indeed a pineapple, will stay with me for some time. The Palace subsequently wrote a charming letter to Richard Dee [the gardener in charge] thanking him for the pine and reporting that Her Majesty had enjoyed it for supper that night.[17]

Hence Richard Dee became one in an illustrious line of gardeners (John Rose, Jacob Bobart, Henry Telende, among others) to supply the British monarchy with this most royal of fruits. Heligan's hotbeds now regularly offer up about fifteen pineapples a year – most of which are consumed by the gardeners themselves, a reward for all the hard work required to coax a fruit from a plant 'in ruder air / Too coy to flourish, even too proud to live'.[18]

The pineapple has long been replaced by other symbols of conspicuous consumption like a platinum ring or a fast car; yet over the centuries, it has acquired such a vast cache of connotations that it would take more than a few tin cans to dent its reputation for being somehow special. It is this that ensures it retains its role within our cultural consciousness: the centrepiece of the turn-of-the-Millennium spring/summer collection of the Paris fashion house Chloe was a range of swimsuits adorned with an artfully-placed signature pineapple (colour plate XIII). The fact is that when displayed in all its fresh glory – crown, leaves and shell intact – vestiges of the pineapple's celebrity incarnation are still in evidence, while whiffs of empire, of sex and of welcome also linger in the air. As Paul Muldoon put it in his 1998 poem 'Pineapples and Pomegranates',

> To think that, as a boy of thirteen, I would grapple
> with my first pineapple,
> its exposed breast

setting itself as another test
of my will-power, knowing in my bones
that it stood for something other than itself alone . . .[19]

Man has always adapted and exploited the exotic to meet his (or her)
needs; the pineapple is no exception.

While our perceptions of the pineapple are partly a cultural
construct, this does not entirely explain its astonishingly constant
image in the West. Is this the result of its Divine Proportions? Its taste
or smell? Or its sheer physical exoticism in comparison to, say, the
rotund kiwi or the yielding mango? As Nature at its least tamed, the
pineapple allows us to cling on to an element of our more primitive
selves. This power to infuse our lives with a tantalising taste of the
exotic means that, in the end, it will always remain king.

Acknowledgements

Many thanks to my wonderful editor Jenny Uglow, as well as Poppy
Hampson and all the staff at Chatto & Windus. My agent Clare
Conville was always supportive, whether through words, deeds or
champagne. Corinna Csáky, Ania Dykczak, Isabel de Bertodano,
Jessie Sklair, Jennie Cox and Jennifer Murphy all spurred me on. I am
grateful to Dylan Ritson for contributing ideas in the early stages of
my research, as well as to Duane Bartholomew for showing me around
Hawaii, answering endless queries and reading a draft of the
manuscript. The Linda D. Russo Foundation and the Author's
Foundation kindly provided travel grants. The staff of the London
Library, the British Library, the University of Hawaii Library and the
University of California Library were also helpful.

A special thanks, for everything, goes to my intended, James Bobin
– obviously.

Finally, thanks to my parents, Chris and Nicola Beauman. They
have always been there for me with ideas, advice, encouragement,
food, books, support, information and inspiration. Innumerable
discussions over everything from commas to colonialism mean that
they have put an awful lot into this book over the years, for which I am
immensely grateful. I dedicate it to them, with much love.

'Someone Put a Pineapple Together' by Wallace Stevens, from *The
Necessary Angel: Essays on Reality and Imagination*, with permission of
Faber and Faber Ltd.

Notes

Two books have been invaluable starting points in my pursuit of the pineapple: J. L. Collins, *The Pineapple: Botany, Cultivation and Utilization* (1960) and D. P. Bartholomew, R. E. Paull, and K. G. Rohrbach, *The Pineapple: Botany, Production and Uses* (2003). General works on the history of gardens and gardening that have been consulted include Susan Campbell, *Charleston Kedding: A History of Kitchen Gardening* (1996); Charles Quest-Ritson, *The English Garden: a Social History* (2001); Miles Hadfield, *A History of British Gardening* (1985); Jane Brown, *The Pursuit of Paradise: a Social History of Gardens and Gardening* (1999); May Woods and Arete Swartz Warren, *Glass Houses: a History of Greenhouses, Orangeries and Conservatories* (1988); and Alice Lockwood (ed.), *Gardens of Colony and State: Gardens and Gardeners of the American Colonies and of the Republic Before 1840* (1931).

Sources are listed in full at their first mention in each chapter; thereafter the author's name or a short title is given.

CHAPTER I

1   Poem 'Figs' in D. H. Lawrence, *The Complete Poems of D. H. Lawrence*, ed. Vivian de Sola Pinto and Warren Roberts (1964) I. 282.
2   While it is generally agreed that the pineapple originates from somewhere in the area of Brazil or Paraguay, within this huge area, there is some debate. According to G. Coppens D'Eeckenbrugge, the diversity of wild and cultivated forms is greatest north of the Amazon river (Orinoco and Negro basins, Amapa, Guianas). This is consistent

with the proposal by M. G. Antoni and F. Leal that the centre of origin was between 10°N and 10°S latitude and 55° to 75°W latitude. See F. Leal and G. Coppens D'Eeckenbrugge, 'Pineapple', in J. Janick and J. N. Moore (eds), *Fruit Breeding* (1996); G. Coppens D'Eeckenbrugge, F. Leal and M. F. Duval, 'Germplasm Resources of Pineapple', *Horticultural Reviews* 21 (1997); and M. G. Antoni and F. Leal, 'Key for Identification of Commercial Cultivars of Pineapple (Ananas comosus)', *Proceedings of the Tropical Region, American Society for Horticultural Science* 24 (1980). Thanks to G. Coppens D'Eeckenbrugge.

3   The available genetic information makes it very difficult to estimate the date that the *Bromeliacae* family first appeared in the form we know today. Email from G. Coppens D'Eeckenbrugge to the author (29 September 2003). See also D. P. Bartholomew 20.

4   For the different varieties of pineapples, see D. P. Bartholomew 13–56.

5   Thanks to Professor Charles Thomas for advice on this. The classic account of the Fibonacci series is Wentworth D'Arcy Thompson, *On Growth and Form* (1917). For more on Fibonacci in nature, see Ian Stewart, *Life's Other Secret* (1998).

6   Anil Ananthaswamy, 'Spiral Pattern Helps Cacti Deal with Stress', *New Scientist* (8 May 2004). Thanks to Robin Weir.

7   My main source for the Tupí-Guaranís in this period is the essay by Alfred Métraux in Julian H. Steward, *Handbook to South American Indians* (1946) III.i. 95ff. For more on pre-colonial life in Brazil, see Frank Solomon and Stuart B. Schwartz (eds), *The Cambridge History of the Native Peoples of the Americas* (1999) III; Leslie Bethell (ed.), *The Cambridge History of Latin America* (1984) I; James Lockhard and Stuart B. Schwartz, *Early Latin America: a History of Colonial Spanish America and Brazil* (1983); and Robert M. Levine, *The History of Brazil* (1999). Thanks also to Professor Leslie Bethell.

8   W. Greenlee (ed.), *The Voyages of Pedro Cabral* (1938) 10.

9   Jean de Léry, *History of a Voyage to the Land of Brazil*, tr. Janet Whatley (1990) 58.

10   Ibid. 65.

11   For more on how wild plants become domesticated, see Jared

Diamond, *Guns, Germs and Steel* (1997) and Michael Pollan, *The Botany of Desire: a Plant's Eye View of the World* (2001).

12 Email from G. Coppens D'Eeckenbrugge to the author (29 September 2003).

13 Carl Sauer, *The Early Spanish Main: the Land, Nature and People Columbus Encountered in the Americas* (1992) 57.

14 Jean de Léry 108.

15 Antonio Pigafetta, *First Voyage Around the World*, ed. Carlos Quirino, tr. James A. Robertson (1969) 7.

16 Andre Thevet, *New Founde World or Antarcticke*, tr. Thomas Hacket (1568) 85.

17 Carl Sauer, *Agricultural Origins and Dispersals* (1969) 141.

18 Jean de Léry 108. Thanks to Jessie Sklair.

19 For the spread of the pineapple throughout South America, see Berthold Laufer, 'The American Plant Migrations', *Scientific Monthly* 28 (1929); Kenneth F. Baker and J. L.Collins, 'Notes on the Distribution and Ecology of Ananas and Pseudananas in South America', *American Journal of Botany* 26 (1939); J. L. Collins, 'Pineapples in Ancient America', *Scientific Monthly* 67 (1948); and J. L.Collins, 'The Antiquity of the Pineapple in America', *Southwest Journal of Anthropology* 7 (1951).

20 Joseph de Acosta, *The Natural and Moral History of the East and West Indies*, ed. Clements R. Markham (1880) 237.

21 Julian H. Steward III.ii. 773.

22 Benjamin Keen (tr.), *The Life of the Admiral Christopher Columbus by his Son Ferdinand* (1959) 254.

23 J. L. Collins, *The Pineapple* (1960) 13.

24 Julian H. Steward III.i. 368.

25 Ibid. V. 102.

26 Joseph de Acosta 318–19.

CHAPTER 2

1 For Columbus's second voyage, see S. E. Morison, *The Second Voyage of Christopher Columbus – from Cadiz to Hispaniola and the Discovery of the Lesser Antilles* (1939) and S. E. Morison and M. Obregon, *The*

Caribbean as Columbus Saw It (1964). For Columbus's voyages in general, see S. E. Morison, *The European Discovery of America* (1974).

2   S. E. Morison (tr./ed.), *Journals and Other Documents on the Life and Voyages of Christopher Columbus* (1963) 234.

3   For the Caribs, see Irving Rouse, 'The Carib', in Julian H. Steward (ed.), *Handbook of South American Indians* (1946) IV.iii. 547–64.

4   Cecil Jane (ed.), *The Four Voyages of Columbus: a History in Eight Documents* (1988) 30.

5   S. E. Morison and M. Obregon ix.

6   Jane 32.

7   Benjamin Keen (tr.), *The Life of the Admiral Christopher Columbus by his son Ferdinand* (1959) 111.

8   S. E. Morison, *Journals* 216. Columbus himself never wrote an account of the pineapple, even though many quote one or all of these sources as being his words.

9   For the way that Europeans sought to translate this new experience into a familiar cultural setting, see Massimo Montanari, *The Culture of Food*, tr. Carl Ipsen (1994) 99.

10   Quoted in Peter Hulme, *Colonial Encounters: Europe and the Native Caribbean 1492–1797* (1986) 1.

11   Quoted in S. E. Morison, *European Discovery* II. 138.

12   Keen 174.

13   F. A. MacNutt (tr.), *De Orbe Novo: the Eight Decades of Peter Martyr d'Anghera* (1912) I. 262.

14   For Spain in this period, see Henry Kamen, *Spain's Road to Empire: the Making of a World Power 1492–1763* (2002).

15   For the relation between the New World and the Old World, see Alfred W. Crosby, *The Columbian Exchange: Biological and Cultural Consequences of 1492* (1972); Anthony Pagden, *European Encounters with the New World* (1993); Antonello Gerbi, *Nature in the New World*, tr. Jeremy Moyle (1985); and J. H. Elliott, *The Old World and the New* (1970).

16   Lucien Febvre and Henri-Jean Martin, *The Coming of the Book: the Impact of Printing 1450–1800*, tr. David Gerard (1976) 248, 262.

17 Quoted in J. H. Elliott 8.

18 Jean de Léry, *History of a Voyage to the Land of Brazil*, tr. Janet Whatley (1990) 108.

19 Jacob Bontius, *An Account of the Diseases, Natural History and Medicines of the East Indies*, tr. Anon. (1769) 148. This is the first English translation, but the original Latin text was first published in 1629.

20 The only surviving original manuscript of Part One of Gonzalo Fernández de Oviedo y Valdes, *Historia General y Natural de las Indias* (1535) is in the Huntingdon Library in San Marino, California (HM 177, Book 7, Chapter 14).

For more on the provenance of the text, see Jesús Carrillo, 'The *Historia General y Natural de las Indias* by Gonzalo Fernández de Oviedo', *Huntingdon Library Quarterly* 65 (3 & 4) 321–44.

No complete English translation of the *Historia General y Natural de las Indias* exists. The only published English translation of the passage on the pineapple is in J. L. Collins, *The Pineapple* (1960) 9–13. All quotes are from this text.

The pineapple is also mentioned in Oviedo's earlier, shorter work, *De la Natural Historia de las Indias* (1526): see Gonzalo Fernández de Oviedo, *Natural History of the West Indies*, tr./ed. Sterling A. Stoudemire (1959) 99.

Thanks to William P. Frank, Curator of Hispanic, Cartographic and Western Manuscripts at the Huntingdon Library, as well as to his assistant, Brooke M. Black.

21 Antonio Pigafetta, *First Voyage Around the World*, ed. Carlos Quirino, tr. James A. Robertson (1969) 5–6.

22 Clements R. Markham (ed.), *The Hawkins Voyages* (1878) in *Hakluyt Society*, 1st Series, LVII. 27.

23 Andre Thevet, *New Founde World or Antarcticke*, tr. Thomas Hacket (1568) 73.

24 Joseph de Acosta, *The Natural and Moral History of the East and West Indies*, ed. Clements R. Markham (1880) 236.

25 Quoted in Nancy Etcoff, *The Survival of the Prettiest: the Science of Beauty* (1999) 15.

26 Ibid. 185.

27 Quoted in Jean Delumeau, *History of Paradise: the Garden of Eden in Myth and Tradition*, tr. Matthew O'Connell (1995) 110.

28 Quoted in William Brandon, *New World for Old* (1986) 12.

29 Nicholas Monardes, *Joyfull Newes out of the New Founde Worlde*, tr. John Frampton (1577) Folio 90.

30 Christopher De Rochefort, *The History of the Caribby Islands*, tr. John Davies (1666) 58.

31 For all the Frans Post paintings that feature the pineapple, see Erik Larsen, *Frans Post* (1967). Albert Eckhout, another Dutch artist, also painted pineapples in Brazil in the mid-seventeenth century – to which Marina Warner's analysis in *No Go the Bogeyman* (1998) 348–73 of the bananas in his paintings might just as well be applied.

32 For Frans Post's interpretation of the New World, see Benjamin Schmidt, *Innocence Abroad: the Dutch Imagination and the New World* (2001) 311.

33 J. L. Collins 10.

34 A. J. R. Russell-Wood, *A World on the Move: the Portuguese in Africa, Asia and America 1415–1808* (1992). It is possible that the Chinese also played a role in the spread of the pineapple around the world, but this is still under discussion: see Gavin Menzies, *1421: The Year China Discovered the World* (2003).

35 Michael Hemmersam, *Guineische und West-Indianische Reissbeschreibung de an. 1639 biss 1645 . . .* (1663) 42.

36 Mia C. Karsten, *The Old Company's Garden at the Cape* (1951) 57.

37 Etienne de Flacourt, *Histoire de la grande isle Madagascar* (1661) 119.

38 Jan Huygen Van Linschoten, *Discours of Voyages into Y East & West Indies*, tr. W. P. (1598) 90.

39 Wheeler M. Thackston (tr.), *The Jahangira: Memoirs of Jahangir, Emperor of India* (1999) 24, 206.

40 Richard Carnac Temple (ed.), *The Travels of Peter Mundy in Europe and Asia 1608–1667* (1919), III.i. 59. In 1623, pineapples were also recorded in the state of Gujarat. Edward Grey (ed.), *Travels in India of Pietro Della Valle* (1891) I. 134. By 1700, they were common in Bengal. Niccolao Manucci, *Storia Do Mogor, or Mogul India 1653–1708*, tr. William Irvine (1908), III. 183.

41 Albert Grey (tr.), *The Voyage of Francois Pyrard of Laval to the East Indies, the Maldives, the Moluccas and Brazil* (1887–90) II. 365; Evert Ysbrants Ides, *Three Years Travels from Moscow Over-land to China* (1706) 183.

42 Michael Boym, *Flora Sinensis* (1656) Plate G.

43 John Nieuhof, *An embassy sent by the East-India Company of the United Provinces to the Grand Tartar Cham or Emperour of China . . . Ingeniously described by Mr. John Nievhoff, Steward to the Ambassadours*, tr. John Ogilby (1669) 264.

44 Athanasius Kircher, *China Illustrata*, tr. Charles D. Van Tuyl (1987) 181–2. The original Latin text was first published in 1667.

CHAPTER 3

1 John Evelyn, *The Diary of John Evelyn*, ed. E. S. De Beer (1955) III. 293.

2 F. Cundall, *The Governors of Jamaica in the Seventeenth Century* (1906) xxx.

3 *Calendar of State Papers (Colonial: North America and the West Indies)*, 12 January 1658.

4 It was certainly possible: while Richard Ligon claimed that pineapples were unable to survive the six-week passage from the West Indies, this is contradicted by the fact that Columbus managed it and he was at sea for seven. Richard Ligon, *A True and Exact History of the Island of Barbados* (1657) 84. Frequent references to the fact that the passage takes about six weeks there and six to seven weeks back are made in the *Calendar of State Papers* for this period.

5 *Calendar of State Papers*, 12 January 1658. On 12 February 1658, this was increased to £400. Little is known about Goodson after this date. He continued to serve in the Navy for some years. At one point he purchased five hundred acres of land in southern England somewhere. A wife is mentioned but no children; but it is not impossible that the John Goodson who was the first English doctor to go to Pennsylvania was his son. He was still living in 1680, but then disappears from the radar.

6 Carew Reynell, *The True English Interest* (1674) 89.

7   See K. G. Davies, *The North Atlantic World in the Seventeenth Century* (1974) and David Armitage, *The Ideological Origins of the Empire* (2000).

8   Quoted in David Armitage, 'The Cromwellian Protectorate and the Languages of Empire', *Historical Journal* 35 (1992).

9   Quoted in Antonia Fraser, *Oliver Cromwell: Our Chief of Men* (2002) 679.

10 Henry Fletcher, *The Perfect Politician; or a full view of the life and actions of O. Cromwell* (1680) 210.

11 R. P. Du Tertre, *Histoire Generale des Antilles* (1667) II. 127. There are numerous examples of this. 'C'est le Roy de tous les fruits' exclaimed the French governor of Madagascar Etienne de Flacourt in an account he wrote of the island in 1661 (Etienne de Flacourt *Histoire de la grande isle Madagascar* (1661) 119). Oviedo called it 'the prince of all fruits', while Peter Martyr commented that it was 'not unworthy of a king's table'. J. L. Collins, *The Pineapple* (1960) 10; F. A. MacNutt (tr.), *De Orbe Novo: the Eight Decades of Peter Martyr d'Anghera* (1912) 262.

12 Christopher De Rochefort, *The History of the Caribby Islands*, tr. John Davies (1666) 58.

13 Sir Walter Raleigh, *The Discovery of Guiana* (1596) 61.

14 John Parkinson, *Theatrum Botanicum: the theatre of plantes, or a universall and compleate herball* (1640) II. 1626. Other complimentary accounts include John Gerarde, *The Herball, or General Historie of Plants, Enlarged and Amended*, ed. Thomas Johnson (1633) 1552 and John Worlidge, *Vinetum Britannicum* (1676) 4.

15 Captain John Smith, *The Generalle Historie of Virginia, New England and the Summer Isles* (1624) 170; Edmund Waller, *Battle of the Summer Islands* (1645) in F. C. Hicks (ed.), *Bermuda in Poetry 1610–1908* (1915) 20.

16 Because Ligon's book was published the same year that Cromwell was presented with a pineapple, Ligon has in the past been erroneously identified as being responsible for bringing into the country the pineapple mentioned by Evelyn. In fact, although he was in Barbados from 1647 to 1650, he had been back in England for seven years by the time the book appeared. Thanks to Karen Ordahl Kupperman.

17 All quotes are from Richard Ligon 82–4.

18 Christopher De Rochefort 58.
19 Nicholas Murray, *World Enough and Time: the Life of Andrew Marvell* (1999).
20 Andrew Marvell, *The Complete Poems*, ed. George deForest Lord (1993) 10.
21 M. C. Seymour (ed.), *On the Properties of Things: John Trevisa's Translation of* De Proprietatibus Rerum (1975) II. 1018.
22 *The Times*, 17 September 2003. Thanks to Luke Singer.
23 Evelyn, *Diary* III. 293. The term 'Queen-pine' refers to a specific variety of pineapple known at this time.
24 For the rest of the petition, see *Calendar of State Papers*, 12 July 1661.
25 Brian Weiser, 'Access and Petitioning During the Reign of Charles II', in Eveline Cruickshanks, *The Stuart Courts* (2000) 203.
26 Ibid. 207.
27 Brian Weiser, *Charles II and the Politics of Access* (2003) 125.
28 *Calendar of State Papers*, 5 August 1661; 12 August 1661; 19 August 1661.
29 Evelyn, *Diary* III. 513. The term 'King-pine' refers to a specific variety of pineapple known at this time – which is why he says that this is the first time he has seen it, since the one he saw in 1661 was a 'Queen-pine', another variety of the same species.
30 John Rose, *The English Vineyard Vindicated* (1666).
31 However, Evelyn's turn of phrase is ambiguous: while he explains that pineapples in general are 'growing in Barbados', this does not mean that the particular pineapple in question did. It is possible that it came from one or other of England's colonies in the West Indies at the time.
32 *Calendar of State Papers*, 11/12 September 1668; 21 September 1668; 21/31 October 1668.
33 John Evelyn, *Elysium Britannicum, or The Royal Gardens*, ed. John E. Ingram (2001) 225 & 413–4. John Evelyn continued to champion the pineapple throughout his writing career. In 1683, he wrote about 'the royal pine – a compendium of all that is delicious to the taste and smell'. This comes in the climax to a passage enumerating the wonders that God has created, of which the pineapple is clearly seen to be the pinnacle. John Evelyn, *The History of Religion* (1850) I. 29.

34   Evelyn, *Elysium* 414. Thanks to Frances Harris, Curator of Manuscripts at the British Library.

35   For the history of the painting, as well as various arguments about the identity of the artist and the house, see Hermia Oliver, 'John Rose's Pineapple', *Hortus* 7 (1988); Lionel Cust, 'The First Pineapple Grown in England', *Apollo* (February 1926); and George Royle, 'Family Links between George London and John Rose: New Light on the "Pineapple Paintings"', *Journal of Garden History* 23/2 (1995).

36   Horace Walpole, *A description of the villa of Horace Walpole at Strawberry Hill near Twickenham with an inventory . . .* (1774); W. S. Lewis (ed.), *The Yale Edition of Horace Walpole's Correspondence* (1983) II. 200.

37   For John Michael Wright, see Sara Stevenson and Duncan Thomson, *John Michael Wright: the King's Painter* (1982). My evidence for John Michael Wright being the artist includes the following points: There is another portrait by Wright of Charles II with the sitter's head in exactly the same position as in the pineapple painting; there is a portrait by Wright of Lady Catherine Cecil and James, 4th Earl of Salisbury, in which a pomegranate is featured in almost exactly the same position as the pineapple in the pineapple painting; Wright was a friend of John Evelyn's, a friend of John Rose's; it explains why he sometimes signed himself 'the king's painter'; on 27 July 1676 he mentioned in a letter to Sir Walter Bagot that 'I am told the King will sitt to my great picture for the Citty this next moneth' but the picture has not yet been traced; and so on.

38   W. S. Lewis, II. 200.

39   Quoted in Stephen Coote, *Royal Survivor: a Life of Charles II* (1999) 207.

40   John Prest, *The Garden of Eden: the Botanic Garden and the Re-creation of Paradise* (1981).

41   John Harrison and Peter Laslett, *The Library of John Locke* (1965) 27.

42   Peter H. Nidditch (ed.), *An Essay Concerning Human Understanding, by John Locke* (1975) 424. Thanks to Dr Hannah Dawson.

43   Christopher De Rochefort 58.

44   Richard Ligon 82; Clayton Colman Hall (ed.), *Narratives of Early Maryland 1633–1684* (1925) 36.

CHAPTER 4

Thanks to Gerda van Uffelen of the Leiden Hortus and Dr Liesbeth Missel of the Special Collections Department of the Wageningen Library for assistance with aspects of this chapter.

1   Samuel Pepys, *The Diary of Samuel Pepys*, eds Robert Latham and William Matthews (1983) VIII. 345 – July 19 1667.

2   See Dale Hoak and Mordechai Feingold (eds), *The World of William and Mary: Anglo-Dutch Perspectives on the Revolution of 1688–9* (1996) and Simon Schama, *The Embarrassment of Riches* (1987).

3   H. Veendorp and L. G. M. Baas Becking, *Hortus Academicus Lugduno Batavius 1587–1937: the Development of the Gardens of Leyden University* (1990) 86.

4   John Aubrey, *The Natural History of Wiltshire*, ed. John Britton (1845) 93. The text was first published in 1691.

5   C. R. Boxer, *Dutch Merchants and Mariners in Asia 1602–1795* (1988) 82.

6   Jan Huygen Van Linschoten, *Discours of Voyages into Y East & West Indies*, tr. W. P. (1598) 90.

7   James D. Tracy (ed.), *True Ocean Found: Paladanus' Letters on Dutch Voyages to the Kara Sea, 1595–1596* (1980).

8   H. Veendorp and L. G. M. Baas Becking 73. While the pineapple in question certainly came from one of the Dutch colonies in the West Indies, West Africa or Brazil, its exact provenance is not known.

9   Mia C. Karsten, *The Old Company's Garden at the Cape* (1951) 57. Jan van Riebeeck was one of the first to champion the rather eccentric idea of importing plants from back home, rather than addressing the needs of native plants, in order to provide supplies for ships on the way to Indonesia or India.

10   D. O. Wijnands, 'Hortus Auriaci: the Gardens of Orange and Their Place in Late Seventeenth-century Botany and Horticulture', *Journal of Garden History* 8/2 & 3 (1988).

11   David Jacques and Arend Jan van der Horst, *The Gardens of William and Mary* (1988) 169.

12 Quoted in Lisa Jardine, *Ingenious Pursuits* (1999) 251.

13 'Hortus Auriaci.'

14 J. D. Dixon (ed.), *The Dutch Garden in the Seventeenth Century* (1990) 19. See also E. de Jong, *Nature and Art: Dutch Garden and Landscape Architecture 1650–1740* (2000).

15 D. O. Wijnands, *The Botany of the Commelins* (1983) 55. In Jan Commelin's *Horti Medical Amstelodamensis* (1697), one of the most beautiful books on horticulture produced in this period, there is an illustration of a pineapple based on a watercolour by Jan Moninckx. The frontispiece, depicting the goddess Flora being presented with flowers by figures representing Europe, Asia, Africa and America, also features a pineapple plant in the foreground of the tableau. It was clearly one of Commelin's proudest achievements.

16 *Journal of Garden History*, 8/2 & 3 (1988) 281.

17 Pieter de la Court, *Byzondere Aaemerkingen* (1737); Richard Bradley, *General Treatise of Husbandry and Gardening* (1721) I. 206.

18 These are dated 1718, 1723 and 1726. Inventory number 31 in the Pieter de la Court Archive in the Leiden City Archives. Thanks to Dr. R. C. J. van Maanen, Deputy Municipal Archivist of the city of Leiden.

19 Richard Bradley I. 208.

20 Ibid.

21 François Legaut, *A New Voyage to the East Indies* (1708) 166.

22 Sue Minter, *The Apothecaries Garden: a New History of the Chelsea Physic Garden* (2000).

23 John Evelyn also admired the underfloor heating at the Chelsea Physic Garden. Following a visit on 6 August 1685, he wrote in his diary that 'what was very ingenious was the subterranean heate conveyed by a stove under the conservatory all vaulted with brick'. See the early pages of Minter as well as Douglas Chambers, 'John Evelyn and the Invention of the Heated Greenhouse', *Garden History* 20/2 (1992).

24 See Mordechai Feingold, 'The Displacement of Cultural Hegemony from the Netherlands to England in the Seventeenth and Early Eighteenth Centuries', in Dale Hoak and Mordechai Feingold.

25 Philip Miller, *A Catalogue of Trees* (1730) vi.

26 Henry and Barbara van der Zee, *William and Mary* (1975) 289.

27 Ibid. 100.
28 *Journal of Garden History*, 8/2 & 3 (1988) 288. By the following year
    when a Dr Grey compiled a list of the plants it contained, the pineapple
    had become a central feature of the Hampton Court collection. *British
    Library Sloane MSS* 3370.
29 Bodleian Library MS. Eng. Hist. c.11 (fol. 19r). Thanks to Greg
    Colley, Assistant Librarian, Department of Special Collections and
    Western Manuscripts at the Bodleian Library.
30 *Calendar of State Papers (Colonial: North America and the West Indies)*,
    14 October 1692. Through the 1680s and 1690s, the pineapple
    continued to be the gift of choice for those seeking to impress those in
    government back home with the treasures of the West Indies. For
    example, in March 1684, Lieutenant-Governor John Witham sent a
    case from Barbados to the civil servant Sir Leoline Jenkins, with an
    accompanying note entreating that he 'hope[s] you may like these (your
    predecessor, Mr Coventry, highly esteemed 'em)'. *Calendar of State
    Papers*, 15 March 1684.
31 J. C. Loudon, *The Different Modes of Cultivating the Pine-Apple* (1822)
    20. My mother's family originated from Breslau: is it possible that my
    ancestors were Dr Kaltschmidt's gardeners? Perhaps a passion for
    pineapples runs in the family . . .
32 The passage continues: 'it, among all the fruits of the universe, has the
    dignified form of the Empire; with the qualities it has for good
    government, the perfect prince, being strict but gentle, being in taste
    the greatest delicacy, being so delicious, so tart and cruel towards
    criminals, towards those that have open cuts and wounds: having both
    rigor and gentleness, the principle of the best kind of government . . .'
    Antonio do Rosario, *Frutas do Brasil* (1702) 1–23. For an analysis of
    this, see Sergio Buarque de Holanda, *Visao do Paraiso* (1969) 230–36.
    Thanks to Jessie Sklair.
33 Robert Halsbrand (ed.), *The Selected Letters of Lady Mary Wortley
    Montagu* (1970) 88.
34 J. L. Collins, *The Pineapple* (1960) 12; Francisco Hernandez, *Rerum
    Medicarum Novae Hispaniae Thesaurus* (1659) VIII. 311.
35 Van Linschoten, 90.

36   Louis Lemery, *A Treatise of Foods in General* (1706) 50.

37   Hans Sloane, *Natural History of Jamaica* (1707) 191.

38   Ibid.

39   Joseph de Acosta, *The Natural and Moral History of the East and West Indies*, ed. Clements R. Markham (1880) 236.

40   J. L. Collins 10.

41   Gulielmi Pisonis, *Historia Natural & Medici Indiae Orientalis* (1658) IV. 195–6. Those that wrote that it caused cholera include Joseph de Acosta and Jacob Bontius. Joseph de Acosta 236; Jacob Bontius, *An Account of the Diseases, Natural History and Medicines of the East Indies*, tr. Anon. (1769) 148.

42   William Bosman, *A New and Accurate Description of the Coast of Guinea*, eds J. D. Fage and R. E. Bradbury (1967) 303; John Nieuhof, *An embassy sent by the East-India Company of the United Provinces to the Grand Tartar Cham or Emperour of China . . . Ingeniously described by Mr. John Nievhoff, Steward to the Ambassadours*, tr. John Ogilby (1669) 264.

43   Christopher de Acosta, *Drogas de las Indias* 347. Thanks to Ned Beauman.

44   There is scarce evidence for the date this happened. While it was certainly some time before 1716, accounts differ about whether it was 1712 or 1714. My guess is the latter. Decker's house on Richmond Green was first known as Fitzwilliam House then later Pembroke Villa. It was demolished in 1840. Ten semi-detached houses now stand on the site on the north-west side of the Green. They are collectively known as Pembroke Villas.

45   Richard Bradley III. 133.

46   *Gentleman's Magazine* (1749) 141.

47   Ibid.

48   Michaelis Friderici Lochneri, *Commentatio De Ananasa* (1716) 2.

49   Richard Bradley I.161 & 206–26; III. 133–45.

50   Ibid. I. 208.

CHAPTER 5

This chapter has been much informed by Roy Porter, *English Society in the*

Eighteenth Century (1990) and Mark Girouard, *Life in the English Country House* (1978).

1 Quoted in Hazel Le Rougetel, *The Chelsea Gardener: Philip Miller 1691–1771* (1990) 58. The Thorndon Hall pinery was 60 foot long and 20 foot wide. See Sir George Clutton and Colin MacKay, 'Old Thorndon Hall, Essex: a History and Reconstruction of its Park and Garden', *Garden History Society Occasional Paper No. 2* (1970) 34.

2 For the pursuit of pleasure in the eighteenth century, see Roy Porter and Marie Mulvey Roberts (eds), *Pleasure in the Eighteenth Century* (1996).

3 John Butt (ed.), *The Twickenham Edition of the Poems of Alexander Pope* (1993) III. I. 128.

4 Bonamy Dobrée (ed.), *The letters of Philip Dormer Stanhope, 4th Earl of Chesterfield* (1932) IV. 1702 – 25 March 1751.

5 Ibid. V. 1905 – 30 June 1752.

6 John Cowell, *The Curious and Profitable Gardener* (1730) 27.

7 B. Faujas de Saint-Fond, *A Journey Through England and Scotland to the Hebrides in 1784*, ed. Archibald Geikie (1907) I. 248.

8 Quoted in E. N. Williams, *Life in Georgian England* (1962) 47.

9 William Speechly, *A Treatise on the Culture of the Pineapple and the Management of the Hothouse* (1779) viii.

10 Philip Miller, *The Gardener and Florist's Dictionary* (1724) I (cited under 'Ananas'); Philip Miller, *The Gardener's Dictionary* (1731) I (cited under 'Ananas').

11 On Philip Miller see Hazel Le Rougetel, as well as Sue Minter, *The Apothecaries Garden: a New History of the Chelsea Physic Garden* (2000).

12 *Museum Rusticum et Commerciale* (1764) I. 143. It was later reprinted in R. Weston, *Tracts on Practical Agriculture and Gardening* (1769).

13 Tom Williamson and Andrea Taigel (eds), *Gardens in Norfolk* (1990) 57. This may have included the cost of stocking the pinery, however, as well as its construction.

14 *Museum Rusticum* I. 143.

15 C. H. Collins Baker and Muriel I. Baker, *The Life and Circumstances of James Brydges, First Duke of Chandos* (1949) 185.

16   Peter Collinson, *Forget Not Mee and My Garden: Selected Letters 1725–1768 of Peter Collinson*, ed. Alan W. Armstrong (2002) 153 – 10 March 1750.

17   William Speechly to the Duke of Portland, 28 April 1781 (Nottingham University archives PwF 8479).

18   John Harvey, *Early Nurserymen* (1974) 204. Originally from Chertsey in Surrey, Richard Woods was also responsible for designing a number of other pineries, including one at Cannon Hall in South Yorkshire, the seat of John Spencer. Following an initial visit on 1 April 1760, by 23 October the same year Spencer was able to record in his diary that he had 'Cutt the first pineapple out of my hothouses'. Fiona Cowell, 'Richard Woods (?1716–93): a Preliminary Account', *Garden History: the Journal of the Garden History Society* 14/2 (Autumn 1986) 91.

19   *Museum Rusticum* I. 143; Elizabeth Hall, 'The Plant Collections of an Eighteenth Century Virtuoso', *Garden History: the Journal of the Garden History Society* 14/1 (Spring 1986) 11.

20   *Museum Rusticum* I. 143.

21   Blanche Henrey, *No Ordinary Gardener: Thomas Knowleton* (1986) 179.

22   Anon., *A Pocket Companion for Oxford* (1744) 26; Thomas Salmon, *Foreigner's Companion through the Universities of Cambridge and Oxford* (1748) 67.

23   George Sherburn (ed.), *The Correspondence of Alexander Pope* (1956) III. 453.

24   Ibid. IV. 117.

25   Ibid. IV. 405 & 420. Ralph Allen then took his lead from Pope and starting growing pineapples himself too in Bath, also with the help of Henry Scott. Ibid. IV. 360 & 429.

26   Richard Bradley, *The Country Housewife* (1732) II. 94.

27   Susan Campbell, *Charleston Kedding: a History of Kitchen Gardening* (1996) 151.

28   W. C. Lukis (ed.), *The Family Memoirs of the Reverend William Stukeley* (1887) III. 29.

29   Quoted in J. H. Plumb, *Men and Places* (1996) 147.

30   Quoted in E. N. Williams 32.

31   Bonamy Dobrée IV. 1491 – 18 January 1750.

32 Abbé Le Pluche, *Le Spectacle de la Nature* (1st edn 1735; citations are from the 1st Eng. edn 1740) II. 153. For more on the pineapple in France, see M. Georges Gibault, *Histoire des Légumes* (1912) 323–9. Voltaire also tried to grow pineapples at his château in Ferney. See Ian Buruma, *Voltaire's Coconuts – or, Anglomania in England* (1999) 21.

33 Louis Sébastien Mercier, *Tableau de Paris*, ed. Jean-Claude Bonnet (1st edn. 1781; 1994) I. 478.

34 To give one example amongst many: in a poem by Laurence Eusden dedicated to Queen Caroline in 1727, it is used as a metaphor for the way all the queen's wonderful qualities manifest themselves:
'. . . As the rich Tastes of Fruits of ev'ry kind
In the delicious Anana we find;
So all the various Glories, that refine,
And, scatter'd, make un-number'd Nymphs divine,
Centr'd at once in Thee . . . shine!'
(Laurence Eusden, *Three Poems* (1727) 25).

35 For more on pineapple cultivation on the Continent in the eighteenth and early nineteenth centuries, see J. C. Loudon, *Different Modes of Cultivating the Pineapple . . .* (1822).

36 Venetia Murray, *Castle Howard: the Life and Times of a Stately Home* (1994) 85.

37 *Gentleman's Magazine* (1825) II. 369.

38 Venetia Murray 88.

39 Ibid. 120.

40 Clare Williams (ed.), *Sophie in London 1786* (1933) 228.

41 Venetia Murray 127. In the end, it seems that Portland's generosity paid off. In 1807 and to everyone's surprise, the Duke of Portland became Prime Minister. The most notable feature of his stint in the role was that he did not once speak in Parliament: having won the general election, he left his ministers to govern the way they wanted. The result, however, was endless rows between two of his most powerful politicians, Castlereagh and Canning, climaxing in a bizarre early morning duel on Putney Heath in which Canning was shot in the thigh (he survived). Portland lasted just two years in the post, then died. Perhaps he missed his pinery just a little too much.

42 Quoted in C. Quest-Ritson, *The English Garden: a Social History* (2001) 163.

43 Blanche Henrey 182. Knowleton soon began to build pineries on commission for other people: in 1758 he built one large enough for 100 plants at Burton Constable, an estate in East Riding of Yorkshire, which included an attached 'Master's Room', complete with fireplace. Ibid. 250. Built for William Constable, the pineapple house at Burton Constable was 200 feet long and heated by fire walls. Constable's first stock of pineapple plants came from Cowick, the estate of Lord Downe near Goole, in April 1758. In the ensuing years he was also supplied with pineapple plants by Londesborough, Castle Howard and Sledmere. Elizabeth Hall 6–32.

44 Blanche Henrey 95.

45 For example, see ibid. 193.

46 Thomas MacKnight, *History of the Life and Times of Edmund Burke* (1860) III. 27.

47 Venetia Murray 97.

48 For Welbeck Abbey in the eighteenth century, see A. S. Turbeville, *A History of Welbeck Abbey and Its Owners* (1938) II.

49 William Speechly to the Duke of Portland, 17 March 1767 (Nottingham University archives PwF 8428).

50 William Speechly to the Duke of Portland, 17 January 1781 (Nottingham University archives, PwF 8471).

51 William Speechly to the Duke of Portland, 4 May 1772; 16 July 1770; 2 November 1776; 26 March 1781 (Nottingham University archives PwF 8444; 8442; 8458; 8477).

52 William Speechly to the Duke of Portland, 12 April 1769 (Nottingham University archives PwF 8435).

53 Quoted in John Harvey, *Early Nurserymen* (1974) 207.

54 Quoted in A. S. Turbeville II. 319.

55 James Ralph, *The Case of Authors by Profession or Trade, State* (1758) 41–2. The passage also upholds the sexual overtones that surrounded the pineapple.

56 W. S. Lewis (ed.), *The Yale Edition of Horace Walpole's Correspondence* (1983) XIX. 106.

57   William Speechly, *A Treatise on the Culture and Management of the Pineapple and the Management of the Hothouse* (1779).
58   R. Weston, *Tracts on Practical Agriculture and Gardening* (1769; citations are from 2nd edn, 1773) 78.
59   David Mason Little (ed.), *Pineapples of Finest Flavour: or, a selection of sundry unpublished letters of the English Roscius, David Garrick* (1967) i.

CHAPTER 6

This chapter has been much informed by Neil McKendrick, John Brewer and J. H. Plumb, *The Birth of a Consumer Society: the Commercialization of Eighteenth-century England* (1982); Roy Porter, *English Society in the Eighteenth Century* (1990); Paul Langford, *A Polite and Commercial People: England 1727–1783* (1989); and Ann Bermingham and John Brewer, *The Consumption of Culture 1600–1800* (1995).

1   Blanche Henrey, *No Ordinary Gardener: Thomas Knowleton* (1986) 230.
2   *Consumer Society* 15.
3   For more on luxury in the eighteenth century, see John Sekora, *Luxury: the Concept in Western Thought, Eden to Smollett* (1977) and Maxine Berg and Elizabeth Eger, *Luxury in the Eighteenth Century: Debates, Desires and Delectable Goods* (2003).
4   Bernard Mandeville, *The Fable of the Bees*, ed. F. B. Kaye (1924) I. 103–5.
5   Ibid. II. 194–5.
6   'Civis', 'Prevalence of Luxury', *London Magazine* XXIII (September 1754) 409.
7   Quoted in *English Society* 273.
8   Quoted in ibid. 186.
9   C. H. Collins Baker and Muriel I. Baker, *The Life and Circumstances of James Brydges, First Duke of Chandos* (1949) 380.
10   Ibid. 186.
11   Quoted in John Harvey, *Early Nurserymen* (1974) 110.
12   *Consumer Society* 9.
13   Richard Weston, *Tracts on Practical Agriculture and Gardening* (1st edn 1769; citations are from the 1773 edn) 78.

14 *Gardener's Chronicle* (20 November 1915) 318.

15 James Justice, *The Scots Gardiners Director* (1754) 122.

16 Blanche Henrey, *British Botanical and Horticultural Literature before 1800* (1975) 377. While the majority of nurserymen specialising in pineapples were based in London, there were exceptions – however, they had to make the extra effort to attract custom, making sure it was an enjoyable place to visit on a day out. A 1767 account of James Clark's nursery at Dorking noted not only a well-stocked shop selling seeds and plants of all kinds, but also a fish pond, pleasant grass slopes surrounded by trees, and a 'convenient' pine stove in order to show off the potential of this marvellous fruit. ('Papers relating to bankruptcy of James Clark, catalogues of his goods and gardener's stock. Dorking, Surrey' in the Public Records Office C110/174)

17 John Harvey, *Early Horticultural Catalogues: a Checklist of Trade Catalogues Issued by Firms of Nurserymen and Seedsmen in Great Britain and Ireland Down to the Year 1850* (1972).

18 See 'The original seed catalogue of James Gordon, Seedsman, of 25 Fenchurch Street in London' in the Lindley Library of the R.H.S.

19 *Early Nurserymen* 84.

20 *No Ordinary Gardener* 138. Gordon had in the past distributed pineapple plants himself, for example, to John Blackburne of Orford Hall near Warrington, the first to fruit the pineapple in Lancashire.

21 E. C. Nelson and A. Brady (eds), *Irish Gardening and Horticulture* (1979) 180. For more on the cultivation of the pineapple in Ireland, see Keith Lamb and Patrick Bowe, *A History of Gardening in Ireland* (1995) 24, 61.

22 Richard Bradley, *A General Treatise of Husbandry and Gardening* (1724) III. 141.

23 George Tod, *Tod's Plans of Hot Houses* (1807).

24 B. Faujas de Saint-Fond, *A Journey Through England and Scotland to the Hebrides in 1784*, ed. Archibald Geikie (1907) I. 60. See also Harold B. Carter, *Sir Joseph Banks* (1988) 338–9.

25 William Robertson, *A Collection of Various Forms of Stoves* (1798) Plate VII.

26 John Giles, *Ananas: or, a treatise on the pine-apple* (1767).

27 Adam Taylor, *A Treatise on the Ananas, or Pine-apple* (1769) 1.

28 Examples include 'On the culture of Pine-Apples. An extract of a letter from William Bastard, Esq., of Kitley, Devonshire . . . Read June 19 1777', *Philosophical Transactions of the Royal Society of London* LXVII. 649.

29 Thomas Hale, *Eden* (1767) 231.

30 Hoh-Cheung Mui and Lorna H. Mui, *Shops and Shopkeeping in Eighteenth Century England* (1989).

31 Quoted in *English Society* 190.

32 Quoted in *Consumer Society* 78.

33 Clare Williams (ed.), *Sophie in London 1786* (1933) 142.

34 Quoted in *English Society* 274.

35 Richard Brinsley Sheridan, *The Rivals*, ed. Elizabeth Duthie (1989) 62 – Act 3 Scene 3.

36 John Forster, *Walter Savage Landor: a Biography* (1869) I. 497.

37 Alfred Spencer (ed.), *Memoirs of William Hickey* (1948) IV. 230.

38 Robert James, *Pharmacopaeia Universalis: or, A New Universal English Dispensatory* (1747) 145.

39 Tobias Smollett, *The Adventures of Peregrine Pickle* (1751), Chapter V. Smollett's literary response to the pineapple is discussed in the article by G. S. Rousseau, 'Pineapples, Pregnancy, Pica and Peregrine Pickle', in G. S. Rousseau and P.-G. Boucé (eds), *Tobias Smollett: Bicentennial Essays Presented to Lewis M. Knapp* (1971) 79–109.

40 Matthew Winterbottom, "Such massy pieces of plate": Silver Furnishings in the English Royal Palaces 1660–1702', *Apollo* (August 2002) 19–26. Other notable representations of the pineapple from the reign of William and Mary include two urns surmounted by a pineapple designed by Edward Pearce in 1686 for Hampton Court Palace (now in the Orangery at Kensington Palace). Thanks to Matthew Winterbottom, Assistant Curator of the Queen's Works of Art, for his advice on this.

41 For further examples of Wedgwood pineappleware, see Robin Reilly, *Wedgwood: the New Illustrated Dictionary* (1995).

42 Alison Kelly, 'Coade Stone in Georgian Gardens', *Garden History* 16/2 (1988) 129.

43 J. J. Bagley (ed.), *The Great Diurnal of Nicholas Blundell of Little Crosby, Lancashire* (1968) III. 69.

44 Margaret Blundell (ed.), *Blundell's Diary and Letter Books 1702–1728* (1952) 39.

45 'Commissioner Mathews, Chatham Dock. Comments on the cost of stone pineapples for his garden. 3 June 1739' in the Public Record Office ADM 106/906/147.

46 For trade with the empire, see James Walvin, *Fruits of Empire* (1997). For the empire in this period, see Lawrence James, *The Rise and Fall of the British Empire* (1994); H. V. Bowen, *Elites, Enterprise and the Making of the British Overseas Empire 1688–1755* (1996); and C. A. Bayly, *Imperial Meridian: the British Empire and the World 1780–1830*.

47 James Grainger, *The Sugar-Cane: a poem* (1766) 30.

48 Peter Mason, *Infelicities: Representations of the Exotic* (1998) 1.

49 For responses to the empire in this period, see G. S. Rousseau and Roy Porter (eds), *Exoticism in the Enlightenment* (1989), as well as Kathleen Wilson, 'Empire of Virtue: the Imperial Project and Hanoverian Culture c.1720–1785', in Lawrence Stone (ed.), *An Imperial State at War* (1994) 128–56.

50 Quoted in Linda Colley, *Britons: Forging the Nation 1707–1837* (1992) 59.

51 Quoted in *Consumer Society* 15.

52 *Britons.*

53 A. C. Fox-Davies, *A Complete Guide to Heraldry* (1985) 208.

54 For more on The Pineapple, see the documents lodged in the building by the Landmark Trust and also Glyn Headley and Wim Meulenkamp, *Follies: a Guide to Rogue Architecture in England, Scotland and Wales* (1990) 469; *Stirlingshire: an Inventory of the Ancient Monuments* (1963) II. 341; and George Mott and Sally Sample Aall, *Follies and Pleasure Pavilions* (1989) 55.

55 J. Mordaunt Crook, *The Dilemma of Style* (1987) 16–31.

56 James Morris, *Heaven's Command* (1973) 6.

57 Barbara Jones, *Follies and Grottoes* (1974) 48.

58 George Walker, *The Vagabond, a novel* (1799) I. 210.

59   Anon, 'Crito: or, A Dialogue on Beauty', in *Fugitive Pieces on Various Subjects* (1761) I. 43.
60   James Thomson, *The Seasons*, ed. James Sambrook (1981) 94.
61   John Henderson, *Letters and Poems by the late John Henderson* (1786) 19.
62   Christopher Smart, *A Song to David* (1763) 18.
63   J. D. Baird and C. Ryskamp, *The Poems of William Cowper* (1980) I. 216.
64   James King and Charles Ryskamp (eds), *The Letters and Prose Writings of William Cowper* (1979) I. 305.
65   Ibid. I. 261.
66   Ibid. I. 305.

CHAPTER 7

Thanks to Patricia Gibbs and Wesley Greene of the Colonial Williamsburg Foundation for assistance with this chapter.

On the history of gardening in North America, see Alice Lockwood, *Gardens of Colony and State: Gardens and Gardeners of the American Colonies and of the Republic before 1840* (1931); Barbara Wells Sarudy, *Gardens and Gardening in the Chesapeake 1700–1805* (1998); Peter Martin, *The Pleasure Gardens of Virginia* (1991); May Woods and Arete Swartz Warren, *Glass Houses: a History of Greenhouses, Orangeries and Conservatories* (1988); and U. P. Hendrick, *A History of Horticulture in America to 1860* (1950).

For eighteenth-century life in the colonies in general see J. P. Greene and J. R. Pole (eds), *Colonial British America* (1984); Cary Carson, Ronald Hoffman and Peter J. Albert (eds), *Of Consuming Interests: the Style of Life in the Eighteenth Century* (1994); R. L. Bushman, *The Refinement of America* (1992); and David E. Shi, *The Simple Life: Plain Living and High Thinking in American Culture* (2001).

 1   John Fitzpatrick, *The Diaries of George Washington 1748–1799* (1925) I. 27.
 2   Griffith Hughes, *Natural History of Barbados* (1750) 230. The list of subscribers to the first edition of this book includes Washington's close friend, neighbour and the father of his brother Lawrence's wife, William Fairfax. It was almost certainly Fairfax's copy that he borrowed.

3   *Diaries of George Washington* II. 150.

4   George Washington to Robert McMickan, 10 May 1774 in *Account Book 2 in the George Washington Papers at the Library of Congress, 1741–1799* (online at www.memory.loc.gov/ammem/gwhtml/gwhome.html). This was not the first time he had placed an order for pineapples. See also George Washington to Lawrence Sanford, 26 September 1769, in ibid.

5   For more on how Washington's background and character predisposed him (perhaps surprisingly) to the pineapple, see Joseph E. Ellis, *His Excellency George Washington* (2004).

6   Louis B. Wright and Virginia Freund (eds), *Historie of Travell into Virginia Britania* by William Strachey (1953) 38.

7   Michael Drayton, *Ode to the Virginian Voyage* (1606), quoted in S. G. Culliford, *William Strachey 1572–1621* (1965) 98.

8   Samuel Purchas, *Purchas his Pilgrimes* (1st edn 1625; citations are from the 2nd edn, 1905–7) XIX. 147.

9   William Hughes, *The American Physitian* (1672) 60.

10   Captain John Smith, *The Generalle Historie of Virginia, New England and the Summer Isles* (1624) 170.

11   Clayton Colman Hall (ed.), *Narratives of Early Maryland 1633–1684* (1925) 36.

12   *Pennsylvania Gazette*, 13 April 1769.

13   Carl R. Lounsbury (ed.), *An Illustrated Glossary of Early Southern Architecture and Landscape* (1994) 275.

14   Author's correspondence with Patricia Gibbs of the Colonial Williamsburg Foundation.

15   *Pennsylvania Gazette*, 28 December 1769 & 19 June 1766.

16   Ibid. 19 June 1766.

17   Author's correspondence with Patricia Gibbs of the Colonial Williamsburg Foundation and with Jennifer L. Aultman, Curator of Archaeological Collections, at Monticello.

18   Quoted in Louise Conway Belden, *The Festive Tradition: Table Decoration and Desserts in America 1650–1900* (1983) 108.

19   *Virginia Gazette*, 21 August 1752.

20   Ibid. 11 August 1768.

21 Philip Vickers Fithian, *Journal and Letters of Philip Vickers Fithian, 1773–1774: a Plantation Tutor of the Old Dominion*, ed. Hunter Dickinson Farish (1945) 155 & 185.

22 Graham Hood, *The Governor's Palace at Williamsburg: a Cultural Study* (1991) 248. This passage on de Botetourt is much informed by this book.

23 'An Account of Cash Paid by William Sparrow for his Excellency Lord Botetourt. By William Marsham. ALS. Orig: Duke of Beaufort and Gloucestershire Records Office, Botetourt Manuscripts from Badminton, ff. 297–329' (Colonial Williamsburg Foundation Library M-1395). The money conversion was calculated using John J. McCusker, *How Much Is That in Real Money?: a Historical Price Index for Use as a Deflator of Money Values in the Economy of the United States* (2002) and John J. McCusker, *Money and Exchange in Europe and America, 1600–1775: a Handbook* (1978). Thanks to Professor McCusker for his advice on this.

24 Quoted in *The Governor's Palace* 118.

25 John Page Jr. to John Norton, 27 May 1769, in Frances Norton Mason, ed., *John Norton & Sons, Merchants of London and Virginia* (1968) 94.

26 James A. Bear, Jr., and Lucia C. Stanton, *Jefferson's Memorandum Books: Accounts, with Legal Records and Miscellany 1767–1826* (1997) I. 78. There is no evidence to suggest that he attempted to grow them at Monticello, even though a range of other exotic fruits adorned the landscape.

27 Marie Kimball, *Thomas Jefferson's Cook Book* (1976).

28 Edward Oliver Fitch (ed.), *The Diaries of Benjamin Lynde and Benjamin Lynde Jr.* (1880) 53.

29 N. M. Miller Surrey, 'The Development of Industries in Louisiana During the French Regime 1673–1763', *Mississippi Historical Review* 9/3 (1922) 230; Georgia's Surveyor General, William Gerard De Brahm, related how 'To return again to the Experiments of Vegitable Productions made in the City of Savannah, the Author in the year 1763 planted the tops of several Ananas (v. g. Pine Apple) which took Root and grew whilst he continued in the Province . . .' in William Gerard De Brahm, *Report of the General Survey in the Southern District of North*

America, ed. Louis De Vorsey (1971) 157; William Guthrie boasted of how 'the tenderest plants of the West-Indies, such as the plantain, the allegator-pear-tree, the banana, the pine-apple, the sugar-cane, &c., remain unhurt during the winter, in the gardens of St Augustine . . .' in Florida. William Guthrie, *A New Geographical, Historical and Commercial Grammar* (1770) 603.

30 Quoted in *The Governor's Palace* 34.

31 Jonathan Swift, *Gulliver's Travels*, Chapter 21. Swift was a close associate of Alexander Pope, an acquaintance of Sir Robert Walpole, and very much a member of the circle of pineapple devotees who featured in Chapters 5 and 6.

32 Quoted in Peter Martin, *The Pleasure Gardens of Virginia* (1991) xix.

33 Quoted in *The Simple Life* 52.

34 *Glass Houses* 84.

35 William Eddis, *Letters from America*, ed. Aubrey C. Land (1969) 57.

36 Marion Tinling (ed.), *The Correspondence of the three William Byrds of Westover, Virginia, 1684–1776* (1977) I. 381 – 15 July 1728.

37 Alan W. Armstrong (ed.), *Forget Not Mee and My Garden: Selected Letters 1725–1768 of Peter Collinson* (2002) 153 – 10 March 1750.

38 Elaine Forman Crane, *A Dependent People: Newport, Rhode Island in the Revolutionary Era* (1985) 60.

39 *Gardens of Colony and State* I. 218. The gateposts remained there until the house was destroyed in the nineteenth century. They were then transferred to form the northern entrance to the grounds of what is now the Redwood Library. Others followed suit: in 1741, a stone pineapple was erected on the gateposts of the Newport home of the wealthy merchant Godfrey Malbone. *Gardens of Colony and State* I. 211. It is now in the cemetery, Fort Adams.

40 *Gardens of Colony and State* I. 217.

41 Gladys E. Bolhouse, 'Abraham Redwood: Reluctant Quaker, Philanthropist, Botanist', in Lorraine Dexter and Alan Pryce-Jones (eds), *The Redwood Papers: a Bicentennial Collection* (1976) 7.

42 Ibid.

43 'Journal of a French Traveller in the Colonies, 1765, II', *American Historical Review* 27 (1921) 70.

44 Quoted in W. Stull Holt, 'Charles Carroll, Barrister: the Man', *Maryland Historical Magazine* 31 (1936) 117.

45 Carroll became known as Charles Carroll, Barrister to distinguish him from the other Charles Carrolls who lived in Maryland at the same time: in addition to him and his father Dr Charles Carroll, there were also the more famous Charles Carroll of Carrollton (a prominent player in the American Revolution) and his father, Charles Carroll. The two families were related but only distantly.

46 Quoted in W. Stull Holt 122 – October 6 1764.

47 For Mount Clare, see Michael F. Trostel, *Mount Clare: Being an Account of the Seat built by Charles Carroll, Barrister, upon his Lands at Patapsco* (1981); Paper 'Mount Clare: Introducing Baltimore to Eighteenth Century Splendor' by Elizabeth Anderson Comer and Kristen L. Stevens presented to the 51st meeting of the Eastern States Archaeological Federation, 2 November 1984; Paper 'Mount Clare: the Georgian Landscape 1750–1780' by Carmen A. Weber presented to the 1986 Mid-Atlantic Archaeological Conference, April 1986. Thanks to Michael Connolly, Assistant Director of the Mount Clare Museum House.

48 Trostel 12.

49 See, for example, 'Letters of Charles Carroll, Barrister', *Maryland Historical Magazine* 38 (1943) 367.

50 Thomas Hale, *Eden: or a compleat body of gardening* (1757) 231.

51 Kimberley Collins Moreno, 'Mistress of Mount Clare: the Life of Margaret Tilghman Carroll, 1742–1817', MA thesis (University of Maryland, 2004) 40.

52 Mrs Gordon B. Ambler (ed.), 'Diary of Mary Ambler', *Virginia Magazine of History & Biography* 45 (1937) 166. The fact that there is little more evidence for the pinery is partly down to the fact that Carroll's collection of letters ends in June 1769.

53 Sarudy 82; quoted in W. Stull Holt 122 – 28 January 1768.

54 Robert J. Brugger, *Maryland, a Middle Temperament 1634–1980* (1988) 85.

55 *Maryland Gazette*, 6 May 1773 & 13 May 1773.

56 D. D. Wallace, *The Life of Henry Laurens* (1915) 28.

57 Edward McCrady, *The History of South Carolina under the Royal Government 1719–1776* (1966).

58 U. P. Hendrick, *A History of Horticulture in America to 1860* (1950) 141; Mrs St Julien Ravenal, *Charleston: the Place and the People* (1906), 158. Watson was also the largest dealer in nursery plants and seeds in the southern region.

59 Henry Laurens, *The Papers of Henry Laurens*, ed. Philip M. Hamer (1968) V. 360 – 13 October 1767.

60 Ibid. VII. 357 – 10 September 1770.

61 Ibid. XV. 399 – 5 October 1780.

62 David Birt, *An American in the Tower* (1988).

63 Johann David Schoepf, *Travels in the Confederacy 1783–4*, tr./ed. Alfred J. Morrison (1968) I. 93–4.

64 Quoted in Waverley Root and Richard de Rochemont, *Eating in America* (1976) 81.

65 Sarah Pattee Stetson, 'American Garden Books Transplanted and Native, before 1807', *William and Mary Quarterly* 3/3 (1946) 343.

66 See, for example, *Public Advertiser*, 22 February 1762.

67 Karen Ordahl Kupperman, 'The Puzzle of the American Climate in the Early Colonial Period', *American Historical Review* 87 (December 1982) 1262.

68 Quoted in Sarudy 143.

69 *Virginia Gazette*, 25 May 1775.

70 *Pennsylvania Journal*, 10 December 1767.

71 *Pennsylvania Gazette*, 16 August 1770.

CHAPTER 8

This chapter has been much informed by Joan Morgan and Alison Richards, *A Paradise out of a Common Field: the Pleasures and Plenty of the Victorian Garden* (1990), Brent Elliott, *The Victorian Garden* (1986) and Tom Carter, *The Victorian Garden* (1984).

1 The Duchess of Devonshire, *The Gardens at Chatsworth* (1999) 26.

2   Kate Colquhoun, *A Thing in Disguise: the Visionary Life of Joseph Paxton* (2003) 35.

3   Ibid. 40. He gave an account to the *Gardener's Chronicle* of the design he most favoured: each pit was 78 feet long and 7 feet wide with a sloping roof. Divided into four compartments to meet the needs of pineapples at different stages of growth, it was heated by a Rogers' Conical Boiler. *Gardener's Chronicle* (1844) 69.

4   Kate Colquhoun 109.

5   R. Glendinning, *Practical Hints on the Culture of the Pineapple* (1839) 1.

6   *Debow's Review* 25/5 (November 1858) 603. The journalist was from the *New York Independent*.

7   Samuel Smiles, *The Life of George Stephenson, Railway Engineer* (1859) 440.

8   Charles Lamb, 'A Dissertation on a Roast Pig', in Charles Lamb, *Elia* (1823) 284–5. These essays are reprinted from the *London Magazine* between August 1820 and November 1822.

9   Quoted in Blanche Henrey, *British Botanical and Horticultural Literature before 1800* (1975) 477; *The Horticulturist* (January 1848) 336; *Journal of Horticulture, Cottage Gardener and Country Gentleman* V (1863) 186.

10 George Eliot, *Felix Holt, the Radical* (1866), Chapter 3.

11 Quoted in Miles Hadfield, *Gardening in Britain* (1960) 300.

12 *Gardener's Magazine* VII (1831) 652.

13 Henry Phillips, *Pomarium Britannicum* (1820) 299.

14 *Chambers's Edinburgh Journal* III (12 April 1845) 232.

15 Freeman Hunt, *Lives of American Merchants* (1858) 546.

16 William Makepeace Thackeray, *Vanity Fair* (1847), Chapter 28.

17 Tom Carter 99.

18 J. C. Loudon, *Different Modes of Cultivating the Pine-apple* (1822) 138.

19 Ibid. 144.

20 J. C. Loudon, *Encyclopaedia of Gardening* (1822) 557 ff.

21 *Different Modes.* During the 1820s and 1830s Loudon made a number of tours of England's gardens with his wife Jane, perhaps to ascertain how many were following his advice. Among the pineapples that impressed him most were those at Hatfield House in 1825, as well as a

crop at Ashridge Park 'that promised a succession during the whole winter'. Four years later Loudon also marvelled at the Duke of Bedford's attempts at Woburn Abbey, while General Popham's at Littlecot Park in 1833 were 'admirably grown'. Priscilla Boniface (ed.), *J. C. Loudon, In Search of English Gardens: the Travels of John Claudius Loudon and his Wife Jane* (1990) 22, 136, 170 & 174.

22 William Griffin, *A Treatise on the Culture of the Pineapple* (1806); George W. Johnson and James Barnes, *The Pineapple: its Culture, Uses and History* (1847); David Thomson, *A Practical Treatise on the Culture of the Pine Apple* (1866). Others published in this period include *The Pineapple Manual* by contributors to the *Journal of Horticulture* (1865).

23 David Thomson 1.

24 Thomas Baldwin, *Short Practical Directions for the Culture of the Ananas, or Pine Apple Plant* (1818).

25 George W. Johnson and James Barnes 9.

26 Quoted in *Encyclopaedia* 580.

27 *Practical Hints.* Another popular system, and the one to which new gardeners tended to turn, was known as the Hamiltonian, based on the methods developed by Joseph Hamilton at Thornfield. Details were published in 1844 to such great acclaim that it went into a second edition just a year later. The main difference was that he recommended that the crowns or suckers be planted in rows plunged directly into a bed of earth rather than in pots, an innovation that was the source of real excitement within many horticultural circles. Joseph Hamilton, *A Treatise on the Hamiltonian System of Cultivating the Pine Apple* (1844).

28 *Gardener's Chronicle* (15 February 1845) 102

29 *Journal of Horticulture* X (8 May 1866) 340.

30 Elizabeth David, *Harvest of the Cold Months: the Social History of Ice and Ices* (1994) 320 & 364.

31 George W. Johnson and James Barnes 65 is a summary of the various discussions that raged in the *Gardener's Chronicle* throughout this year on this subject. Joseph Hamilton's treatise is *On the Hamiltonian System.*

32 *Gardener's Chronicle* (4 November 1843) 772.

33 Ibid. (9 February 1850) 84.

34 Ibid. (23 March 1850) 182; *Encyclopaedia* 592; *Gardener's Chronicle* (4 March 1843) 138.

35 Elizabeth Gaskell, *Ruth* (1853) Volume 2, Chapter 2.

36 Charles Darwin, *Journal of Researches into the Natural History and Geology of the Countries Visited during the Voyage of the H.M.S. Beagle round the World . . .* (1st edn 1839; citations are from the 1871 edn) 407.

37 Charles Dickens, 'A Flight', in Charles Dickens, *Reprinted Pieces* (1858). Charles Dickens was familiar with the English home-grown pineapple. Amongst others, his friend, the great Victorian philanthropist Baroness Burdett-Coutts, grew pineapples in her hothouses on her Highgate estate in North London, Holly Lodge. According to Hans Christian Andersen, who visited the hothouses while he was staying with Dickens in 1857, they were 'in such luxuriant spendour as I had never before witnessed'. *The Eclectic Magazine of Foreign Literature* (February 1871) 183.

38 *Gardener's Chronicle* (2 January 1847) 3.

39 Diary of Harriet White Paige (June 1839) in CD-Rom *North American Women's Letters and Diaries* (2001).

40 Beverly Seaton, *Language of Flowers* (1995) 188.

41 *Practical Hints* (1839) 1.

42 Kathryn Cave (ed.), *The Diary of Joseph Farington* (1984) VII. 2622, 2635 & 2794; VIII. 3111; X. 3531; XII. 4372 & 4405.

43 Ibid. XII. 4372.

44 Ibid. VIII. 3111.

45 Henry Phillips, *Pomarium Britannicum* (3rd edn, 1823) 291.

46 *Gardener's Chronicle* (28 October 1843) 759.

47 Ibid. (11 November 1843) 787.

48 Quoted in Asa Briggs, *The Age of Improvement* (1979) 472.

49 *Gardener's Chronicle* (6 January 1844) 8.

50 Thanks to Simon R. L. Carter, Assistant Curator, Works of Art at the House of Commons.

51 William Makepeace Thackeray, *Pendennis*, ed. Peter L. Shillingbury (1991) II. 62–3.

52 Ibid. I. 382.

53 Quoted in Ina Ferris, *William Makepeace Thackeray* (1983) 48.

54 *Journal of Horticulture* (1875) 288. An American magazine printed an account of a dinner party at Cyfarthfa Castle held a few days before Christmas: 'I have not only some of the most elegant dinners of London and Paris to compare it with, but also a Chicago game-dinner of fifty dishes to which I once sat down; and comparison can no further go. The Welsh dinner distanced them all: it was an expression of the limit of civilization in this direction – a dinner not merely provided by vast wealth, quite careless of cost, but adorned with luxurious piles of the rarest exotics grown in my host's conservatory, and including pheasants shot on the estate, and great pine-apples, oranges, peaches, the most luscious grapes, fruit of the rarest perfection and in profuse abundance, all reared in the hot-houses belonging to the castle, and served by men whose ancestors had been servants under the same roof.' *Appleton's Journal* (January 1878) IV. 32.

55 *Journal of Horticulture* XXII (1872) 455.

CHAPTER 9

1 Henry Phillips, *Pomarium Britannicum* (1820) 299.
2 Henry Mayhew, *London Labour and the London Poor* (1851) I. 84.
3 *The Times* (10 August 1850) 5.
4 Ibid. (22 March 1852) 3.
5 Henry Mayhew I. 84.
6 *The Times* (19 August 1847) 5.
7 Ibid. (11 September 1849) 6.
8 *Illustrated London News* (17 July 1847) 36.
9 Charles Dickens, 'The Streets – Morning', in *Sketches by Boz* (1839; citations from Penguin edn, 1995) 70.
10 Henry Mayhew I. 82.
11 Charles Dickens, *A Dictionary of London* (1879) 81.
12 John Timbs, *Curiosities of London* (1855) 498.
13 Charles Dickens, *David Copperfield*, Chapter XI.
14 All quotes from Henry Mayhew about the pineapple are from Henry Mayhew I. 79–86.
15 *The Times* (23 August 1856) 6.

16 Richard Bradley, *The Country Housewife and Lady's Director*, ed. Caroline Davidson (1980) II. 94; Elizabeth Raffald, *The Experienced English Housekeeper* (1769) 202; Richard Dolby, *The Cook's Dictionary* (1833) 429–30.

17 Isabella Beeton, *Book of Household Management* (1861) 741.

18 Henry Mayhew I. 84.

19 *The Times* (23 August 1856) 6.

20 For the early history of the Bahamas, see William H. Sears and Shaun O. Sullivan, 'Bahamas Prehistory', *American Antiquity* 43/1 (1978); Michael Craton and Gail Saunders, *Islanders in the Stream: a History of the Bahamas* (2000) I; William F. Keegan, *The People Who Discovered Columbus: the Prehistory of the Bahamas* (1992); and D. J. R. Walker, *Columbus and the Golden World of the Island Arawaks: the Story of the First Americans and their Caribbean Environment* (1992). For more on the arrival of the pineapple in the Antilles, see also Sven Loven, *Origins of the Tainan Culture, West Indies* (1935) 405.

21 *Calendar of State Papers (Colonial: North America and the West Indies)*, 19 July 1701.

22 *Calendar of State Papers*, 30 June 1729.

23 *Calendar of State Papers*, 14 January 1735.

24 Quoted in Howard Johnson, *The Bahamas in Slavery and Freedom* (1991) 56. For more on the Bahamas in the eighteenth and nineteenth centuries, see Craton and Saunders II; Paul Albury, *The Story of the Bahamas* (1975); Daniel McKinnen, *A tour through the West Indies in the years 1802 and 1803, giving a particular account of the Bahama Islands* (1804); Surgeon Major J. T. W. Bacot, *The Bahamas: a Sketch* (1869); and Charles Ives, *The Isles of Summer; or Nassau and the Bahamas* (1880).

25 L. D. Powles, *The Land of the Pink Pearl; or, recollections of life in the Bahamas* (1888) 96.

26 George Johnson and James Barnes, *The Pine Apple: its Culture, Uses and History* (1847) 11.

27 Ibid.

28 J. T. W. Bacot 88.

29 Thomas C. Harvey, *Official Reports of the Out-islands of the Bahamas* (1858) 67.

30   *The Times* (6 July 1846) 5.

31   Ibid. (22 July 1856) 9.

32   *Gardener's Chronicle* (19 August 1843) 575.

33   *The Times* (31 July 1873) 5.

34   For the pineapple in the Azores, see Captain Godfrey, 'St Michael's and its Fruit Gardens', *The Floral World and Garden Guide* (1873) 125, as well as James H. Guill, *A History of the Azores* (1993).

35   *The Times* (8 February 1873) 6.

36   J. Robson, 'The Pine Apple', *Journal of Horticulture* XXII (6 June 1872) 455.

37   Marcel Proust, *Pleasures and Regrets*, tr. Louise Varese (1988) 123.

CHAPTER 10

1   Philip Morin Freneau, *Poems Written Between the Years 1768 & 1794*, ed. Lewis Leary (1795; facs. edn 1976) 132.

2   Quoted in Hugh Brogan, *Penguin History of the United States of America* (1990) 256.

3   For specific examples, see Ian M. G. Quimby, *American Silver at Winterthur* (1995) 268, 351, 429, 439 & 447; Kathryn C. Buhler and Graham Hood, *American Silver in the Yale University Art Gallery* (1970) II. 119–20, 128–9, 140–1 & 193–4; Jennifer F. Goldsborough, *Silver in Maryland* (1983) 107, 111, 129, 175, 183, 199 & 201; Deborah Dependahl Waters, *Elegant Plate: Three Centuries of Precious Metals in New York City* (2000) II. 299 & 423. Many thanks to Jennifer F. Goldsborough.

4   *Gardener's Magazine* (1836) XII. 293.

5   David John Jeremy (ed.), *Henry Wansey and his American Journal* (1970) 74.

6   J. C. Parsons (ed.), *Extracts from the Diary of Jacob Hiltzheimer of Philadelphia, 1765–1798* (1893) 243. See also Eleanor Young, *Forgotten Patriot: Robert Morris* (1950) 56.

7   Bernard M'Mahon, *American Gardener's Calendar* (1806.) For M'Mahon, see L. H. Bailey, *The Standard Cyclopaedia of Horticulture* (1925).

8   *Genessee Farmer* (25 June 1836) quoted in T. P. Thornton,

'Horticulture and American Character', in Walter T. Punch, *Keeping Eden: a History of Gardening in America* (1992) 190.

9   Charles A. Barker, *American Convictions: Cycles of Public Thought 1600–1850* (1970) 383.

10   For Boston men, see T. P. Thornton, *Cultivating Gentlemen: the Meaning of Country Life among the Boston Elite 1785–1860* (1989).

11   *Horticultural Register and Gardener's Magazine* (1 December 1837) 465.

12   *American Gardener's Magazine* (1835) 272.

13   Ibid. (1837) 347.

14   *Horticultural Register and Gardener's Magazine* (1 December 1837) 465. Haggerston's pineapples were displayed at the 1837 annual exhibition of the Massachusetts Horticultural Society, the first ever to be displayed there. *Horticultural Register and Gardener's Magazine* (1 October 1837) 385.

15   *American Gardener's Magazine* (1835) 350.

16   Ibid. (1837) 27.

17   Ibid. (1836) 36.

18   Perkins gave an account of the heating system he developed for a greenhouse he built in 1831 to the *New England Farmer* (30 November 1831): 'With hot water not above 190 deg. of Fah. left by the gardener at 8 o'clock in the evening, heated by Anthracite Coal and with the dampers nearly closed, the state of the house if ordinarily tight, will be found in the morning within a few degrees of the state in which it was left twelve hours before.'

19   Carl Seaburg and Stanley Paterson, *Merchant Prince of Boston: Colonel T. H. Perkins, 1764–1854* (1971) 391.

20   *Horticultural Register and Gardener's Magazine* (1 October 1837) 385.

21   *Magazine of Horticulture* (1838) 1.

22   *The Horticulturist and Journal of Rural Art and Rural Taste* (1851) 438.

23   *The Horticulturist and Journal of Rural Art and Rural Taste* (1856) VI. 234. In July 1855 John Tucker's gardener, William Thompson, exhibited a collection of pineapples at an exhibition of the Pennsylvania Horticultural Society (James Boyd, *A History of the Pennsylvania Horticultural Society* (1929) 141). The *Delaware County Republican* reported that at a meeting of the Pennsylvania Horticultural Society in

May 1857, John Anspach's gardener, George Lazenby, received a prize for the best pineapples in the state (*Delaware County Republican*, 22 May 1857).

24 *American Farmer's Magazine* (September 1858) 549.

25 *American Gardener's Magazine* (1838) 417. For an account of how to grow a pineapple in the United States in this period, see (for example) *The Horticulturist and Journal of Rural Art and Rural Taste* XV (October 1860) 458–61.

26 *The Horticulturist and Journal of Rural Art and Rural Taste* XV (October 1860) 461. For more details on the technological development of greenhouses in America, see U. P. Hendrick, *A History of Horticulture in America to 1860* (1950) 223 & 267.

27 May Woods and Arete Warren Swartz, *Glass Houses: a History of Greenhouses, Orangeries and Conservatories* (1988) 140.

28 Ann S. Stephens, *Fashion and Famine* (1854) quoted in *Glass Houses* 138.

29 Letter from Sarah Butler to Benjamin Franklin Butler (September 1862) in *North American Women's Letters and Diaries* CD-ROM (2001).

30 *The Horticulturist and Journal of Rural Art and Rural Taste* (September 1859) 394.

31 See, for example, P. Henderson, *Gardening for Pleasure* (1875) or William Corbett, *The American Gardener* (1821).

32 *The Horticulturist and Journal of Rural Art and Rural Taste* (May 1865) XX.151. This was in contrast to England where in 1823 Henry Phillips commented that 'We consider the principal cause of the ease with which this fruit is grown amongst us, is the liberal and spirited manner by which the growers have, from time to time, laid their improved plans before the public by their well-directed pens.' Henry Phillips, *Pomarium Britannicum* (3rd edn 1823) 291.

33 While the literature had been a problem since the previous century, garden writers continued to highlight it: 'English authors have often misled our horticulturists; we often adopt their examples without reflecting that the temperature of our winters and those of England are entirely different.' *American Gardener's Magazine* (January 1836) 2. For example, in England it was often recommended that the rafters used in

the pineapple house should be as light as possible; but it was pointed out that 'one of our heavy winter's snows on [these] rafters of fir poles, would make an end of the house and all inside of it'. *The Horticulturist and Journal of Rural Art and Rural Taste* (September 1859) 394. Published information on the subject of the pineapple remained relatively scarce even towards the end of the century. A letter to *Gardener's Monthly* in 1880 from a reader in Tracy City in Tennessee asked plaintively about pineries in the country, 'I have in vain endeavoured to get any information on the subject. Here, where I live, fuel could be had for the hauling, and I think a market for the fruit could be made without trouble, since it bears shipping well. Is there any good book or publication on this subject?' M'Mahon's book is suggested in response to his inquiry, but 'We have no doubt, with the new light gained since it was written, pine culture could doubtless be made even easier.' *Gardener's Monthly* XXII (December 1880)370.

34 U. P. Hendrick 223.

35 *Plough, the Loom and the Anvil* (January 1850) 441. This magazine later changed its name to the *American Farmer's Magazine*.

36 *Plough, the Loom and the Anvil* (March 1850) 570.

37 *The Family Magazine* (1837) 396.

38 Nathaniel P. Willis, *Dashes at Life with a Free Pencil, Part II: Inklings of Adventure* (1st edn 1836; citations are from the 1968 edn) 6.

39 Robert B. Leuchars, *A Practical Treatise on the Construction, Heating, and Ventilation of Hot-Houses; including conservatories, green-houses, graperies, and other kinds of horticultural structures . . .* (1851) 36. This passage compares the altitude of the sun in relation to the slope of the greenhouse's roof in London and in Philadelphia.

40 *The Horticulturist and Journal of Rural Art and Rural Taste* (1 May 1851) 220.

41 Ibid.

42 For more on horticulture in the South, see U. P. Hendrick.

43 *The Horticulturist and Journal of Rural Art and Rural Taste* (September 1873) 268.

44 *Pennsylvania Gazette* (17 July 1776).

45 J. H. Ingraham, *Steel Belt* (1844), Chapter 2.

46 Joyce Appleby, *Inheriting the Revolution: the First Generation of Americans* (2000) 75.

47 *Frederick Douglass' Paper* (22 April 1853). Not surprisingly, it tended to be the British who were most impressed. For example, in 1818, James Flint saw pineapples 'plentiful beyond example' in Philadelphia market. R. G. Thwaites, *Early Western Travels* (1904) IX. 61.

48 Caroline M. Kirkland, *The Evening Book; or fireside talk on morals and manners with sketches of western life* (1852) 145.

49 Waverley Root and Richard de Rochemont, *Eating in America* (1976) 112.

50 Henry Thoreau, *The Journal of Henry Thoreau*, ed. Bradford Torrey and Francis H. Allen (1984) XIV. 274 – 26 November 1860.

51 Quoted in Root and de Rochemont 130.

52 Emmeline Stuart-Wortley, *Travels in the United States etc during 1849 and 1850* (1851) 43. As far away as Charleston, South Carolina, similar fears surfaced. 'It was too bad that dread of the cholera made them all forbidden goods,' observed one journalist of the pineapples he saw in the markets there. *Frederick Douglass' Paper* (22 April 1853).

53 Quoted in Surgeon Major J. T. W. Bacot, *The Bahamas: a Sketch* (1869) 88.

54 Letter from the US attorney for the State of New Jersey to the Secretary of the Navy (5 September 1863) in the online database *The Making of America* at http://cdl.library.cornell.edu/moa.

55 Letter from Thomas Rowland (December 23 1861) in *The American Civil War: Diaries and Letters* CD-ROM (2001)

56 Belle Boyd, *Belle Boyd in Camp and in Prison* (1998) 150.

57 For example, throughout the summer of 1866, the *Delaware County Republican* featured advertisements for pineapples placed by Morrison's ice-cream, cake and confectionary store on Market Street in Chester, Pennsylvania. *Delaware County American* (26 May 1865 & 4 July 1866).

58 Oscar Edward Anderson, *Refrigeration in America: a History of a New Technology and Its Impact* (1953).

59 George Ripley and Charles A. Dana, *The American Cyclopaedia* XIII (1873–6) 528.

60   Eliza Leslie, *Seventy-five receipts for pastry, cakes, and sweetmeats* (1828) 88.

61   Eliza Leslie, *The House Book* (1837) 235, 240, 241, 470 & 476.

62   Jean Pfaelzer, 'Leslie, Eliza' in *American Dictionary of National Biography* CD-ROM (1999)

63   See the recipes from American cookery books of the nineteenth and early twentieth centuries available from the online database *Feeding America* at http://digital.lib.msu.edu/projects/cookbooks.

64   James Gates Percival, *The Poetical Works of James Gates Percival* (1865) I. 332.

65   *Gardener's Monthly* XIX (February 1877).

66   Quoted in Sandra Oliver, *Saltwater Foodways: New Englanders and Their Food, at Sea and Ashore, in the Nineteenth Century* (1995) 182.

67   *Gardener's Monthly* XXIII (January 1881) 18.

68   *Garden and Forest* 6/298 (1893) 470.

69   Ibid. 10/485 (1897) 230.

70   Mark Windegardner (ed.), *We Are What We Ate: 24 Memories of Food* (1998) 58.

71   Richard Hawkins, 'The Baltimore Canning Industry and the Bahamian Pineapple Trade, c.1865–1926', *Maryland Historian* (Fall/Winter 1995).

CHAPTER 11

This chapter is based primarily on the huge number of miscellaneous pamphlets, prospectuses, brochures, newspaper cuttings, advertisements and labels held in the Dole archives at the University of Hawaii at Manoa. See the finding aid prepared by Susan M. Campbell available in the Special Collections Reading Room, Hamilton Library, University of Hawaii at Manoa. The source of all advertisements quoted in this chapter is the 26 volumes of (uncatalogued) scrapbooks in the Dole archives. Where a source is not given, the reference is to be found somewhere within them.

   For the period up until 1921, see the 26-page supplement published by the *Pacific Commercial Advertiser* on 9 February 1921 which provides a complete and accurate account of the pineapple industry in its earliest days, as well as revealing interviews with Captain John Kidwell and James D.

Dole. This forms the basis for most secondary accounts of the pineapple industry in its earliest days, of which the most useful was an unpublished manuscript by the director of the Pineapple Research Institute, E. C. Auchter, *People, Research and Social Significance of the Pineapple Industry of Hawaii* (1951) and an unpublished manuscript by the editor of Pineapple Research Institute publications, Gus M. Oehm, *By Nature Crowned: King of Fruits: Pineapples in Hawaii* (1953). Richard A. Hawkins, *Economic Diversification in the American Pacific Territory of Hawaii, 1893–1941* (PhD thesis, University of London 1986) was also consulted.

1   Edward O. Wilson, *The Future of Life* (2003) 44ff.

2   In 1527 three Spanish ships sailed from Mexico on their way to the Moluccas to provide reinforcements to the settlement there. Of these, two were shipwrecked. At the same time, Hawaiian folklore has it that during the reign of Kealilokalea, son of the Chief Umi, there was a shipwreck on the south coast of Kona. Since Kealilokalea was born in about 1500, it makes sense that the two coincided. Alternatively, the culprit may have been the Spanish adventurer Juan Gaetano who is said to have landed in 1555. It is possible that the Chinese also played a role in the introduction of the pineapple to Hawaii: see Gavin Menzies,1421: *The Year China Discovered the World* (2003) 442.

3   J. C. Beaglehole (ed.), *The Journals of Captain Cook on his Voyages of Discovery* (1999) III.i. 120, 195 & 235.

4   John Gascoigne, *Science in the Service of Empire: Joseph Banks, the British State and the Uses of Science in the Age of Revolution* (1998).

5   Agnes C. Conrad (ed.), *Letters and Journal of Francisco de Paula Marin* (1973) 209. See also Ross H. Gast, *Don Francisco de Paula Marin: a Biography* (1973) 51–2.

6   *Proceedings of the Royal Hawaiian Agricultural Society* (1853), quoted in E. C. Auchter 7.

7   Quoted in Gus M. Oehm 36.

8   *Pacific Commercial Advertiser* supplement (9 February 1921) 11.

9   For John Kidwell, see Richard A. Hawkins, 'An English Entrepreneur in the Hawaiian Islands: the Life and Times of John Kidwell, 1849–1922', *Hawaiian Journal of History* 31 (1997) 127–42.

10   *Paradise of the Pacific* (December 1911) quoted in Gus M. Oehm 304.

11   Quoted in Richard Dole and Elizabeth Dole Porteus, *The Story of James Dole* (1999) 34.

12   For James Dole, see Richard Dole, Elizabeth Dole Porteus and Henry A. White, *James D. Dole: Industrial Pioneer of the Pacific* (1957). For Dole the company, see F. J. Taylor, E. M. Welty and D. W. Eyre, *From Land and Sea: the Story of Castle and Cooke of Hawaii* (1976). The extensive interview with him in the *Pacific Commercial Advertiser* (9 February 1921) about the early days of his company is also useful.

13   University of Hawaii, *Women Workers in Hawaii's Pineapple Industry* (1979) II. 1ff. See also Caroline Manning, *The Employment of Women in the Pineapple Canneries of Hawaii* (1930).

14   *Women Workers* II. 842.

15   *Economic Diversification* 549; *The Employment of Women* 1 & 6. See also Robert C. Schmitt, *Historical Statistics of Hawaii* (1977).

16   *Women Workers* I. 94.

17   Ibid. I. 108.

18   Jan K. Ten Bruggencate, *Hawaii's Pineapple Century* (2004) 140.

19   Victor Terras, *Vladimir Mayakovsky* (1983) 10.

20   Letter from the H. K. McCann Company to the Advertising Committee of the Association of Hawaiian Pineapple Canners (5 September, 1925) 3 in *Dole National Advertising Scrapbook Box 2: 1925–6*.

21   Richard A. Hawkins, 'The Pineapple Canning Industry during the World Depression of the 1930s', *Business History* 31/4 (1989) 49–66; Richard A. Hawkins, 'The Hawaiian Economy in the 1930s: the Successful Adjustment of an American Territory to the Great Depression', *Journal of American and Canadian Studies* 12 (1994) 47–67.

22   See the collection of advertisements held in the Advertising Archives, 45 Lyndale Avenue, London NW2 2QB.

23   Duchess of Devonshire, *The Garden at Chatsworth* (1999) 105.

24   Denis Mackail, *Greenery Street* (1925; citation from the Persephone Books edn 2002) 113.

25   *The Times* (11 September 1946) 2; (22 October 1946) 2; (5 February 1947) 8; (20 February 1947) 8; (20 April 1947) 8 .

26 'The Pineapple Canning Industry' 49.

27 James Joyce, *Finnegans Wake* (1st edn 1939; citation from the Penguin edn 2000) 170.

28 E. C. Auchter, *The Pineapple Industry: a Brief Review of Its History, Research Achievements and War Job* (1946); Gwenfread Allen, *Hawaii's War Years 1941–5* (1952) 285.

29 Dorothy Atkinson Robinson, *'It's All in the Family': a Diary of an American Housewife* (1943) 116.

30 *The Times* (29 October 1947) 2.

31 US Department of Agriculture Economic Research Service, *Food Consumption, Prices and Expenditures (Agricultural Economic Report No. 138)* (1968) 69 & 70.

32 Wallace Stevens, *The Necessary Angel: Essays on Reality and Imagination* (1960) 83–7.

CHAPTER 12

For the most current news on the pineapple, see the newsletter of the Pineapple Working Group, *Pineapple News*, at http://agrss.sherman. hawaii.edu/pineapple/pineappl.htm; the archives of *Food News* at www.agra-net.com; the archives of *Fresh Produce News* at http://www.freshinfo.com; and the websites of the pineapple companies themselves.

1 David Silverman, 'Letter', *New Statesman* (11 December 2000) 62.

2 Mike Leigh, *Abigail's Party* (1983) 15 & 33.

3 Nigella Lawson, *Forever Summer* (2002) 105.

4 For the international pineapple industry between about 1960 and 1980, see Claude Py, J. J. Lacoeuilhe and C. Teisson, *The Pineapple: Cultivation and Uses* (1987). For the international pineapple industry in recent years, see D. P. Bartholomew, R. E. Paull, and K. G. Rohrbach, *The Pineapple: Botany, Production and Uses* (2003) and *Economic Research Service of the United States Department of Agriculture – Fruit and Tree Nuts Outlook – FTS-307 (November 21 2003)* (available at www.ers.usda.gov/publications/fts/nov03/fts307.pdf). For the pineapple industry in Hawaii between about 1960 and 2000, see Jan K.

Ten Bruggencate, *Hawaii's Pineapple Century: a History of the Crowned Fruit in the Hawaiian Islands* (2004).

5   For market research on consumers' response to the pinapple, see 'Pineapples Compete in Prickly Market', in *Fresh Produce News* (21 October 1997); 'Split Industry Faces Up to Great Pineapple Paradox', in *Fresh Produce News* (6 November 1998); 'Give Consumers the Chance to Choose', in *Fresh Produce News* (8 October 1999); 'Pineapples Continue Strong Performance', in *Fresh Produce News* (2 October 2003); 'Pineapple Potential', in *Fresh Produce News* (29 April 2004); 'Pineapples on Course', in *Fresh Produce News* (4 October 2004).

6   Erich Hinrichs, *Ananas* (1996) 119.

7   Girolamo Benzoni of Milan, *History of the New World, shewing his travels in America, from 1541 to 1556*, tr. Rear-Admiral W. H. Smyth (1897) 88.

8   United States Department of Agriculture, *Economic Research Service* (available at http://www.ers.usda. gov/data/foodconsumption) (last updated 21 December, 2004); Department of Food, Environment and Rural Affairs, *Basic Horticultural Statistics for the United Kingdom (2004)* http://statistics.defra.gov.uk/esg/publications/ bhs/2004).

9   Robert Frank, 'Going for "The Gold" Turns Pineapple World Upside Down', *Wall Street Journal* (7 October 2003) 1 & 14, as well as the various stories that appeared in *Food News* at the time. Thanks to Robert Frank.

10 *Fruit and Tree Nuts Outlook* 17; 'Can Costa Rica Remain No. 1 Pineapple Exporter?' in *Food News* (7 December 2004).

11 Marilyn Berlin Snell, 'Pineapple Republic', *Sierra Magazine* 87 (March/April 2002), available at www.sierraclub.org.

12 www.agrofair.com.

13 'Sweet Pineapple Variety Transforms Fresh Market' in *Food News* (10 September 2003).

14 'Pineapples on a Roll', in *Fresh Produce News* (25 April 2003) and 'Pineapples Drive Ghana', in *Fresh Produce News* (15 January 2004). See also the report 'Ghana: Sustainable Horticultural Export Chain', an insight into the problem areas confronted by the Ghanaian horti-

cultural sector with particular focus on pineapples, at www.lei.dlo.nl.

15 Dickon Poole, *Pineapple Market Monthly Report* (April 2005). Thanks to Dickon Poole at J. P. Fruit.

16 *The Pineapple: Botany, Production and Uses 5–6;* Food and Agricultural Organisation of the United Nations, *Statistical Database*, available at http://faostat.fao.org/.

17 Tim Smit, *The Lost Gardens of Heligan* (1999) 153–70 & 270. Thanks also to Philip McMillan Browse and to Lorna Tremayne.

18 John Armstrong, *The Art of Preserving Health* (1744), lines 334–40.

19 Poem 'Pineapples and Pomegranates' in Paul Muldoon, *Moy Sand and Gravel* (2002) 25.

Index